PAUSE

# Pause

SONIA S. ROBINSON

Copyediting by Elizabeth Kovacs.
Cover design by Meredith Bogardus.
Cover design inspired by photography taken by Anna Sanders.

ISBN/SKU: 979-8-9931656-0-8
EISBN: 979-8-9931656-1-5

# Dedication

*To my boys, Major & Max,*
*for being key ingredients of my life's recipe.*


*To my parents, Johnny Lynn and Susan Jeanett,*
*for teaching me the recipe.*


*To my great-grandparents and grandparents,*
*for passing down the recipe: family, hard work, and faith in God.*

# Contents

# Author's Notes

This book is based on actual events. Some details have been intentionally omitted or modified to protect private and confidential information. I use the real names of select individuals only. Other names have been redacted or changed to protect the privacy of individuals who crossed my path and became a part of my personal story. It is an invitation, if you will, for those not named to share their story and perspective in their own book.

Relationships are hard work, careers are challenging, and human emotions only add to the complexity. The intent of this book is not to disparage or disrespect any character or workplace mentioned. While my story is dramatic, I intend to dramatize the surprises of life rather than the individual participants. I hope that my story will inspire women, mothers, cancer patients, and female executive leaders to understand the recipe for living a great life.

Furthermore, I hope the stories shared in these pages resonate with aspiring and experienced female leaders, serving as an effort to reframe a role that often leaves many of us, including myself, unprepared: leadership. Leadership is hard work.

I, the author, am not a special person. My story is not unique. There are millions of stories just like mine, undocumented by people just like me. It's a story about how our upbringing informs our decision-making and emotional responses for better or worse. A story about life's lovely and dark surprises that equally take our breath away. Lastly, it's a story about the universal recipe, curated by my great-grandparents and passed down over three generations, with three critical ingredients.

Like sourdough bread, you need a starter, a sourdough "mother", to enjoy the fruits of your labor in the kitchen. Requiring equal parts of flour and water to feed the sourdough starter until it is ready to be mixed with the rest of the ingredients. Sourdough bread involves time and patience before it is prepared for the oven. Even after pulling the bread from the heat and removing it from the safe cocoon of its Dutch oven, the waiting isn't over. The bread needs to sit and rest.

Standing in our kitchen, the wait was over. The bread knife was used to saw off three pieces of bread. One for me, and one for each of my boys. "This is amazing," Max said. "You did good, Mom." I hadn't done anything special; I just followed the recipe taught by the Sourdough 101 class instructor. The training paid off. It was delicious.

I poured in the ingredients to feed the sourdough mother, as a portion of her had been discarded and incorporated into the mixing bowl along with the other ingredients. Preparing to make another loaf, I worked in the kitchen to bake bread for lunch, which my family and I would have together around my mom's table after church. Our family tradition is to break bread together on Sundays.

Each new generation adds a special touch to the process, to the recipe. The ingredients are simple: family, hard work, and faith in God. They are essential to living, not merely surviving, life. This is a story about a woman, daughter, sister, mother, and executive leader all rolled into one beautiful life, with a dash of spice that only I could add to my recipe: pause.

# Prologue

*Setting the scene for the climax of my story: It was the fall of 2017 when the realization that my career was over hit me following a personal battle with breast cancer, as the bell rang signifying chemotherapy was over, and I was cancer-free. Two endings collided, and my life fell apart as a result. My boys, two sons from a marriage that ended in divorce before the cancer diagnosis, were now nine and five. They had no clue what their mom was fighting, and neither did she.*

I wanted to quit. As I sat across the table from my boss, I noticed his lips were moving, but I was consumed with an internal fight. Was he even talking to me? Tears were ready to explode from my eyes, and the downtown coffee shop was buzzing with conversation. In my head, I kept repeating to myself over and over, "Don't cry. Don't cry." "Breath in...one, two, three, four. Breathe out...one, two, three, four," I told myself, trying to slow my heart rate down and keep the flush from exposing the truth.

My career in executive leadership was taking off. It was a career I had worked so hard for following a divorce from my husband. It was a career that would provide financial stability, access to healthcare, and help me keep my boys in the safety and comfort of their childhood home. My career was over, and I wasn't the only one who knew it. The gentleman sitting across from me in that coffee shop, my boss, knew it too. We didn't understand each other's reasoning or the evidence that supported our respective narratives and defended our positions.

I wasn't so sure my boss knew the recipe, a recipe that had been taught to me my entire life. The ingredients were an equal mix of family, hard work, and faith in God. It was a recipe I knew well, thanks to the careful teachings of my great-grandmother, Mamie.

# Part I: Family

The first part of this book pays tribute to my big, beautiful, and loving family. Not everyone is mentioned. The book would be far too long. I was blessed with the gift of family and many memories to turn into stories. Most of the stories are funny, like the time the leftover lingerie party penis pasta made its way to a family lunch. My baby cousin, Rebecca, brought it as her food contribution to the meal. All of the grandchildren chipped in to lighten the load for Granny Evelyn, our matriarch, who worked hard in the kitchen to prepare a feast that would feed her family. The night before, all of my girl cousins had hosted a lingerie party for the youngest girl in Granny Evelyn's gaggle of grandchildren, Dana.

To make the story of a lingerie party food favor even funnier, our Granny invited friends from church to join us that particular Sunday. She had no idea her granddaughter's pasta salad was rated R for the less mature adults, like her grandchildren. By now, all the grandchildren were aware that the pasta in the bowl placed next to the potato salad was in the shape of little penises. We couldn't take our eyes off Ms. Jean, the invited guest, as she raved about the pasta salad, bite after delicious bite.

Granny Evelyn is no longer with us. She died peacefully in her own bed, free of any medical accessories and not in the care of hospice, on Christmas Eve 2024. Her family would fill her house one last time to celebrate the holiday with her, only she was no longer there in spirit. She was spending eternity with the love of her life, my Granddaddy Wayne. Their grandchildren still roar with laughter retelling the story of penis pasta around their own kitchen table with their children and my grandparents' great-grandchildren.

Other stories are somber with grief, recalling a comment I heard in my early twenties when my career was just taking off. At yet another family gathering, a bit of wisdom was served on the side as we broke bread together. Susan, my dad's first cousin and a mother of three, spoke with deep conviction. Her words were pure wisdom, the wisdom of a protector and nurturer. She said, "I would live in a house with dirt floors if it meant my family was here with me."

Coming from her, I believed it. I just didn't know life's surprises would cause me to speak the exact words a decade later. Her two daughters would battle their own unique cancers. One was diagnosed with triple-negative breast cancer. The other was diagnosed with an aggressive brain cancer. One daughter would live. The other fought like David against a Goliath she was unable to slay.

Thank you, Susan, for your wise words. The true meaning of her words was revealed to me through life's beautiful and dark surprises. She understood the recipe that my great-grandmother, Mamie, had taught her children. With each generation, the recipe was passed down as our family, ever evolving through birth and death, sat around the kitchen table to break bread together.

# Chapter 1

# Grandmother

My early childhood memories of my great-grandmother, Mamie Chapman Fowler, primarily revolved around the kitchen. She was always in the kitchen, making this, stirring that, and preparing for yet another family meal around her table. Perhaps I was too busy to notice her outside of the kitchen, as I was often engaging with my newest imaginary friend, playing fetch with a dog that always seemed to be around, or leaping from the shed and screaming, "You didn't find me," as my sister and cousins often played hide-and-seek. At the same time, the adults socialized in the kitchen with Grandma.

Out of eight great-grandparents, only one missed out on the opportunity to meet me and participate in my early childhood. Grandpa Gifford, my mom's maternal grandfather, was the first to die at age fifty-five. His bride, my Gramma Ruby, would die many years later from Parkinson's disease. Our family moved Gramma Ruby from Chicago, Illinois, back home to Estillfork, Alabama, when her disease progressed to the point that she could no longer live independently. Her daughter, my Granny Evelyn, became her caregiver along with one of my mom's baby sisters, Nancy. Surrounded by the love and care of family, Gramma Ruby was well taken care of until the end of her life.

Grandma Mamie lived the longest out of all of my great-grandparents. The will of a mother aligned with her mission to live a long life and fulfill her purpose on this Earth: to outlive her son. While she was my great-grandmother, she was the mother to six children. My great aunts and uncles seemed always to be around, even though three of them lived elsewhere. When giving birth to Carl, my great-uncle, something went terribly wrong. He suffered a stroke while in the womb, which damaged the nerve on the right side of his brain, leaving him paralyzed on his right side and causing seizures to be a part of everyday life.

It was 1946, a time when home births were common. My great-grandmother gave birth to a son at home. A son whom she knew, as soon as he was placed in her arms, was not like all the other babies she had given birth to. Ultrasounds were not used at the time, but became more widely used in the 1970s. Doctors could not prepare a new mother for the possibility that her baby could be different from most babies.

A forever child, never evolving beyond a toddler's temperament, Uncle Carl's tantrums rivaled those of any child. He did not have the body of a child; he was tall and strong, even with his physical limitations. Stomping his left leg as his temper raged and dragging his right paralyzed leg forward to gain his footing, he would stomp again. His left arm pierced the air like a sword. His right arm, paralyzed since birth, was drawn up tight to his chest like a shield. We kids would scatter, seeking the disguise of our hiding places, thinking he wanted to play hide-and-seek with us. As expletives spewed from his mouth, he would take a lap around the yard, only to return to his mother, who patiently and quietly waited for the episode to end. I'm not sure where Uncle Carl learned those dirty words, because I never heard them spoken aloud by any adult family member when I was a kid.

"Carl, it's time to listen to your music. Go on, go get in your chair and turn your music on." Compliant, he listened to his mother as if she had a superpower when it came to calming him down. Grandma Mamie lived to be ninety-three years old, holding on to her responsibilities as a mother until she took her last breath. Reminiscing with family, no one could recall a time they heard Grandma Mamie raise her voice or express frustration toward her different son. She comforted, nurtured, and protected him with her quiet nature.

Year after year, my mental and emotional development evolved, while Uncle Carl was stuck. Even though he was thirty-six years older than me, mentally and emotionally, he would never outgrow me. I surpassed him in ability and maturity.

Christmas was Uncle Carl's favorite holiday, and visiting Santa Claus was not a request. It was a demand. He had to see Santa to tell him how good he had been, knowing the gifts of new music tapes and vinyl records would multiply under the tree. And they did. A fresh addition to his ever-expanding music collection every Christmas, birthday, or any special occasion calling for gifts. Music was his escape. It was his world, and in his world, he made sense. Our family kept his world joyful with each new gift of music.

Careful not to disturb my Uncle Carl's familiar environment when his mother passed away, even though he was a fifty-eight-year-old man, his little sister became his primary caregiver. My Great-Aunt Gail kept his routine as close to normal as possible after Grandma Mamie passed. He was able to stay in the home where he and his mother had lived. Aunt Gail had been staying with them when Grandma's health began to decline, and she was no longer able to help Uncle Carl when he fell, needed assistance in the bathroom, or needed help preparing his food. His other brothers and sisters jumped in to help.

Great-Aunt Gail, following the recipe her mother had taught her, ensured Uncle Carl lived an extraordinary life without his mother there to comfort and calm him. He lived eight more years under the loving care of his siblings and extended family. Uncle Carl passed away in 2012, surrounded by the people who loved him most: his family. I was thirty-two years old when he passed and bore witness to the care and concern his entire family had for him. Each of us was taught to show up for family, always—even if tantrums ensued.

For thirty-eight years, Uncle Carl attended school and held a job at The Arc of Jackson County. He and his school friends were all given simple jobs that they could complete on their own or with little assistance. Even with his disabilities, he was expected to put in the hard work. Work gave him purpose. Occasionally, he would join us around the table for Sunday lunch at his older sister's house, my Granny Ruth's kitchen table.

Boastful about his hard work from the previous week, even my Uncle Carl, disabled from childbirth, understood the importance of hard work. He didn't earn very much money, but he made up for it with the pride he took in a job well done.

On Sundays, he was in church with his family at Mt. Nebo Baptist Church, located in Hollytree, Alabama, unless a seizure or tantrum kept him home. Gospel music was his favorite genre, and he had a deep love for Jesus. What I consider the most impressive detail of my Uncle Carl's life is that, when he was born, the doctors told his parents that he would not live past the age of sixteen.

As one of his older sisters, my Great-Aunt Gladys, shared this detail, she added, "It just proves what loving care can do for someone." He surpassed sixteen and lived to be sixty-six. The recipe had somehow carefully accounted for physical and mental limitations, and Uncle Carl followed the recipe: family, hard work, and faith in God.

From the outside looking in, it was a hard sixty-six years. But to my Uncle Carl, it was his life, and he had a recipe. A recipe his mother and my great-grandmother knew well and carefully taught to all of her children, including my Granny Ruth.

# Chapter 2

# Mama & Daddy

Digging ditches with just his hands and a shovel was how my daddy's career began. He loved to talk about his work. The City of Huntsville Public Works Department, in Huntsville, Alabama, laid the stepping stones perfectly for him to advance from digging ditches to leading a crew of Day Laborers. Around the dinner table each evening, he would share details of the latest road or sewer project he and his team were working on. It was fitting for him. Daddy was a natural-born leader who loved to create and build with his hands while using his words and actions to mentor young men and women.

During the summer months, under sleepy eyes and in the darkness of night, Dad would load my sister, Amanda, and me into his '70s-model maroon two-door Chevrolet Malibu. Amanda was riding shotgun, and I sprawled across the back seat. It was a time when seatbelts were optional, but the risks were ever present. Granny Ruth, his mother, would be on the back porch, ready to greet us as the sun peeked over the horizon. Amanda and I would stand on the back porch with Granny and wave goodbye to Daddy as he backed down the gravel driveway, off for another day of hard work.

Daddy would work a full day in the city and drive forty-five minutes home to our little white house in Estillfork at the head of Paint Rock Valley, Alabama. No time for rest, he would take a short break for dinner. Mom always had dinner ready when he arrived home. One of her many family responsibilities. Once dinner was over, out the door he went, hopping on his tractor to tend to the field that sat parallel to my early childhood haven. He came from a line of farmers, and he found joy in cultivating row crops. Located a few miles from the Tennessee state line, we had a large yard that was perfect for my entertaining imagination. Clouds of dry dust from Daddy's tractor boiled in the air as I tooled around in the barn, coaxing our horses up to the fence for a pat on the head.

My mom spent her career as a caregiver. To date, she's never earned a dime for her caregiving work. Her compensation was reflected in the thousands of photographs neatly organized in tattered photo albums. Memories to last her a lifetime. Money was a tool to live life, always coming and going, but memories were forever.

Mom always had a camera in hand, snapping candid shots as well as staging my sister and me for more formal images. She wanted to be a mother. A career outside of the home wasn't her goal. Selfishly, I'm glad my mom didn't pursue a career outside of the house. She was the ever-present steadiness to my perfect childhood, just like Grandma Mamie was to Uncle Carl. Always in the periphery, available to kiss a skinned knee, clean up a spilled drink, or remind me to be careful as I swung from the monkey bars.

Content with W-2 jobs, she would settle into a work schedule here and there only when her family needed the extra money. The oldest of five, her maternal qualities took hold early as she kept a watchful eye on her younger, more mischievous siblings throughout their childhood.

My parents served as an example for my sister and me, an equal partnership providing for their family. The lessons my parents taught me over the years are countless. There is one lesson that stands out: always show up for the people who love you the most—your family. For some, family may not be defined by blood relatives; rather, it may be defined by meaningful friendships.

The weekly routine was the same. Daddy left for work before the sun rose, only to come home in the evenings to work in the field or check the livestock. Mom was fulfilling her responsibilities of laundry, house cleaning, and taming two girls. Our house was always clean. Dinner was on the table as soon as Daddy came home from work. We would sit down at the kitchen table to eat together, and our conversation would fill the room.

It wasn't disappointment, but rather an acknowledgment that Daddy longed for a son. However, my parents decided on man-to-man coverage rather than zone defense when it came to the number of children they would have together. He was a girl's dad, with no son to take fishing or teach the discipline of farm life to. But that didn't stop him from influencing my tomboy behavior. Hair either cut short or pulled back in a ponytail, he nicknamed me "boy." I was his boy and the boy he wanted.

Like a shadow, I tagged along to check the cows, feed and brush the horses, and attend the cow sale, among other farm boy responsibilities. If a cow or calf was in distress, I would be right next to my daddy observing his extensive veterinary skills.

This was knowledge learned not from a formal collegiate education but through generations of farmers passing down the knowledge required to make this lifestyle a success. In the pasture behind our house, Daddy would hoist me up on a bareback horse for a short walk or include me in some project he was working on in the barn.

I held my mom in the same high regard as I held my daddy, but I aspired to be like my daddy—his boy, a career man. Daddy eventually phased out the nickname "boy" and began using "son," short for Sonia. It was a reminder that I was still his boy and of his realization that I was evolving into a young lady. Grit and toughness, complemented with styled hair and makeup.

As his responsibilities at work evolved, so too did the dinner table conversations. By the time I was in middle school, he was coaching and mentoring young men who were just starting out their careers in public works. Only these young men had the equipment to dig ditches. Innovation minimized the need for hand-to-shovel combat in the ditches. I prepared for college as my dad advanced his career into senior leadership. Twenty years into his decorated career, with just a high school education, he would set a goal and give himself a timeline to achieve it, only to continue that process until he was appointed by Mayor Loretta Spencer as the Deputy Director of Public Works for the City of Huntsville.

His experience far outweighed any theory or ideology taught in a textbook. Yet, not having a college degree did come with its limitations. These limitations were often placed by superiors who held a coveted diploma. My dad was just a simple country boy who wanted to make an honest living to support his family. Sure, he worked a lot, but I never noticed because he didn't miss out on his girls' busy sports or social schedule. He was a constant in my daily life, always present and always within the proverbial arm's reach.

My dad learned the role of husband, father, provider, and protector from my grandfathers. My mom knew her role as wife, mother, caregiver, and protector from my grandmothers. Granny Ruth was a realist, firm, and no-nonsense. Children were meant to be seen, but not heard, certainly not in church. A fresh switch from a backyard tree resting underneath her church pew, ready to strike a little shoulder if a sound was made, was proof she meant business. Her husband, my Granddaddy Carl, was the complete opposite. He was laid back and unbothered by surprises. Always telling jokes or sharing a story, being around Granddaddy Carl was always fun and full of adventure.

Granny Evelyn, my mom's mother, was an empath. She always felt emotion so profoundly, and she hurt for other people. Nothing made Granny Evelyn happier than having a house full of guests, family or not. Everyone was welcome, and she was going to feed them. She was energetic and generous with her praise. Granddaddy Wayne, my mom's father, did not appreciate anything or anyone that could potentially burn daylight. With little tolerance for tomfoolery, he would occasionally satisfy us grandkids with a ride on his tractor. Proof that he loved us, but playtime had no place in the life of a busy farmer. Even while taking us for a spin on the tractor, he was fulfilling a task.

They were a threesome: my dad, his dad, and his father-in-law, spending most Saturdays together tending to farm responsibilities. While they were working, my mom, sister, and I would often visit family. We'd go on playdates with cousins, trips to town, or house cleaning sprees. I would remain close to all of my grandparents well into my young adult life. Four loving adults teaching me the recipe with their words and actions.

# Chapter 3

# Child

For all the work hours my dad put in with a physically demanding full-time job and a physically demanding side hustle as a farmer, on Sunday mornings church was nonnegotiable. Arriving ahead of any other parishioner, my parents would consult over a songbook. Daddy led the congregational singing, and Mom played the piano. Over the years, my daddy's role in the church would evolve. Accepting the call to preach, he has shepherded our congregation for nine years now. Mom is still playing the piano.

Folding the corners of the songs they had selected together, the morning worship session was planned. As Mom's fingers floated over the ivory keys, my dad's beautiful tenor voice lit up the sanctuary. Our small congregation joined in, harmonizing with the lead singer, a mix of soft alto and deep bass voices singing along to a strong voice—my daddy's voice.

The last song was our cue. All the kids darted toward the Sunday school classroom where Ms. Leona would greet us. She did well to settle us into a routine. First, we studied the Bible verse she had selected. Then we would practice reciting it. She always allowed time for play, circulating between our favorite activities. "Duck, duck, duck, duck" and screaming "GOOSE" as my feet kicked into high speed, barely escaping the hand reaching out to tag me. Red Rover was another all-time favorite for the small group of kids, stair-stepped in age. A mix of school friends and cousins filled the churchyard.

Ms. Leona expected us to be able to recite our Bible verses on demand from memory. She would tease us with short verses, only to torture us with longer ones. The twenty-third Psalm would undoubtedly be my demise. Afraid she might banish me from her class if I didn't master it, I practiced for a week until Sunday rolled around again. Confident, I recited the passage. I had mastered it, and to this day, I can recite it from memory as if Ms. Leona were here with me. Her kind smile and soft hug were always an indication that she was proud and pleased.

Amanda, my older sister and only sibling, and I never thought about what we would do after church. Mom already packed our change of clothes. Every Sunday after church, our routine was precisely the same. We would hop back in the car and drive a quarter of a mile to our grandparents' house. Granny Ruth would have lunch already prepped and ready to be finished. Muscle memory kicked in as Amanda and I gathered plates, utensils, and napkins to set the table. That was our Sunday lunch responsibility. A responsibility we held almost every Sunday for over thirty years in our grandparents' house after church on Sunday. Daddy and Granddaddy Carl would seek refuge in the living room to catch up on their crops and discuss repairs that needed to be done around the house or barn as a new week came into focus.

Our lunch bounty was dished and placed on the table as everyone took their unspoken assigned seats. Granddaddy Carl was at the head of the table, with my daddy sitting directly across from him at the other end, engaged in a healthy debate on who was actually at the head of the table.

My sister and I were on one side of the table, and Granny Ruth and Mom were on the other side. Granny routinely cooked one of my all-time childhood favorites: a big pot of pinto beans, hand-cut fried potatoes, cornbread, and fresh picks from her garden. The smell of pinto beans still takes me back to that table all these years later. This was our Sunday routine. The consistency of family around the kitchen table, with conversation filling the room. Every Sunday, my family and I sat around my grandmother's table. A continuation of the recipe her mother, Mamie, had taught her throughout her childhood.

Sunday afternoons were leisurely, with nothing on the agenda after church and lunch. Mom would take her afternoon nap. Daddy would relax on the couch, watching TV, or go outside. Weather permitting, I would be outside, caught up in some pretend world.

As a kid, it seemed so strange that a creek would be named Dry. I've passed by that creek hundreds of times, and I've never seen it completely dry. Each passing season, the creek maintained the proper water threshold, even when reduced to puddles only deep enough to incubate the summer tadpoles. Other times, the creek would rise. Winter storms and spring showers coaxed the water from the safety of its own bank, creeping across the field bottom. Sometimes the water from Dry Creek would be brave enough to cross the road. Travelers slowed their pace but remained confident in successfully navigating the parts of Dry Creek that had now swallowed the asphalt underneath.

The floodwaters never seemed to faze my daddy. Watching him navigate the flooded road only elevated him more into hero status in my eyes. He was fearless as he drove slowly through the Dry Creek water. Dry Creek, such an odd name for a creek that never seemed to run dry, I would ponder in the back seat, buckled with a seat belt. It's as if the creek were somehow tied to the greater universe, with each season rising and falling by nature. The creek was following a recipe all its own.

Spring brought the creek to life. Water from spring showers flowed freely and filled the deep fishing holes. My dad and I would crane our necks as we passed by on the way to church. Mt. Nebo Baptist Church stood beaming just over 100 yards away. We had moved out of Paint Rock Valley when I was in the second grade. Daddy's promotion at work required that he live within the limits of Madison County. Our Sunday trip to church changed directions. Instead of driving south from the north end of the Valley, we now moved down the winding road of Highway 65 North. Dad would turn the car off of Highway 72 and over the train tracks as he drove his family to church every Sunday of my childhood.

Dad took me wading in Dry Creek a few times, which brought me to another strange thought: wading in a dry creek. We would catch redeye bass, yet another peculiar name until I saw my first one. Then the name made perfect sense. These little red eyes were on prominent display, unique to this fish, which was endemic to the Coosa River system tributaries in Georgia and Alabama.

The first time I caught one, I studied it, but I needed help from Daddy to safely remove it from the hook and release it back into Dry Creek's water. When I finally got the hang of it, I tried to be as gentle as possible when removing the hook in preparation for releasing a strange-named fish back into a strange-named creek. We would wade Dry Creek all the way until the tributary opened up into the Paint Rock River. Walking back to our car parked on the side of the road, we could see our beautiful church ahead.

Although there is evidence that Mt. Nebo was founded in the mid-to-late 1840s, the Alabama Baptist Historical Society has no records to prove the exact date. Mt. Nebo was one of ten churches to form the Tennessee River Baptist Association in 1853. The church building that stands today was built in 1913. My family is part of a church with 158 members, a church I have attended my entire life, becoming a member at the age of thirteen.

All of my grandparents attended and were members of Mt. Nebo. Granddaddy Carl sat on the left in the second pew. Granny Ruth sat on the opposite side of the church, on the second row from the first pew. Granddaddy Carl had a spit cup under his pew. He had given up smoking, only to continue his nicotine addiction with tobacco chew or snuff, as he called it. And, of course, Granny Ruth had a switch under her pew. The church was a revered place, and she ensured that the children in the church understood how to behave. We kids understood what the switch was capable of inflicting if we were disrespectful in a revered place such as the church.

Mt. Nebo would become my sanctuary, a steady constant in my life as I too rose and fell with the seasons of life, just like Dry Creek. Mt. Nebo became the place of reflection, prayer, and balance. This place soothed my mind and helped balance my ambition and wanderlust. I accepted Jesus Christ into my heart at the young age of thirteen. I was a child of God, proof that I was comprehending the recipe.

I spent most of my childhood summers just up the road at Granddaddy Carl and Granny Ruth's house. I was feral, roaming all over the hillside, in lockstep with Granddaddy if he was home from work or the field. Otherwise, I would help Granny around the garden and house. Upon reflection, those days were some of my best days as a child. Breaking beans on the front porch or bottle feeding peewee calves, time with my grandparents was time I cherished.

Granddaddy Carl was a Deacon at Mt. Nebo, and he drove the church bus. I would ride shotgun as we picked up the elders, Ms. Lucille and Ms. Molly. We were often the second vehicle to arrive in the church's gravel parking lot on Sunday morning, a trait my granddaddy passed on to his son. Mom and Dad would already be in the sanctuary, consulting over the songbook, as Granddaddy and I assisted two elderly women to their spot on the pew.

The church represents my heart's home. The majority of my Sundays have been spent inside its walls. All four of my grandparents' funerals were held in this place. With each of them, the church house was filled, bursting with people standing around the perimeter, on the porch, and spilling onto the lawn. Each funeral was an indication of a life well-lived, a perfect recipe followed step by step.

It will be here that my parents will lie in state, and one day, I, too, will lie at the altar for those who love me most to bid farewell. It is here that I said "I do", my marriage lasting only ten short years. Divorce wasn't a word that I ever expected to use to describe myself; after all, I had been raised in a Southern Baptist church. But life surprises us. That's precisely the point. Even in our short marriage, my husband and I had two children, both boys, Major and Max.

Mt. Nebo would also be the place where I would meet a very special woman who would later fill an essential role in my life. Again, life surprises us. Priority number one was my relationship with God. I didn't question it; I could see and feel His impact on my life. My spiritual life was deeply personal and rarely on display. Occasionally, you might find me kneeling at the altar in prayer on Sunday mornings, but most of my time spent in conversation with God was spent in solitude.

I didn't pray traditional prayers or start each conversation with God as a prayer. More often, it was a conversation in my head that felt one-sided. Yet, if I were still long enough, I would see the signs of His ultimate presence, especially when it came to my family and hard work. There were two critical ingredients in the recipe I had been taught.

# Chapter 4

# Granddaughter

Throughout elementary, middle, and early high school, this would be my normal. All three of the men in my life were working to provide for their families. Age and health issues caught up to my Granddaddy Carl first. By the time I was driving, he had slowed down and was spending more time around his house. I knew I could usually find him in one of two places: the local store where he and his buddies sat around telling tall tales, or on his front porch, generally whittling a piece of wood until all that was left were wood shavings under his feet.

He lived an overly simple life. His family was the core of his being, with God first, followed closely by family. Beyond the people he loved most, he didn't have a care in the world. We still laugh at one of his favorite stories, retelling it in our own words now. It involved me and a public tantrum witnessed by what felt like everyone in the store.

When my small body morphed into a possessed figure, he tried to reason with the demons and failed. Scooping up my body from the floor and dodging the uncontrollable limbs, the lady at the checkout counter giggled as she acknowledged the special bond between a grandfather and his granddaughter, asking, "Is that your daughter?"

As my granddaddy told it, he responded with, "No, if she were mine, I would have already tanned her hide." Even a terrifying toddler could not shake this man. He had the wisdom to know that this, too, shall pass without the need for a spanking. My Granddaddy Carl never raised a hand or a switch to me. Corporal punishment was not in his nature. Large in stature, he was a gentle giant.

When Granddaddy died in 2015, he left a void in my life. He was a steady, larger-than-life figure for thirty-five years. It was the first and most devastating loss I had experienced in my adulthood. His death prompted me to get my very first tattoos.

Following in our daddy's footsteps, my sister and I sang in church often. Granddaddy Carl loved to hear me sing "His Eye Is on the Sparrow." He was a sparrow serving a higher being, and he would smile as I sang, "You did good, Catherine," calling me by my middle name.

On my left side, just below my left breast, are the words "His eye is on the sparrow" in black ink. Time has faded the ink to a cloudy, bluish-black. Preaching at his funeral, our Pastor shared a story about the headstone that would sit at my granddaddy's grave, marking his eternal resting place.

"There are two dates on your headstone," Brother Mark began. "Your birth date and your death date. In between those two dates is a dash, and the dash is the most important because it represents the life you lived." He concluded with, "Make the most of your dash. Live your dash. Live your dash for our Lord and Savior."

My second tattoo would be a thick, short line on the inside of my left ankle—a dash and a constant reminder to live mine for the glory of God. I didn't always follow that mantra, but even when my decisions didn't follow the gospel, my family loved me. Now, I was only left with memories of a man who was larger than life. I wasn't his child, a child he would have disciplined in that store the day I threw a fit; I was his grandchild, and he loved me, this I knew. What I didn't realize was that my tattoos would become more symbolic to me, and not just because they reminded me of my grandfather.

# Chapter 5

# Sister

Our bond is one that time could only forge, like water slowly carving out winding rivers until a masterpiece like the Grand Canyon is created. A sister, a childhood companion, and a built-in best friend. Naturally, my sister and I were polar opposites. She was the people-pleasing, non-combative, and sweet little girl, while I was the defiant, hardheaded, and challenging little "boy."

An early memory I have of our differences comes from the school bus. We still lived in the Valley, and the school bus was our regular transportation to and from Paint Rock Valley School, now a historic building with its welcoming rock exterior walls transformed into a communiversity in partnership with Alabama A&M University and the Jackson County Historical Association. The class of 2018 would be the final graduating class to walk across the stage in the old hardwood-floored gym.

On this particular bus ride, one of the boys had a sucker. A treat he had hidden away to enjoy on the ride home from school. No one expected what he would do after finishing his sugary treat. I didn't see him do it, but when I realized what had happened, I stood with my purse over my shoulder. I was a little girl, after all, and carried the accessories to prove it.

Exploding from my bus bench, I came to my sister's rescue, swinging my purse over my head. It was full of rocks because even though I was a little girl, I was my daddy's little "boy." When this boy finished his sucker, he had buried the stick in the back of my sister's long blonde hair. The sticky residue, activated by his spit, was now matted in her hair. I was livid. The only person who could terrorize my sister was me, and I communicated that fact with my protective action.

We lived in a small, tight-knit community. The bus driver knew who I was, and he knew my parents. That didn't matter; I could take my punishment. I didn't get in trouble for swinging my purse filled with rocks around my head in a threatening manner. No one was going to treat my sister like that. I had stood up for her. My parents understood the bond between sisters because they had the recipe and were teaching it to us.

My sister and I differed in our ambitions. She was determined to follow our mom's lead. She wanted to be a mother. I, on the other hand, was determined to follow our dad's lead. I wanted a career outside of the home. Amanda didn't go to college, but I did. She worked W-2 jobs until she landed a job in the procurement department at a familiar, highly regarded workplace.

After all, Dad had a successful career working for a municipality. Throughout our childhood, we both learned that a job with a government municipality was a means to a simple and good life. That was it, she would build her career by working in city government, just like our dad had done.

Amanda was always sick when we were little. The seasonal common cold seemed to metastasize in her body, leaving her in bed, unable to play, with strep throat. Year after year, the same cadence would continue. Maybe I was too mean to let the common cold germs attack my body with such force.

After she had my niece, Anna, incontinence became embarrassing, and she could not control the liquid dripping between her legs when she sneezed or even walked. I did my fair share of hazing, the only person authorized by blood to deliver jokes about incontinence to my sister. We would always laugh together because she knew I would have my own experiences with the embarrassing symptoms caused by age and the wear and tear of vaginal childbirth.

After consulting with her obstetrician, it was decided she would have surgery: a hysterectomy and a bladder tack all at once. The doctor explained the complications, like any procedure, there were potential risks. He assured her that this was a routine procedure, and she would recover just fine. She did.

Kidney stones also ran in our family, and my sister got the brunt of that physical ailment, too. She recovered from surgery just fine, only to recognize the familiar pain in her left side. She had a kidney stone, and it hurt badly. Arriving at the emergency room, she told the receptionist, "I have a kidney stone." Anyone who has ever experienced the pain of a particle the size of a grain of sand grinding in the ureter as it made its way to the bladder understands. After triage, they wheeled her back. A quick pregnancy test confirmed she could have some pain medicine before being taken back to imaging to determine the size and location of this painful grain of sand.

The imaging informed the doctor that this particular kidney stone was too big for her to pass using fluids alone. The emergency room doctor scheduled her to have a lithotripsy, another routine procedure commonly used to crush kidney stones that are too big to flush out with fluids. The shock waves were like a jackhammer pounding her kidney to crush the stone. No one could have foreseen the damage that procedure would do to her left kidney, not even the doctor who ordered it or the doctor who performed the procedure. They did what their training had prepared them to do: remove the kidney stone as safely as possible to relieve a young woman's agony. Risks were clearly and appropriately communicated to her by the medical professionals. When you are in that much pain, you take the risk.

# Chapter 6

# Liar

With surgery and a lithotripsy behind her, Amanda was feeling better. Most women experience significant improvement or are even cured of incontinence after a bladder tack or bladder sling surgery. Still, Amanda began having more frequent urinary tract issues: bladder infections, kidney infections, one after the other, just like the strep throat from her childhood.

Now in her mid-thirties, she was still always sick. Rather than missing school, she was missing work and spending days in bed, unable to tend to her duties as a wife and mother. After numerous doctor visits, no one had answers for her, and she began to think it was all in her head. No one believed the amount of pain she was in. No one understood why she was missing so many workdays. No one knew why she was taking antibiotics upon antibiotics due to an infection that wouldn't go away.

By now, her squeaky-clean personnel file, because she was a people pleaser, had a stack of doctors' excuses. It just didn't seem real. She had to be lying about her symptoms. No one could be this young, in this much pain, and missing this much work. She was a fraud who needed to be found out.

Finally, she was referred to a new urologist, a young doctor who was thorough in his investigation of her symptoms and complaints. He was meticulous in his investigation of her pain and infections. The mental and emotional toll of disbelief still wreaked havoc in her workplace. Then the new doctor discovered the source of all her urinary tract system problems.

The mesh that had been implanted to hold her bladder up and cure her of incontinence was defective, and it had grown into the healthy tissue of her bladder. To make matters worse, the lithotripsy used to rescue her from the pain of a kidney stone had significantly damaged her left kidney. Imaging revealed that her left kidney was much smaller than her right kidney and was only functioning at ten percent.

There was one problem left to figure out: the infection. She was always on antibiotics, and her new doctor found out why. Her left kidney and bladder were infected with methicillin-resistant Staphylococcus aureus (MRSA). A deadly infection that, if not treated immediately and aggressively, could kill my sister.

We now had all the clues to solve the mystery of why my sister was always so sick. She would have to have her left kidney removed and her bladder sling replaced. Another surgery, only this time, the complications explained to her wouldn't just be for acknowledgment. She didn't get better. Recovery from surgery did not come. By now, I had two little boys and a demanding career. I wasn't there to rescue my sister. She was hurting, and she was not getting better.

The MRSA was still wreaking havoc on her body. She was in and out of the hospital, missing more days of work, and littering her squeaky-clean personnel file with more doctors' excuses.

Still, on days when she didn't feel well enough, she continued to get up and go into her office to do her job well. No performance concerns, no explicit feedback that her performance was less than satisfactory. Amanda's colleagues and supervisors never told her she was not performing her duties and responsibilities. They only gave her praise and support, as anyone would expect when someone is sick and still shows up to work, despite the limitations of a body that barely allowed her to get out of bed. Amanda put in the hard work.

"We're placing you on paid administrative leave." Amanda's jaw dropped as her new boss stated this matter-of-factly. Amanda's new boss was an outsider who had recently relocated to Huntsville from Auburn, Alabama, to fill a director position left vacant when her long-time supervisor retired. This new leader did not have the historical awareness of my sister's medical crisis and how hard she had worked to keep things normal for her children, maintain a routine paycheck, and retain access to health insurance.

The new director, a people leader, continued to explain that Amanda had missed a significant amount of work. She had reason to believe that my sister had falsified doctors' excuses, which had tarnished her personal file. An investigation would need to be conducted, and Amanda was neither welcome in the office nor entitled to perform her duties until the investigation was complete.

My sister, the docile people pleaser, did as she was told. Her new boss instructed her to call each morning she was out on paid leave to check in. This was a trick to catch her out of compliance with the paid administrative leave demands and a cause for immediate termination with cause. Each morning for three entire months, Amanda made the call in a polite and respectful tone. Each passing workday, she sat at home on paid leave, while her colleagues were forced to pick up the slack for three months over an unproven, falsified doctor's excuse and a team of colleagues who knew her history but were silenced when they tried to come to her defense.

Over those three months, her colleagues and perceived friends slowly retaliated with harsh and critical comments. The care and support she had once received from them were eroded by this new leader, who was supposed to be trained and effective. This leader's command-and-control demeanor wasted taxpayer dollars. It bred hate and discontent among the very team she was hired to lead.

Hopeful that she would return to work soon, Amanda followed the instructions provided by the Human Resources Department. As the days passed, reality began to sink in: she would never be asked to return. After twenty years, five more years until she was eligible for retirement, she had been terminated for cause, all because she had been so sick for way too long for anyone to believe her. The doctor's excuses, piled in her now flawed personnel file, were seen as proof she had made it all up and had been telling lies about her medical condition.

My proverbial purse of rocks swung over my head as I encouraged her to fight, to use her voice, even if it meant she lost. She had to fight for herself this time. This was the sucker stick she had to remove. Amanda followed the grievance process outlined in the employee handbook, and she let her voice be heard. A twenty-year career was over. The grievance committee concluded she had falsified one doctor's note out of many: a note from the urologist who had arguably saved her life.

"We can no longer see you as a patient," the office receptionist informed her. During the investigation, someone from my
sister's place of employment had called the doctor's office to in-
form them of the suspected forgery. That accusation alone was
enough for the office to dismiss her, a defensive step to protect the business. Who could blame him? I would have done
the same if I were in this doctor's position. The litigious nature
of our society had evolved, and it was apparent on billboards
and television commercials. Lawyers were making money, as evidenced by the millions of dollars spent on advertising their services and promoting their victories. Lawyers and lawsuits had
their place, people needed protection, and the workplace was
often ripe with opportunity.

Not only was she devastated that she had lost her job, but
she was even more devastated to be called a liar. And now, she
didn't have a doctor for when a bladder or kidney issue flared
up. No one believed that she had been sick. No one believed her,
and she fell into a dark depression. My sister, my best friend,
was hurting, and I came to her rescue. I encouraged her to file a
claim with the EEOC. She did, and it was denied. By this time, I
was settled into executive leadership. Looking through the lens
of a Chief Executive Officer, I questioned my sister: "Did you
lie? Did you forge a doctor's excuse?" And she was confident in
her response, "NO!" And I believed her.

Having witnessed the revolving door of doctor's office visits,
it seemed far-fetched that she would lie about this. Surely
something, somewhere, had been lost in translation. Why would
a new manager, a trained leader, conjure up some bizarre story
with shallow evidence? As I walked through the scenario, I

landed on a more reasonable explanation for the mysterious forged doctor's excuse.

Doctors' offices were notorious for turnover. New nurses and office personnel were hired, only for them to leave, and the process of new people cycling in would start all over again. The person who had given Amanda the excuse, the excuse in question, no longer worked in the office and wasn't there to confirm or deny the evidence. All of the other excuses, some from this same office, had been validated.

Indeed, Amanda missed a significant number of workdays. As a leader, I could empathize with the new manager's perception that the productivity and value she was bringing to the team were lackluster. But even then, working in city government wasn't known for making people rich. Salaries were low, but the benefits package was flashy. Paid time off, sick leave, and excellent insurance benefits made the trade-off for a lower wage attractive. The benefits package was a key factor in recruiting and retaining talent.

Amanda exhausted her paid time and sick leave for several years in a row, often being gifted extra hours by her work colleagues because they, too, knew she was ill. Why would her colleagues be so kind, extend an olive branch, and then retract their support later? The human behavior didn't align with the recipe we had been taught. They didn't know the recipe, and that was the only explanation.

The work Amanda was doing in government procurement was never going to scar the earth. It was a W-2 job, a means to earn a living and lead a good life, as she had been taught. She had never received a poor performance evaluation. Her work had always been satisfactory. Now, I love my sister, and I've seen her get into trouble with my parents because of her mouth. But she's a people pleaser who loves people, never meeting a stranger, just like our daddy. I concluded that my sister did not deserve to be treated that way. I wanted to share this recipe with others so they, too, could learn about the critical ingredients of family, hard work, and faith in God.

"Chin up, sis," I encouraged her. "You fought and let your voice be heard. You stood firmly in your truth." Slowly, she regained her confidence and started applying for a new job. Her children were now in high school and getting ready to embark on their own adult lives. Amanda now had the time, space, and health to give more of her time and energy to her children. She, too, had been following the recipe given to us. Life had surprised her in ways no one had ever warned her about. But why had we not been warned? Didn't our great-grandparents, grandparents, and parents have these experiences so they could teach us how to navigate a cruel world, how to defend our truth, and how to hold firm to our beliefs?

Amanda's workplace experience was not unique; her medical issues may have been, but this type of behavior from managers and leaders happens in all workplaces. It was not my place to review the performance of a person I did not know or had never met. That responsibility fell on the shoulders of this manager's supervisor. As I write this story, I have confirmed that the manager in question still holds her leadership position, and the workplace and my sister's former colleagues continue to be under her influence.

My opinion was shaped by my experience and my sister's words. I hoped that this manager had gleaned the lessons, realizing that she had gaps in her leadership ability, especially when it came to helping an employee transition out of a job. I was thankful for the scenario because it helped me settle into deep thinking about how I would help transition an employee out should the need arise.

My sister's circumstances continued to reveal more and more gaps in the transition from individual contributor to manager or leader. To give her new manager, this outsider, the benefit of the doubt, I told myself she was doing her job, just not very well from my perspective.

I, too, had been a young manager and made mistakes when it came to leadership, people leadership. My transition from individual contributor to leader was messy, and I lacked the awareness and training required to successfully lead people, even if it meant they had to be led out of a job. Her manager could have taken a different path, one that was less dehumanizing. She could have chosen to lead with empathy, respect, and kindness instead of apathy, disrespect, and brutality. Had she been taught this barbaric leadership style? And if so, by whom?

Still another thought taunted me. It's tough to uncover the factual truth of some situations and scenarios. Human nature, the psychology of our brain, grounds us firmly in our own narrative and agenda. Sometimes, extreme measures are taken to protect our position, regardless of whether it is right or wrong. Amanda's manager wasn't a terrible person; she was just human.

My sister accepted a position with a school system that paid minimally. This left Amanda with time in the afternoon and evening for a part-time role. I suggested she speak to one of my colleagues about filling in as needed in my organization's customer support center. It was challenging to find and retain exceptional part-time customer support representatives, especially during the 3:00 p.m. to 6:00 p.m. evening hours. It would be temporary, but it would provide an opportunity to earn a little more money, and she would fulfill a meaningful part-time role at my company. Her pay was fifteen dollars an hour, the same as anyone else working in that role. She did not report to me, but rather to a director, and we set a firm boundary that we would not discuss work around the Sunday lunch table with family. Those conversations were reserved for much greater topics about the recipe we had been taught.

In the afternoons and evenings following her day job, she set up a home office and fielded phone calls and responded to emails as a temporary customer support representative. Amanda did her job well. When a full-time customer service representative (CSR) position opened up, she asked me if she should apply. After all, I was the CEO of the organization. I told her I would not be involved. As a leader, I understood the implications of nepotism. It is a common practice in the workplace for positions with hiring power to choose unqualified friends or family over qualified candidates. It was not my place, and I was not the hiring manager. As CEO and a leader, I trusted my team to make the best decisions for the team they managed. They were responsible for their key performance indicators and allocating resources to achieve them. I was firm, and Amanda navigated this on her own, never speaking of it or of work again outside of regular business conversations with my team, which focused on typical business challenges and opportunities.

Just as she had done when exploring the temporary job, my sister consulted with the hiring manager, who encouraged her to apply. After the interviews were complete, Amanda was offered the job. My sister didn't have to prove her worth to me. I knew her worth. She had to prove it to others. Amanda had to do the hard work herself. That's how we were taught. Daddy always told us that if we were in the right, things would work out as they were supposed to, implying that God was in control. He was much better than my sister and me at following and comprehending the recipe.

Now, my sister is happy, and her health has improved dramatically. Amanda has transitioned to a new career at another premier workplace, where she has an incredible leader who coaches and mentors her daily on the job. Our daddy was right, because he knew the recipe better than we did.

# Chapter 7

# Wife

Studying the mortgage refinance application, I hesitated at the relationship status. Slowly putting my pen down on the paper, I checked the box next to "divorced." It's a word I never expected to use to describe myself. It was embarrassing. The disappointment was paralyzing. I had committed the ultimate cardinal sin, declared by Southern Baptist doctrine and the direct word of God. Marriage was a sacred commitment between a man and a woman and God. Specifically, this act would land me smack in the middle of hell. I didn't talk about it with anyone.

On top of my personal disappointment was the weight of my parents' disappointment and the weight of my Granddaddy Carl's death. Our divorce would be final the same year Granddaddy Carl passed away. Still, we did not talk about it. My mom tried, but I shut her out, trying, on my own and certainly without God, to collect all the details of the chain of events and decisions that led to this point. I knew my fate. Eternity would be spent at the right hand of the devil and not my loving Savior, Jesus Christ. I would never see my Granddaddy Carl again. He would not know me in heavenly eternity. I was doomed, and like a rebellious teenager, I withdrew from God and family.

My relationship with God was over, and distance grew between me, my mom, my dad, and my sister. If I were going to hell, I might as well embrace a whole life of sin. I had punched my eternal ticket and cut back to only going to church when the boys were with me, thinking that raising my boys in church would somehow minimize my punishment. On a quest for something tangible to prove that I was successful and worthy, I sought titles and salaries instead. My marriage was over, but I still had my career, and it was taking off. I was there for the wild and energizing ride that would take me all the way to the top in just a few short years. After all, hard work was a part of the recipe, and I didn't think it mattered if I added more of it to my version. The other two ingredients had been minimized anyway.

Later in my career, I would be reminded of the decision I had made to end my marriage, leaving my children to be shuttled back and forth week after week. During small talk with a new colleague in my new job, he mentioned he was going to visit his dad at the beach. This was my first job back in the paid workforce following my first pause, which will be explained later in the book. I politely asked questions to keep the conversation going. "My parents divorced when I was a kid," he informed me. As he continued, his following statement would pierce my heart. "My parents ruined my childhood," he said. "I hated going back and forth."

My mind immediately went to my boys and their childhood. My pursuit of a career and my decision to end a marriage had certainly ruined it. The four of us—my ex-husband, our two boys, and I—had adjusted to this co-parenting, two-home situation, and we were doing well, I thought.

They would pack up on Sunday afternoon to be driven to one of their homes, where they would spend a week, only to pack up on the following Sunday to go back to their other home. Week after week, this was the delicate dance. Jason and I were trying to keep things as normal as possible, just as my Great-Aunt Gail had done for Great-Uncle Carl when Grandma Mamie passed away. But our situation was very different from their situation. Grandma Mamie wasn't divorced. She and my Grand-daddy Joe were married for over fifty years before he passed away. The boys would not be under one roof in the steady presence of both parents, and this realization broke my heart.

Our divorce didn't come with shouting matches or arguments over money. We didn't use our words as passive-aggressive knives to cut the other person down. Our marriage ended with little fanfare and little emotion; it simply came to an end. I knew Jason loved me, and I loved him. And I knew, together, we had messed up the recipe. We've now been divorced for as long as we were married. We excel at co-parenting. Redemption for our sin or redemption for the recipe, I'm not sure.

When Jason and I began planning for a baby, we never discussed my being a stay-at-home mom. I wanted a career, just like my dad, and my boys had two grandmothers who were more than eager to take on the role of caregiver. Collectively, my mom and mother-in-law, Brenda, curated a schedule that would give them both equal access to their precious grandchildren. Furthermore, the boys' grandfathers were also equally involved in the child-rearing of the grandchildren. My daddy took on the name Big Daddy with great pride. My father-in-law, Gary, would become one of my boys' best friends, their Papa. That's what I wanted. I wanted my children to have the experience I had as a child—time with their grandparents, which allowed me to pursue my career outside the home.

After all, at the time, I still had all of my grandparents, the boys' great-grandparents, and my relationships with them were some of the most cherished in my life. I could focus on my career, knowing my children were being nurtured by the very people who raised their father and me. With our shortcomings, Jason and I were good people. Our parents had done a good job, even though we sometimes messed up the recipe.

As I doubled down, I was sure to put in the hard work in the office, and I began traveling more and more. Gone for days at a time, our marriage was neglected in the process. When I was home, I made up for lost time away from my boys, not my husband. By the time Jason announced he was moving out, there was nothing left to save. Our marriage was over.

Being the man he was, he called to tell me that when I got home from a work trip, his things would be gone. To avoid causing alarm, he wanted me to be aware. Jason didn't want to disrupt the boys; therefore, I would keep the house. The house, our house, meant stability for our two boys. We would work through the specifics at a later time. But for now, the best thing was for him to move out. Our divorce would be finalized, and we would establish a new routine.

We never argued. We never even raised our voices to one another. We accepted our fate and placed the boys at the center of our individual worlds. Our marriage may have failed, but as parents, failure was not an option. Both of our families rallied around us, all focused on the boys. Divorce was complicated when children weren't involved. The division of a unified life, vowed until death do us part. Add children into the mix, and things could get messy. The mess never came. We agreed to joint custody, Sunday to Sunday. We would both have equal time with our children and do our absolute best to keep things as normal for them as possible. The boys' family would be within arm's reach should they need the comfort and advice of a trusted adult.

The distance between my mom and me was closing, and she became my most trusted advisor, my escape when I needed to vent or complain. Never overstepping with too much opinion, she would redirect her focus to my boys. I'm not sure if Jason did the same with his mother, but we never confronted one another if we disagreed on the facts of this new life or how the other was choosing to live it.

When we did talk, the conversation was about the boys and nothing else. We were sure to keep each other informed with details on a need-to-know basis. Parenting topics included who would buy school supplies, how we would split certain expenses, and what to do if either of the boys was sick. Our roles were no longer that of husband and wife, but of mother and father.

I can and will speak to Jason's paternal qualities. He's an extraordinary father. Our boys are a beautiful mix of our characteristics, both physically and personality-wise. I will always love Jason in a way that I will never love another human. As the father of my children, he is my life partner, even if we couldn't make our life together work. Sure, I'll never vent my frustrations about his less-than-desirable qualities in front of our boys. He, in return, gave me the same respectful consideration. Our dirty laundry was not the concern of our children. After all, I couldn't help but think that my need for achievement, my intense focus on building a career and climbing the corporate ladder, made up the majority of the dirty pile of memories.

I had followed the recipe, or so I thought: family, hard work, and faith in God. It wasn't supposed to be this way. Somehow, somewhere, I had screwed up the ingredients. The failure of our marriage was surely due to my misinterpretation of the recipe that had been handed down to me from my great-grandparents, grandparents, and parents. An important step had been missed somewhere along the way.

Speaking for only myself, the butterfly effect of my decisions was something that I could not easily wrap my mind around, unsure of the damage or improvements the decision to divorce would have on all of us, especially our boys. As time passed, I found myself pondering whether I would be fortunate enough to experience various forms of love throughout my lifetime. Jason and I were high school sweethearts, and he was my best friend. Proposing on New Year's Eve, surrounded by our friend group at the time, it was an easy yes.

Jason would be a great father, and I wanted to have my children with him. Not fully understanding what "unequally yoked" had meant, I had grown up hearing it in church and reading about it in the Bible. Neither of us could see around the corner to know what lay just ahead. A life surprise was waiting for me after the divorce. This surprise would have me longing for the strong embrace of a man who intimately knew my curves and the scars that would soon tattoo my body. These new tattoos would not be black ink, but rather a pinkish tone to match my skin tone.

Even with the challenges that came with a young marriage, we battled through. It would take me years to process and eventually discard one hurtful and devastating reality: this may not have been forever love, or the forever love that I had envisioned for my life. Given my nature, the "boy" of my childhood, my grit and toughness carried me through our ten-year marriage. I buried the emotions that had bruised me so profoundly. Emotions that only I could process. Hard work that only I could do. And it took me longer than I care to admit to forgive. To forgive myself.

I was lonely. I felt alone in my marriage, and it was not Jason's fault. The blame was mine to carry alone. Over eight years, the buried emotions lay dormant until my career filled the void. The specific details remain cryptic, like a social media post. As the reader, you are given the freedom to inject your own narrative and story as you continue to read mine.

The gift of perspective came only through time and lived experiences. Another nugget of wisdom helped me process what had transpired throughout our ten-year marriage. We were both young, busy with the routine of young love and babies. I didn't feel depressed, and postpartum depression never came up in conversation. I was sure I didn't have postpartum depression. However, as I reflect on my behavior and the way I felt during those brief years, it now makes sense. The responsibilities, including daily tasks as a wife, mother, and budding executive leader, piled up faster than I could process them appropriately. I didn't have the lived experience to draw from. This was a new world, different from anything I had ever experienced in my life. I had hit a ceiling in my own emotional and mental house.

If I worked harder, everything would be okay. The hard work from the recipe was the answer. There was no blame to assign to any other individual involved, including myself. Jason and I had failed to keep our marriage together because we lacked the awareness that patience was key to just about any recipe. We didn't give ourselves time and space to collect the fruits of our labor. The fruits of our young love would have come in due time.

Ten years after our divorce, my love for Jason had evolved. The love shared in our short marriage was beautiful, carefree, and ultimately unable to overcome my intrinsic desire for success and achievement. We were too young, and the wisdom of age and experience eluded us. But it was love. We had just mixed the wrong amount of key ingredients at the wrong time, resulting in a recipe with a bitter taste.

Together, we created two humans whom we both love unconditionally, our boys. Our divorce made room for a very special person to come into all of our lives, someone none of us knew we needed. Had it not been for the divorce, the four of us might not have had the opportunity to feel the impact of her love.

I want my boys to know that I am proud of how their dad and I navigated our divorce. Establishing a healthy co-parenting relationship requires considerable effort. Still, we did so responsibly and respectfully with the two of them at the center of our individual worlds.

The "my parents ruined my life" comment from a new colleague would come full circle as Major and I stood in our kitchen talking. The topic was a hard one. I wanted to know how he felt about divorce and being shuffled between two homes now that he was sixteen and driving. Continuing our conversation, he said, "Divorce was annoying, and I don't like going back and forth." I had never been taught how to respond to a statement like this. As I carefully prepared my response, choosing my words wisely, I encouraged him by saying, "Hunny, we can talk about this. You, your dad, and I can sit down together and talk through this to come up with a solution that gives you the ability to live your life the way you would like to. We could adjust the co-parenting schedule, or you could choose to designate one home as the primary residence."

A hard realization came over me as Major and I talked in the kitchen that day. He was a sophomore in high school, now sixteen—the exact age my Uncle Carl wasn't supposed to surpass due to his medical condition, which had been present from birth and forced on him by no one. Here was my handsome and quietly confident son, using his voice to speak his truth.

The following words I would speak to him had to be crafted with greater caution than the previous statement I had made. "Major, you are sixteen, and you only have two more years of high school remaining until you will be eighteen and free to make your own decisions without the careful guidance of your dad and me," I said calmly without emotion. Taking a deep breath and preparing to finish what I had to say, Major interjected as he looked at me and smiled, "I can do this for two more years."

Major had given me an escape route; he allowed me to keep the emotion tucked away and hidden from sight. The brutal thoughts rolling around in my head were questions I had asked myself in silence. What if he chose his dad's house as his primary residence? My time with him was already cut in half due to my decision to divorce his dad, and I wanted as much time as possible with him before he graduated from high school and moved on into his adult life. The other question bubbled in silence. What would I do when my baby boy, the center of my world, left home to begin building his own adult life?

My sixteen-year-old son, forced into two homes, with his parents not under the same roof, had given me an escape route, so I didn't have to pour my heart onto the floor beneath us. Even in his youth, he possessed the wisdom to give deep thought to complex topics and to realize that time would pass quickly. Two years would be over before he knew it, and he didn't want to lose precious and limited time with either of his parents. That day in our kitchen, as our conversation filled the room, he proved to me, his mother, that he understood the recipe and its key ingredients: family, hard work, and faith in God.

The need-to-know topics and demeanor of our co-parenting situation dissipated over the years. Our conversations have grown in substance, mainly due to life's unexpected events. With each beautiful and dark life surprise that hit us, we unpacked personal and private details, preparing the other parent for a conversation just in case the boys sought the other's careful counsel. We were a unified team in raising two boys and wanted to make sure we set each other up for success in doing the job and doing it well. I was no longer a wife; I was a mother.

# Part II: Hard Work

The following chapters will take you, the reader, on a journey through the first half of my career—the first twenty years. Sifting through memories and old journal entries, there were so many stories to evaluate and select for the precious words in this book. My goal was to curate a recipe that combines fun, challenging, and unbelievable stories about hard work and what it can yield. Writing this section was healing, and it allowed me to document lessons learned and nuggets of wisdom acquired along the way.

# Chapter 8

# Apple Pie

Before launching my career, I attended the University of North Alabama in Florence, where I initially studied to become a journalist with a focus on television news reporting. In my "Introduction to Journalism" class, I realized something I had never thought about: my Southern accent, while endearing to some, would not translate well on the news. We had all seen enough news coverage of tornadoes in the South to know how country folk described a twister. I would not change my accent for a job. By now, I was used to people asking me to say "apple pie" or "donkey" in my southern twang. I was a Southern belle, and so it was settled: the degree I would pursue would be a Bachelor of Science in Communications with a focus on Public Relations.

The time to apply for a senior internship came fast. In my second-to-last semester at college, my advisor, Lisa Darnell Frazier, coached me through the process of researching and applying for available internships. Lisa would become a lifelong trusted advisor.

The internship research led me to inquire with organizations within industries that I found interesting: healthcare, sports management, and economic development. In fact, I did three internships, one in each of those industries. The compensation from all three experiences was simply experience. This was back in the early 2000s, when unpaid internships were pretty standard, and I didn't mind. Living with my parents, I worked a paid job in tandem with an unpaid internship.

Two days a week, I worked an unpaid marketing internship at Crestwood Medical Center. I fell in love with the work environment and the people in the department overseeing the internship program. It was here that I met my early career mentor, Lori Light.

Three days a week, I worked a paid job. Over three summers, when I returned home from college, I worked in an orthodontist's office. My sister, Amanda, helped me get the job. The unofficial title was "Model Picker," and the official title was "Laboratory Assistant." Summers were busy for orthodontic offices. An uptick in patients, mostly school-age children, required a perfectionist orthodontist to seek additional help in his laboratory, and hiring a college student was economical for his small business budget. My responsibility was to prepare and carefully manicure small plaster statues of an individual's teeth. Using a substance similar to the plaster of Paris, each little model would begin once a patient assistant placed two metal trays filled with a puffy pink molding cream on the counter in the lab. The trays were small enough to fit comfortably in a patient's mouth and had shallow crevices where the puffy pink cream hugged each tooth. All the tiny details of a patient's gum tissue were hidden, ready for the plaster to reveal its unique patterns.

The orthodontist taught me a lot about attention to detail and presentation. He desired teeth models completely free of imperfections. "The finished product needs to look just like the inside of someone's mouth, smooth and clean," he would coach. In solitude, I sat in the file room behind the laboratory where the plasters were made. In the uniform of scrubs, hand-me-downs from my sister, who had also worked in the same office years before, the models underwent their transformation from unmanicured plaster to polished, tiny statues.

Using the same tools that my teammates used when assisting the doctor in applying braces, I smoothed the rough edges left behind from the plaster mold. The office had a small team, with the orthodontist outnumbered by the young women, and we all wore the same color scrubs. Each day in the office, a different color of scrub was worn. The orthodontist would be in dress slacks, a long-sleeved button-up dress shirt, and a tie. He was professional and had the uniform to prove it.

I picked around plaster teeth just like a dental hygienist would do in a real mouth. With a small bowl of water and a dental tool, I would mix and place a tiny amount of plaster to fill in air bubbles left behind by the puffy pink molding substance used to capture the shape. I loved the work. It was artistic, and I was good at it. Once a masterpiece had been finished, I would place the bottom and top models of teeth in a container labeled with the patient's name, signaling to the team they were ready for their debut.

On a patient's second consultation visit, the orthodontist would know that a beautiful model of the patient's teeth was waiting for them as they were seated in the private consultation room. He had confidence that the piece of artwork was ready for him to present. Sometimes I could hear his excited voice as he began to describe the optimal plan that would give a particular patient a beautiful set of straight teeth.

Every patient would see a final mold of their teeth to compare with this model at the end of their treatment, when the braces would be removed. One minor task performed by a seasonal college student made the orthodontist look professional and prepared, which gave his patients confidence in his ability to do the job they were hiring him to do.

He thanked me for my work often and was always kind with his words. Here I was, a proud "model picker," earning gas and book money. He would undoubtedly have moments of intense emotion, but he was a great boss with high expectations for his team. Even the tiniest detail, such as an air bubble beside a tooth on a plaster statue that would only be visible to one patient, mattered to him. He wanted the patient experience to be perfect. Knowing his team was responsible for most of the customer-facing responsibilities, he treated them exceptionally well. This was my first experience in the paid workforce, and it was a great experience.

On the days I worked as an unpaid intern, my uniform transformed from scrubs to dress clothes and high heels. My direct supervisor, Jaclyn Robinson, treated me with the same respect and kindness as the orthodontist. Because we were close in age, I learned a great deal from Jaclyn about marketing, physician relations, and public relations. Translating the ideology and theory learned in college courses, Jaclyn taught me how to apply them. She was a great teacher.

Furthermore, she was helping me prepare for the launch of my career. It's a scary and unpredictable reality that almost every college graduate faces: landing a job. Not just any job, but a job that makes the investment in college worth it—a good-paying job within your field of study. Jaclyn was also faithful in her spiritual life and spoke freely about her relationship with God.

When my internship came to an end, Jaclyn and I stayed in touch well into my last semester at college. I spent considerable time researching job opportunities. When I came across a chance to work at a large orthopedic physician's office in Huntsville, one I was familiar with due to my internship at Crestwood, I sent it to her for feedback. "Sonia, I was offered that job. My role at Crestwood will be vacant in a few weeks." She was my early career champion who gave me the courage and helped me shape my voice for this significant step in my career—landing my first dream job.

As Jaclyn advanced in her career, I was just getting started. I got the job at Crestwood, the role she had once held, and the role I had interned under. What piqued my interest, though, was how this young woman navigated upward mobility so early in her career. What was her secret? She was polished, professional, and excellent at her craft, and I wanted to be just like her. Our professional relationship evolved as we became peers in the workplace, and our friendship took root.

For eight years, I enjoyed an incredible work experience and environment. Lori Light, my boss, was a larger-than-life professional woman whom I admired and respected greatly. She was my work mom. Lori cultivated a small yet high-performing team of four individuals, including herself. She led by example and carefully coached her team to do their jobs and do them very well.

If we were under the pressure of a high-stakes project, she was our calm and steady voice guiding us along as we each fulfilled our assigned responsibilities. We were each assigned a hospital department to provide marketing and public relations support as each department worked to reach its independent goals. Each person on our team was given an equal opportunity to lead a project that Lori felt aligned with our strengths, knowing that together, our team would fill in the gaps. Lori was grooming us for our next move in our young careers. She had the wisdom to know that the growth and development of subordinates was a key role of a great manager and leader.

To this day, I'm not sure why my colleague, Veronica Carter, was assigned to lead the public relations project promoting colon cancer awareness. Veronica's newly assigned project—one championed by the clinical manager overseeing the hospital's special procedures department, which involved colonoscopy and endoscopy procedures—provided us with plenty to laugh about as we all jumped in and followed her lead in implementing a plan she had curated. Together, we put all the pieces of the plan in place until the big day arrived. The project Veronica was leading involved a giant replica of the human colon. Housed under a tent in the hospital's parking lot, we stood in awe of what we had accomplished as a team: a giant colon appropriately named CoCo the Colossal Colon. CoCo the Colossal Colon became a media sensation in the early 2000s after Katie Couric, former anchor on NBC's *Today Show*, highlighted the exhibit during one of her news stories following the death of her first husband.

Our small but mighty team supported and encouraged one another, and we all prayed for each other. This job came with an entry-level salary and an introduction to the business world. Veronica, now a lifelong friend, did a phenomenal job bringing colon cancer awareness to our community in a big and bold way. She brought in a giant colon with informational exhibits of each colon disease, including cancer. CoCo the Colossal Colon allowed visitors to crawl through an oversized model of the human colon that measured forty feet long and four feet tall to see colon diseases such as Crohn's disease, diverticulosis, and cancerous and non-cancerous polyps.

Our team's collective goal was to increase awareness and utilization of a lifesaving procedure, as measured by the number of colonoscopies our hospital performed on an annual basis. With Veronica leading the effort, our team accomplished the goal. Veronica had been supported and encouraged, even if a few jokes were made. Led by a supportive and encouraging woman, mother, and badass professional, we thrived as young professionals. It would be Lori who piqued my interest in leadership. Jaclyn wasn't the only professional woman I aspired to be like; I also wanted to be like Lori.

With the encouragement of two mentors and friends, I submitted my application to the University of North Alabama's online Executive MBA program and was accepted. Six years after completing my undergraduate work, and with a new baby at home, I was back in school. Only this time, it wouldn't be Communications or Public Relations that I would study, but Business.

My time at Crestwood exposed me to business operations specific to the healthcare industry, including hospitals. At one point, I considered pursuing a Master's Degree in Healthcare Administration. Instead, I returned to school to pursue a Master's

of Business Administration. Taking advantage of the tuition re-
imbursement program, my current employer helped cover the
cost of this next step in my higher education.

Some of the online classes were less challenging than others.
Statistics kicked my ass as I repeated a mantra I had often heard,
"Cs earn degrees." I would earn my MBA with a GPA in the 3s,
the exact number not easily found in the files of my memories.
Over time, specific data points lose their luster. My GPA was of
no concern to me, my current employer, or a potential new employer. In my experience, I have developed the ability to articulate the value I could bring to the table, should I deem it time
to take the next step in my career. I loved my job at Crestwood,
and I especially enjoyed working with and for Lori. If I were to
leave, it would have to be for a position in a workplace I highly
regard—one that would provide me with upward mobility into
executive leadership.

# Chapter 9

# Upward

Interest in leadership began well before I was settled into my career. Involved in high school sports, I also served as the President of the Class of 1999 at Madison County High School and as the President of the Anchor Club. Fast forward to my early career, and I was eager to volunteer my time with the North Alabama Chapter of the Public Relations Council of Alabama (PRCA), the Rotaract Club of Huntsville, and Leadership Greater Huntsville.

Community relations was a key responsibility in my role at Crestwood, and I was encouraged to volunteer in our community. Lori managed her own docket of community relations and volunteer work. Through volunteer work, I expanded my professional and personal network. I met so many like-minded young professionals, and a small group of them would become instrumental in my career and life. A handful would become lifelong friends. It was as if God were handpicking people and placing them directly in my path with perfect timing.

Talking on the phone with a young lady I had become fast friends with, she mentioned a job opportunity. "It's perfect for you, Sonia. You should apply," she said. Intrigued, I knew the Chief Executive Officer at this particular company. We had volunteered together, and his company was well-regarded in our community. The phone rang. I really didn't expect him to answer. When he did, we had a short conversation. Agreeing to meet at his office, portfolio in hand, to discuss the Director of Marketing position, I was prepared to showcase the incredible work from my tenure at Crestwood. In just a few short weeks, I would be sitting in a new office space, meeting my new team. It was April 2011 when I leaped into my second dream job.

Honestly, I don't know if the deadly tornadoes that tore through North Alabama that April foreshadowed a new season of life—a season of turmoil and destruction. But I jumped into this new job and doubled down on my career. I was following a recipe that required a lot of hard work, and my efforts continued to pay off.

Quickly rising through the ranks, I quietly kept my impostor syndrome off-stage. "Off-stage" was a term I learned in a training session at Walt Disney World. For a short time in college, I worked as a custodial hostess at Walt Disney World in Orlando, Florida. While attending UNA as an undergraduate, I enrolled in the program. It was a fascinating experience, but it was cut short due to my anxiety following the terrorist attacks on September 11, 2001.

Sharing student housing with five roommates, I had slept in that morning because I wasn't scheduled to work. The ring of the phone woke me up. It was my mom. She broke the news, and I bolted for the living room to turn on the TV. My roommates, who were home, joined me as we sat on the couch, speechless. Unbeknownst to me, two of my roommates were calmly ushering guests out of the Disney parks. Walt Disney World was evacuating—something that rarely, if ever, happened in "the happiest place on Earth." Our country was under attack.

The next day, I reported for my shift at Magic Kingdom, mentally flipping a coin to decide whether I would be assigned to restroom duty, pan-and-broom duty, or garbage duty. Standing at the time clock, the cleaning crew was instructed to report to the meeting room before proceeding to the park. Our manager proceeded to coach us on what to do if we spotted an unattended bag or a suspicious package in the park. Anthrax was also a concern.

In 2001, Disney Parks used powdered soap in all of its restrooms. It was an interesting substance. Pumping the release valve under the soap dispenser, a small amount of powder residue would fall into your palm. Water would activate the powder, and it would become a soapy, bubbly, refreshing gel. Just one day after the deadliest terrorist attack on U.S. soil, this powder became a threat to paranoid park guests.

Our manager proceeded to educate us on anthrax and what we should do if there were a threat. I wanted to raise my hand and kindly say, "Excuse me, I'm just a college kid. I'm just a custodial hostess in the happiest place on Earth. I'm not a bomb or anthrax expert, and I'm not sure I can do this. I clean toilets because I don't like seeing a dirty public restroom."

Regarding dirty public restrooms, when on restroom duty at Disney, I had only two restroom locations to tend to, a standard assigned number due to the extremely high expectations. Every thirty minutes, the expectation was that both restrooms would be cleaned, only to start the thirty-minute cycle over again. Clean restrooms weren't only an expectation of our manager, but also a specific expectation of park guests. Custodial hostesses were expected to keep the restrooms spotless at all times. I would never be thanked so much for a job well done. Park guest after park guest, as sweaty, tired moms exited the restroom, would almost always say "thank you" as they passed by me.

Only on this day had I been thrown into a bomb squad and covert ops. I read the body language of my teammates and knew I wasn't the only one who thought this wasn't what we had signed up for. Yet, we remained silent. Upstairs in the park, I obsessively scoped the crowd. All the bags looked suspicious. Relief would fall over me when I saw a frantic dad running up to snatch a forgotten bag, a suspiciously unattended one. To a custodial hostess who had just received thirty minutes of bomb squad training, every bag was a threat, whether it was unattended or in someone's possession. Individuals with tiny, clear earpieces would suddenly appear outside restrooms—another powdered soap anthrax scare that would leave a restroom shut down for an investigation.

A few weeks passed, and I finally admitted to my parents that I wanted to come home. I had been homesick since I left, but I was managing with the help of my friends and family. My parents were planning to be in Orlando for my birthday in October. Could I hold on until then? On the phone with my mom, I could hear my dad in the background: "Tell her to come home."

My manager could sense something was wrong, too. He asked to speak with me, and I shared my concerns with him. He explained the options, and I ultimately decided to self-terminate and cut my Walt Disney World college program experience short. If my memory serves me correctly, the manager's name was Rosco—a fitting name for his jovial demeanor. Rosco was a good manager and kind with his words when I shared my reason for leaving. I needed to be in a place where I felt safest, at a time when the world didn't feel safe. I needed to be home. Living with my parents, I finished that semester of college working retail rather than cleaning toilets at Walt Disney World. At the turn of a new year, I returned to UNA's campus and resumed my role as a Resident Assistant for my final year of college.

In my new role, after eight wonderful years at Crestwood, I held various strategic responsibilities, including public relations, marketing, sales, business development, customer service, human resources, and back-office operations. In the fall of 2014, our team began building out our sales operations. From the ground up, we had an audacious goal of $15 million in new revenue in less than twelve months, and we accomplished that goal. The associated research and planning led us to build a sales pipeline and nurture sequence strategy to curate relationships with C-suite executives and organizational influencers through a value-based, consultative sales and marketing model.

Due to my relationship with our customers, I transitioned from sales and marketing into customer success to start up and lead a new customer support and account management center. Our visionary leader spearheaded the establishment of a customer support center in under forty-eight hours. He blew my mind with what he was able to accomplish with focus and lots of coffee. He had a vision for our support services, and rather than being a CEO, he jumped in as an individual contributor to bring that vision to life. The customer support team expanded to 24 agents, responsible for a total book of business valued at $40 million. Our primary goal was to retain customers and deliver exceptional support as measured by national key performance indicators.

Although my Walt Disney World work experience was cut short, I retained the disciplined customer service principles I was taught during training sessions. After all, the happiest place on Earth was created by the Cast Members, and we were all empowered and expected to deliver exceptional guest service.

As a custodial hostess, my job was essential. Cleanliness was our top priority, and we kept our designated areas in the park spotless. Beyond cleaning, we were expected to engage with guests. A custodian was on par with Mickey Mouse in terms of the overall guest experience. In fact, our custodial training primarily focused on customer service. We received very little training on how to clean. A skill I thought everyone had until my boys became teenagers. Parents, if you want your children to learn how to clean, teach them. Otherwise, ship them off to Disney, where I know for a fact they will be trained well.

# Chapter 10

# Service

As we designed our customer service operations, we applied the "Disney" principles I had learned. We wanted to be the Walt Disney World of customer support centers. We gathered our customer support team in the front vestibule for an all-hands meeting. The agenda held space for me to coach them on exceptional customer service. I wanted our team to be empowered to go above and beyond, just like my managers at Disney had empowered me.

The session began as if I were onstage at an improv show. Pretending to pan and broom, I demonstrated the responsibility of walking my designated area in the pretend world of Disney's Magic Kingdom. I was sweeping up pretend debris left behind by pretend park guests. Tomorrowland and Toontown were my two assigned areas in Magic Kingdom. Custodial hostesses were issued little brooms and matching pans. For an entire shift, I would meander from Space Mountain to the Speedway and into Toontown. Loop after loop, sweeping up the smallest piece of trash left by a happy guest. My feet were blistered from the number of steps taken in the hot Florida sun. It was unacceptable for any trash, regardless of its size, to be visible to Disney park guests.

As I continued my pretending, I began the heroic tale of a custodial hostess in the most magical place on the entire Earth. One particular day, I spotted a family, and they were so happy. Standing at the ice cream cart, the dad handed a Mickey Ears ice cream to his son. His face lit up. Adults have the awareness and childhood experience to know that the Florida heat is not kind to frozen treats. Adults know speed is the key, and you have to eat it fast to save it. The young son had not yet developed this awareness. Trying to savor each bite in between excited hand gestures and giggles, the ice cream was melting faster than his little mouth could lap up.

I wasn't close enough to know if it sizzled when its creamy shape hit the concrete. However, this family was in direct view, and I was witnessing a Disney vacation on its way to ruin. The tantrum that erupted from the child's small body left his parents scouring for a hiding place.

Witnessing this happy family at the happiest place on Earth quickly transform into an unhappy family now in hell, I imagined the dad thinking to himself, "Why did I waste the money on this trip?" The mom thinking, "Why did I believe we could really pull this off?" It was all lies. Disney was not the happiest place on Earth. The melted ice cream and screaming kid were all the evidence these parents needed to make up their minds.

I drew upon my custodial training and sprang into action. Like a superhero, my eyes surveyed the landscape, searching for the nearest ice cream cart. With no cape to adjust, I tucked my pan and broom under my arm and darted over. I had to save the day. It was what I had been trained to do.

As I approached the ice cream cart, my fellow cast member, whom I did not know and had never met, greeted me with a smile. "I need a Mickey Ears," I said, and she opened the insulated metal door of the ice cream cart she was responsible for. The cold air rose to meet the hot air, condensing into fog and then dissipating. Handing over the Mickey Ears ice cream, she turned to pick up a clipboard and added a tick mark. Each tick mark symbolized a job well done. After all, the ice cream cart cast member was responsible for the inventory left under her careful management, and we were in the happiest place on Earth. A place where Mickey Ears ice cream tick marks on an inventory sheet meant happy guests and recovered vacations. The two of us had been trained exactly the same way to provide an exceptional guest experience, even if it meant giving a Mickey Ears ice cream to a person who worked as a custodian.

As I approached the distressed family, I prepared myself to stoop down to the child's eye level, just as I had been trained to do. Our Disney trainers coached us to get on eye level with the park's littlest guests, as it was both a sign of respect and a way to communicate trust. I held out the ice cream. His little hands reached out cautiously. Then the smile came. Mom and Dad's shoulders relaxed. This was indeed the happiest place on Earth. A custodian earning ten dollars an hour and living in an apartment with five roommates had saved the day. More evidence that hard work paid off.

My superhero custodian story set the tone for the key takeaway of the coaching session with our team. Everyone was empowered to replace the melted ice cream. As customer service representatives, each phone call, email, or chat was an opportunity to help someone. It didn't require death-defying action. It didn't take a lot of money. It didn't take roller coasters, elaborate shows, or 3 o'clock parades. It didn't even require Mickey Mouse or princesses. Heroic customer service only required empathy. Our customer service team was empowered to take action. Their voice and chosen words were their Mickey Ears ice cream. Each satisfactory call and email resolved was marked with a tick, serving as an indication of a job well done.

As I stepped into the role of Vice President of Customer Success, I was offered equity as part of my overall compensation package. Honestly, I didn't know much about corporate structure or equity. Sure, it sounded cool, but holding equity in an organization wasn't a career goal I had established. Signing the equity agreement, I filed it away. The hard copy was placed in my personal safe at home. A digital copy was added to my personal personnel folder on my personal computer. That was equity—just a piece of paper to file away.

As a young manager, I was terrible. I had no clue how to develop and lead a team effectively. Although I delivered a compelling presentation on Mickey Ears, it did not necessarily translate into being a good people manager.

Every manager will have their first managerial role, and mistakes will be made. I reflect back on that experience through the lens of wisdom and realize that while it was painful, it was necessary. With each painful experience as a young people manager, and the piece of paper stating I was an owner in this organization, I continued to fumble around in the dark for the light switch. It would click on eventually. When he called me into his office, I was expecting our normal mentoring session. Not my boss, but another visionary leader in our organization. I will refer to him as "Mentor" in this book.

Mentor was a busy executive, but he managed to carve out time to mentor our entire leadership team. He held a handful of bi-weekly or monthly one-on-ones, with the cadence determined by the individual's needs. During this particular session, he explained distributions and how equity worked. We discussed different scenarios and decisions I could make. Armed with the general awareness of what an equity event meant, my jaw dropped when I reviewed my bank statement online. I chalk it up to dumb luck. This country girl, who had to work hard for her grades in school and who was often asked to say "apple pie" with her southern twang, had found herself in a very different world.

By now, my ex-husband and I had established a manageable co-parenting relationship. I always used the "single mom" title cautiously because he was an equal parenting partner and a great dad. I wasn't a "single" parent, but I was single and the head of my own household with two dependents. My ignorance of equity had provided financial stability. The majority of the cash from the equity event was invested in a plan for me. A small amount was tucked away in two Alabama 529 College-Counts plans. Another small amount was added to my growing emergency fund. It was the responsible thing to do. Eager to grow and advance my career, I rarely spent time doing anything other than working. I put the money away, out of sight and out of mind, and got back to work. Perhaps another foreshadowing of what was coming—a life surprise no one could have predicted would happen to me.

By now, my travel schedule had lightened. Still, when I wasn't on the road, I was at my desk in either my home office or our office at the workplace. Never thinking to ask for help, such as requesting an administrative assistant, I put in ten to twelve hours a day. My brain was young and could handle the workload, and I just thought that was what successful people did. They worked long, hard hours. After all, my dad and both of my grandfathers had taught me the value of hard work. I was following the recipe, and my family was proud of my early career success. Yet another example of hard work paying off. I was following the recipe perfectly.

# Chapter 11

# Alone

As usual, Granny Evelyn's house was packed, and food over-flowed from the kitchen counters onto the dining room table. It was Mother's Day in 2017, and our family had gathered for our traditional Mother's Day feast at my grandparents' house. The house was loud and full of people talking over each other. Granny and Granddaddy's children, grandchildren, and great-grandchildren were all gathered in their home to break bread, just as the recipe called for.

I let the cat out of the bag and quietly announced that I would be going in for a diagnostic mammogram and ultrasound the next day, right after Mother's Day. No cause for alarm. Lumps are found all the time, only to be declared benign. After all, my Granny Evelyn was a recent breast cancer survivor. What were the chances that one of her granddaughters would be diagnosed in her thirties and so soon after her experience? The odds were in my favor. It would be okay, and I would report back with an all-clear in less than twenty-four hours.

We enjoyed our lunch and time with family. Mom insisted on taking a picture. Granny Evelyn, Mom, Amanda, and I all smiled. Granddaddy's cow pasture in the background and the Paint Rock River flowing behind the tree line. It was Mother's

Day, and my mom loved taking pictures to commemorate any special occasion. I do love this characteristic about you, Mom! Thank you for taking all the photos, because it's so much fun to sit on the bed in my old bedroom at my childhood home and flip through memories with you. It's even sweeter when my niece, Anna, joins us.

The morning of my diagnostic mammogram and ultrasound, I woke up energized for a meeting I had with a potential new customer. The meeting was in the afternoon. I would head into town for my mammography appointment, meet up with a colleague, and then, together, we would close a meaningful deal with a high-profile customer.

Shuffling hangers as I browsed my full closet, I selected a favorite outfit: the Ann Taylor denim button-up blouse and the Ann Taylor rose pink skirt with a flowery layer of cotton lace. Perfect for a mammogram because the blouse was easy to get on and off. Strapping on nude-colored heels, out the door I went, calling my mom before I put the car in drive. "It's going to be nothing, Mom. There is no need for you to come with me." Besides, as soon as the imaging was complete, I would need to get to this crucial meeting. After all, my career was meaningful, and I wanted the satisfaction of hard work paying off. Mom complied with my request. I went alone to have my breasts inspected and get confirmation that this lump I could feel with my fingers was nothing. It felt like a little pinto bean just beneath the skin of my left breast.

Six years had come and gone since I had left my dream job at Crestwood Medical Center in March 2011; however, I still knew several of the technicians and the nurse manager at the Women's Center. We exchanged some small talk about our kids and what we had been up to. I was then ushered into the dressing room and handed a darling, flowery short gown. I loved this about Crestwood. Little details like a hospital gown that could double as a blouse, something normal in a place where no woman felt she belonged. I certainly didn't belong here in this hospital gown, even if it was cute.

The mammography technician had gotten the images she needed. "I'm going to consult with the radiologist to confirm we do not need any more angles." Out the mammography room door she went, and I sat alone replaying the key points I wanted to make in the critical afternoon meeting I had on my calendar. My career, which became my anchor after the divorce, was all I thought about.

"The images were good. Let's get you moved over to the ultrasound room," she instructed me. "By the way, after your ultrasound, the radiologist would like to speak with you." The physicians in our medical community, or at least those I had encountered, had an excellent bedside manner. I was sure the radiologist spoke to all mammography first-timers; it was good bedside manner.

In the ultrasound room, the tech and I chatted about our tattoos. "What does this one on your side mean?" I shared the story of how my Granddaddy Carl loved to hear me sing in church, as well as the message from his funeral about the "dash" on tombstones.

With the ultrasound complete, I sat back up on the exam table, adjusting the short, flowery gown. The radiologist walked in and introduced herself. This was the moment she would tell me that I was free to go. The lump was of no concern to her trained eye.

"It looks suspicious, and I've already consulted with your obstetrician. Expect a call from her this afternoon." Shocked, I sat silently looking at her. "Do you have any questions?" I sat in silence. I simply had no words to speak to this woman I had just met, who had delivered news I was not expecting.

Changing back into my denim button-up blouse, I felt the tears forming and fought them back. Mom should have been here. I was alone, processing devastating news. Another devastating reality following a disastrous divorce, and I immediately regretted my decision not to bring my mom with me. However, I still had a meeting to attend before I could fall apart.

The meeting attendees and my colleague knew nothing of my morning ordeal. Once the key points had been made, the decision-maker requested time to discuss the content with his extended team. My colleague and I walked out. As we were leaving, the decision-maker said, "I'll be in touch." I would never talk to him again. The deal would never close. A high-profile customer was lost all because of me, because I had more critical meetings on the horizon.

In the building's foyer, my colleague and I conducted a quick retrospective of our performance. Pleased, we were about to say our goodbyes when my phone lit up. It was my obstetrician's office. "Sorry, I have to take this. Bye." We shook hands. He said goodbye and walked out the door. Answering the phone, I found a nearby chair and sat down. "Hello, this is Sonia."

"Hi Sonia, I'm so sorry." Our conversation consisted of my questions and her answers. My OB-GYN recommended a breast surgeon, and I gave her the green light to schedule an appointment with him to determine the next step: a breast biopsy. There was still hope that this was nothing, and the biopsy, another routine medical procedure, would prove that this lump was not cancerous. Now I had to call my mom to break the news, and I knew what she was going to say.

"I should have gone with you," she said as she began to process the news. "You should not have been alone, Sonia." Firm in my belief that this was still nothing for us to be concerned about, I consoled my mother. "I'm fine, it's fine. I'll see the surgeon tomorrow." Continuing, she didn't need to say it, so I told her, "Yes, Mom, you are coming with me."

Just like that, my mom and I began to forge a more profound, sweeter connection. She was the court reporter in the trial between her daughter and breast cancer. With a notebook and pen in tow, she documented details from every doctor's appointment. Details that I would surely forget or not even comprehend in the first place. A new emotional and mental ceiling had been reached, and my brain struggled to keep all the details organized to make the best decision for me at the time with the information I had. My mom knew this. Her wisdom and understanding of the recipe had prepared her for this. The two of us just didn't expect the role reversal in our particular situation. Mom and I knew that it should be her processing all the details. It should be my mom trying to make the best decisions with the information she had at the time, and I should be the one by her side, scribing each and every detail explained by a medical professional.

I followed the breast surgeon's instructions. After the surgical biopsy, since a needle biopsy would risk puncturing the medical-grade balloon that was already present, the doctor instructed me to call his office the following day at three o'clock in the afternoon. Because the lump was too close to the current saline balloon in my left breast from a previous elective procedure (to be explained momentarily), a surgical biopsy was necessary for my particular situation.

The day after my biopsy, I rose as always and put on my professional uniform. Out the door I went to the office to get my work done, knowing I was planning to leave early. I wanted to be at home, off-stage, when I made the call to my surgeon's office, just in case the news was not what I had expected. This was not cancer, and the surgeon would deliver that news when I called his office. I just knew that at three o'clock on that particular Friday afternoon, this would all be behind me.

Now, at home, I returned from the office a few minutes early, and as instructed, when the clock hit three, I dialed the breast surgeon's office number. The nurse who answered the call, in a kind voice, said, "Hi, Ms. Robinson. Yes, the doctor is expecting your call. Is this a good number for him to reach you?" Confirming my cell phone number, I ended the call. Pacing my kitchen floor, my phone lit up with the surgeon's number. Answering, he said, "Sonia, we have a little cancer." As he shared the details of the biology of my cancer and the options to consider, my parents walked through the threshold of my front door. They were scheduled to pick my boys up from school, knowing I had an important phone call on my calendar for three o'clock that Friday afternoon.

By my demeanor, my parents knew instantly that the news was cancer. I didn't have to speak a word. The boys were always rowdy when they came in from school. Their way of shaking off the stillness of a school day. After a quick exchange, I escaped to my bedroom, and my mom followed me. Lying down on my bed, I curled up into a fetal position. My mom slid onto the bed next to me and wrapped her arms around me. Here we were, my mom and I spooning in my adult bed just like she had done in my childhood bed when my sister or I was sick. I would never be alone again, and my mom made sure of it. Together, we would put in the hard work to navigate breast cancer. Breast cancer, she knew, should be in her and not in her thirty-six-year-old daughter. My mom was heartbroken, and so was I.

# Chapter 12

# Surgery

Confident that surgery would be the cure, my surgeon gave me two options. Option one: clear the margins with a lumpectomy coupled with radiation. Option two: a double mastectomy. Both possibilities seemed extreme to this thirty-six-year-old divorced woman and mother of two young boys. Perhaps I should just clear the margins and do nothing else. That was an irresponsible decision, and I knew it. My boys were eight and four years old. Divorce was eighteen months in the rearview. I had to be aggressive. Surgery, a double mastectomy, was scheduled for June 26, 2017, only forty short days from the day I received confirmation of my breast cancer diagnosis.

I had to prepare my body and mind for recovery so I could return to my career and continue with my life. The days leading up to my surgery were hyper-focused, consisting of a mix of BodyPump, a full-body weight-resistant HIIT-style workout, three times a week, and running at least three miles three times a week. My plastic surgeon said I needed to be strong. Core strength would be essential. Drains would be inserted, and two tubes would protrude from the sides of both breasts. For up to two weeks, medical drains would be in place, and my upper body would be useless. All the hard work of sitting up, standing, or repositioning a heavy body would be the responsibility of my legs and core.

Chemotherapy was not part of the treatment plan. My medical team was confident that we had caught it early. Six to eight weeks following surgery, I would be back to normal, and all of this would be a distant memory. Once healed, the scars would be the only proof that breast cancer had attacked me in my thirties.

With my mom riding shotgun, we were off to another doctor's appointment. This particular appointment was the last visit with my breast surgeon before he would perform the double mastectomy. His nurse explained the numbing cream. "Apply it to your left nipple, making sure to cover the entire area. Place a piece of cling wrap over it. On the day of surgery, contrast will be injected around your nipple, and you will want that nipple to be good and numb, trust me."

Looking at myself in the mirror, breasts exposed, I applied the cream to my left breast. The breast where the palpable lump resided and where the cling wrap was used. Before putting on my shirt, I snapped a picture. Here I was, with cling wrap on my boob, and I couldn't help but laugh. The cling wrap I kept in my kitchen pantry, used to wrap up leftovers from dinner, was now being used to keep numbing cream in place on my left breast so that I wouldn't feel tiny needles entering my skin. The small needles that would inject dye into the sensitive skin just so a radiologist could confirm that no cancer cells had spread to my lymphatic system. This was my reality. A divorced, cancer patient, relying on her mom to be her caregiver rather than a husband. I didn't have strong, loving arms with the intimate familiarity of each curve to embrace me. Instead, I had the soft and gentle arms of a mother wrapped around me like a home-made quilt.

Leaving for the hospital on the day of surgery, I was surprised when both my parents showed up at my house together. A serious yet comical situation had distracted us for a week now.

Ronald, a registered two-thousand-pound four-year-old Black Angus bull, had escaped the pasture. My dad's cow pasture. He'd been spotted near a friend's house on Dug Hill Road, just over the hill from my parents' house in Brownsboro. Dad had taken his truck and cow trailer over, hoping to coax Ronald into the trailer without anyone getting hurt. It was a serious situation fraught with risk for drivers on the road, animal control personnel, and bystanders. My dad felt a sense of urgency, and he had friends there to help keep an eye on the large, wandering animal.

Several attempts had been made. Early in the morning on the day of surgery, the day of his thirty-six-year-old daughter's double mastectomy, my daddy was bound and determined that Ronald would be captured. He went back to his truck and trailer, parked at his friend's house on Dug Hill, hoping to end the standoff with his bull, Ronald. He took his gun and enough bullets, just in case.

Ronald was right where the truck and trailer sat in a clearing between trees. When Ronald saw my dad, they made eye contact, and the bull walked right into the trailer. He had been safely captured. The bull had saved his own life through his docile compliance after witnessing the farmer's determination. I'm not sure if Ronald the bull had the awareness or cranial horsepower to know that my daddy was prepared to shoot him to end this escapade. Nonetheless, Ronald was on his way to the cow sale. Daddy and I wouldn't make this cow sale trip together. Instead, Granddaddy Wayne and Granny Evelyn, two people who knew the life of a farmer better than my daddy, volunteered to drive Ronald to the cow sale, freeing up Daddy to be at the hospital with me. Ronald would never escape from my daddy's pasture again, and my grandparents made sure of it.

Mom, Dad, and I sat in the hospital waiting room, nervously chatting about Ronald's adventure, trying to keep our laughter low in consideration of the other patients and hospital staff. Other anxious patients and their family members.

Back in triage, we continued to keep the mood light. Humor has always been our family's go-to coping mechanism in times of challenge. With medical workers in and out of the room preparing me for surgery, one of them handed me a pair of khaki-colored hospital non-slip socks. If you've ever been in the hospital, you know how unappealing yet practical those hospital-issued non-slip socks can be for a person. I scoffed and turned down the khaki socks, reaching for the pink, non-slip socks Mom had brought for me. Fitting for the occasion, the day my breast tissue would be cut from my body in an attempt to remove breast cancer, I had pink, non-slip socks to wear.

Daddy picked up the pink socks before I could get my hands on them and stood at the foot of my hospital bed. He didn't look up. He didn't say a word. He put my pink, non-slip socks on my feet. Perhaps he was trying to manifest himself into the hospital bed to somehow take my place. That quiet moment was shared with my daddy. No words were spoken, just a father caring for his child in a way he had always done. He was putting my socks on. Only this time, shoes weren't required for my destination: a cold and sterile operating room.

It was time to go. We said our final "I love yous" and shared a final hug. Thankfully, I had met a friend, a lawyer, the week before to create my living will. Should something happen in the operating room, I had the document prepared. It was the responsible thing to do in my position. A thirty-six-year-old divorced woman, mother of two young boys, and a breast cancer victim. The living will, my living will, gave control of my tiny estate to my parents. The only verbal instruction I gave them was, "If something were to go wrong, please ensure my boys are taken care of." Surgery came with risks, and they had been appropriately explained to me by a professional medical team.

I lay back on the hospital bed and watched the fluorescent lights pass one after the other as a nurse wheeled me through the hospital corridor of Huntsville Hospital Women's & Children's. I had cancer. I was being wheeled into the operating room, where these rogue cells in my body would be removed and replaced with a new pair of medical-grade balloons to keep my body in the shape I was accustomed to. Two mounds on my chest, a physical indication that I was a woman.

Five years earlier, I had elected to have breast augmentation. After having my second son, I jumped on the trend of declaring that once breastfeeding had concluded, I would trade the saggy, small sacks for a brand new set. Electing to breastfeed my boys was a personal decision I made after learning so much about the benefits from the childbirth instructor Jason and I had during my pregnancy with Major. She was a beautiful Australian woman who had practiced attachment parenting with her own children and taught the practice to other young, soon-to-be mothers.

A recommendation made by this breastfeeding expert became my guide to the practice of attachment parenting. I purchased the book *The Attachment Parenting Book: A Commonsense Guide to Understanding and Nurturing Your Baby*, published in 2001 by authors William Sears, M.D., and Martha Sears, R.N.. The benefits of the nutritious milk my body would create, paired with intimate skin-to-skin contact with my baby, would serve my babies well. It was the responsible thing to do as a mother.

Breastfeeding was a magical experience for me, and both of my boys took to my breasts with ease and familiarity. It was also challenging work. Layer in a high-demand career on top of it, and the challenge of pumping, storing, and freezing enough liquid to sustain my babies for a year seemed impossible. I stopped breastfeeding three months after the birth of both my boys.

With Major, I had the opportunity to take an extended maternity leave. My career was at a place where I could leave my work responsibilities comfortably in the hands of my colleagues at Crestwood. After Max was born, I took a shorter maternity leave, as my career at a new workplace was in a more demanding phase, requiring me to return to the office sooner.

I was happy to get back to work. Part of my responsibilities involved attending conferences, and a conference was coming up right as I would be returning to the office with milk bags attached to my chest wall. My team didn't pressure me to attend the conference. In fact, I was the one who agreed to go. My team knew I had a new baby at home, and they would not even consider me for the position otherwise, because my colleagues respected my current situation as a professional woman. A colleague had already been selected and would take my place. The day before she was to depart and drive to Birmingham, Alabama, to set up our company booth for the conference, she fell ill with pneumonia. She was so sick that she didn't have the strength to get out of bed, let alone drive two hours and attend a two-day conference. Volunteering to take her place, I said, "I'll go. After all, I could use two nights in a hotel room alone." My new baby refused to sleep. It was as if Max knew his mother and father desperately wanted sleep, and he aimed to take that longing from us each and every night.

Jason and I were struggling as young, sleep-deprived parents. Our mothers were both happy to stand in and love on their new grandson as I represented my company at a conference. Still breastfeeding at this time, I made a plan. It would be okay to supplement with formula for two days if the frozen milk supply ran out. I took my high-powered breast pump with me so I could pump and maintain a healthy milk supply while away from my baby, packing all the accessories to pump, package, and safely store the collected liquid for transport back home to my baby. The baby who refused to sleep at the same time his mom and dad sought the benefits of sleep.

For two nights, I got eight hours of sleep. It was heavenly. And for two days, I tried to find a private space at a conference with hundreds of people around to pump my engorged breasts. After a couple of hours of working at our conference table, the group dispersed for lunch, and I took a break. Trying to find a private space, I was left to pump while sitting on a toilet in a public restroom at a convention center.

The relief of the breast pump drawing milk from my breasts, even if I was in a bathroom stall in a public restroom, was much needed, and I didn't mind. Sitting alone on the toilet, I chuckled to myself, knowing that if I hadn't placed the round cotton pad with a thin layer of plastic backing inside my bra, the front of my shirt would have shown round, wet spots on full display as I greeted conference guests. An embarrassing situation had been avoided.

To be clear, I did pump and dump that precious harvest of milk my incredible body had worked so hard to produce to provide nutrition to my baby. Of course, I pumped and dumped because I was pumping my breast milk on a toilet in a public restroom. I set a reminder on my phone, as if I needed one, so I wouldn't forget to sanitize the breast pump when I returned to my hotel room that same evening. The hotel room that had given me what I longed for: rest. Rest after the hard work my body was putting in to care for and feed another human, my baby boy. Even if Max had his own sleep pattern and preferences, I loved that little boy. I wanted to do everything in my power as his mother to provide the best nutrition for his growing body and brain.

As I was being wheeled into a sterile operating room on the day of my double mastectomy, I was thankful for the choice I had made to have breast augmentation surgery years prior. Saline, medical-grade balloons already filled two mounds on my chest. Once the breast surgeon was finished with the mastectomy, the plan was for the plastic surgeon to follow right behind and complete the reconstruction. One surgery, and I would be done. Even better, I wouldn't have to go through the painful process of spacers to expand my chest wall to make room for the balloons. One surgery, no chemotherapy, and I would be back to living an everyday life with my career intact. I wouldn't miss many days, and my colleagues were incredibly understanding, respecting my need to rest and recover.

"Doctor, I don't care what you have to do. Please get those balloons in there, even if you have to punch them in." I did not want to have any more surgeries, and my plastic surgeon was confident the reconstruction would go well. He was prepared with not one but two sets of new saline, medical-grade balloons, just in case his math and measurements were off a little.

The surgery was over. The two mounds on my chest proved that my plastic surgeon was successful in meeting my demand. Cancer was behind me. Entering my hospital room, my breast surgeon's smile met mine. His smile served as confirmation. A sweet perfume circulated through the air from all the flowers decorating my hospital room. Each flower stood at attention as if confetti would shoot from its petals. Listening intently, still a little fuzzy from the anesthesia of surgery, I focused on his mouth to make sure I heard him correctly. The mood quickly shifted, and the flowers withdrew. There would be no confetti. The pathology report declared this was not over.

# Chapter 13

# Poison

I couldn't shake the need to comfort her. She was my mother, and she was hurting. The roles we played were backward, and she knew it. It should have been her in the hospital bed and me in the chair holding her hand. It wasn't supposed to be this way. The cancer had spread to my lymph nodes. Recovering from a double mastectomy now meant processing news that none of us had expected.

Chemotherapy was now a recommendation, and I had another big decision to make as a divorced mom of two young boys with a career that was taking off. At my age and in my position, I should have been on an *Eat, Pray, Love* adventure like Elizabeth Gilbert. Instead, I was alone, trying to decide whether or not I should elect to poison my body rather than learn Italian with a handsome Italian man.

Hopeful that the drains would be ready to come out sooner, Mom loaded me into her car for transport to my first post-operative appointment with my plastic surgeon. "Looks like we have one drain that can come out." Once the doctor's assessment was complete, the nurse began preparing the materials she would need to remove the drain. This was a good sign. The healing process was textbook.

Naive about how the nurse was going to get this tube out of my body, she moved closer to me. "Take a deep breath in. NOW EXHALE!" I didn't black out, and the pain of this tube ripping and tearing to escape my body did not render me speechless. I yelled "SHIIIIIIIIIIT!" It was over no sooner than it had begun. I apologized for the expletive. The nurse assured me that they had heard and seen much worse. She scheduled me to return in a week so she could continue the torture and remove the other three drains. All of the drains would be gone by week two; it was textbook.

Four medical devices in total. These tubes wound down to bulbs where liquid would collect. Twice a day, unsure if I could strip them on my own, my mom and I would sit in my bathroom. Her gentle hands took one tube at a time. Between her thumb and index finger, she carefully coaxed the fluid slowly down the tube until it was deposited into a small, clear bulb. Once the tubes were clear of liquid drawn from my healing body, Mom would continue her work.

Unscrewing the bulbs, she poured the cloudy liquid into the bathroom sink and reattached the bulbs. The process took fifteen to twenty minutes total. My job was to tuck the bulbs back into the pockets of my post-surgical vest. It was a white tank top that fit more like a loose sports bra, with a zipper in the front because I could not lift my arms high enough to pull anything over my head. The vest was complete with two perfectly sized pockets where the bulbs would be housed until the next stripping session. Yet another tactical piece of clothing, much like the ugly, non-slip, hospital-issued khaki socks and the darling, flowery hospital robe.

With the bulbs placed in their individual homes, resting just below each breast, we would repeat the process before bedtime for two weeks. With each drain-stripping session, we would make a joke or reminisce about memories. Curious, my youngest son, Max, would sometimes observe this unusual exchange between his grandmother and his mother. He was only four at the time and could not wrap his little mind around the fact that he had to be so careful around mommy because she had boo-boos. My oldest son expressed little interest. After all, at the age of eight, he was now the man of the house. His mom was a weak and fragile figure recovering from a double mastectomy. It wasn't supposed to be this way.

Granny Evelyn didn't have to do any of this. Eighteen months before my diagnosis, Granny received her own diagnosis. The only difference was that she was in her late seventies, and I was in my mid-thirties. The biology of our tumors was the same: HER2 negative, BRCA1 & 2 negative, ER/PR positive. Translation: we did not have any genetic markers, no genetic indicators connecting the lineage of our cancer.

When I received my diagnosis, I didn't even mention my granny's breast cancer history. Cancer wasn't going to kill my Granny Evelyn, and her treatment plan consisted of just clearing the margins—no radiation or chemotherapy. She had surgery to remove the tumor and the surrounding tissue to rid her body of all the cancerous cells. She would be just fine, and she was. I knew Granny Evelyn would have happily taken my place, too. She was a strong woman, able to withstand life's surprises. Granny Evelyn had the wisdom and the recipe.

While chemotherapy had been discussed, it was not part of my original treatment plan. After surgery, the sentinel node shifted chemo from a "not necessary" to a "highly likely" status. Mom and I would add more doctor's appointments to our weekly operating rhythm. She sat scribing notes while I pondered another big decision: whether or not I should move forward with chemotherapy. I didn't have the appetite to eat. I didn't have love in my life from a man, and my self-love was at an all-time low. But I was sure praying a lot.

Up until now, the focus had been on building physical strength to expedite recovery. Life was waiting, and more importantly, my team was embarking on a transformative strategy for our workplace and the customers we served. Our leader's vision was contagious, and we were all in. As planned, I would take two full weeks off after the double mastectomy. Once my drains were removed and my upper body regained mobility, I would return to my computer and work from home until I was strong enough to resume my office work with my colleagues. It was not in my nature to miss work, and my team had observed my ability to lead and execute. I did my job well. The feedback I received regarding my performance was consistently positive, accompanied by encouraging words.

My personnel file was, and had always been, squeaky clean. Sure, I had periods of stress-induced tantrums leading up to and after my divorce, but my boss and colleagues were incredibly understanding, more than most. They helped me navigate that torturous period in my life with encouraging words and actions. Only now, I had doctors' excuses piling up just like my sister's personnel file. Both of us were weighed down by life surprises beyond our control, as well as the control of our boss and colleagues.

My sister and I both experienced a medical crisis, although in very different scenarios, that caused us to miss work and diminished our ability to perform at an extremely high level day in and day out. I just didn't know that the process of recovery, specifically the process of healing, and the time it required were seen as unacceptable. No one had ever told me that, and my boss and colleagues had never used their words or actions to make me feel like a failure for needing time to rest and recover from a life surprise.

I wasn't sure I could make the trip, but my boss indicated that he wanted me to attend our off-site strategic planning session. Once a year, he planned an off-site, usually in a city elsewhere, to get us out of our comfortable environment. Just forty-three days after surgery, I flew first class to Denver to meet up with my team. He had assigned us an insurmountable number of books to read in preparation for our off-site. My boss was an avid reader, and he expected his leadership team to read often as well. I loved that about him, his eagerness to teach us through his own disciplined actions and behaviors. Of course, we all complained about the number of books. After all, bosses were not immune to jabs from subordinates once outside of earshot.

In a futile attempt to comply, I skimmed through the books, searching for pages I could at least reference if called upon. Still, my mind was elsewhere. I was haunted by the question I had to answer sooner rather than later. After consulting with an oncologist, I was under a deadline to decide: would I have the courage to elect chemotherapy as part of my cancer treatment plan, or would I decline the poison?

The first night in Denver, I held on as long as I could before retiring to my room with the goodies I had purchased from a dispensary earlier in the day. A marijuana novice, and unsure of what to expect once I ate a gummy, I wanted to be off-stage and in the safety of my locked hotel room.

Lying in bed, the self-talk chatter continued. I knew we had to be aggressive. Alone in my hotel room, the one-sided conversation began, knowing ears much greater than mine were on the listening end. I didn't want to look back later in life with the regret of not doing everything in my power to reduce my risk of recurrence. God had given me this brain and filled it with knowledge to navigate life's surprises. But He also made it clear: I had to do the hard work and use what I'd been given productively and responsibly. I was young and strong. My boys were now nine and five years old. That night, I would decide to move forward with chemotherapy. It was the responsible thing to do in my situation.

When the gummy kicked in, my mind drifted back to my first experience with weed. Sitting on the balcony, taking in the view of the beach, one of my best girlfriends coached me through my very first inhale, a little over a year before this nightmare of breast cancer had begun. I laughed out loud as I recalled the experience.

The details of that story will not be shared in this book. I can't believe I just admitted to illegal drug use publicly in a book I was writing for my boys, and a book that my parents were likely to read.

To my parents, "Sorry, Mom and Dad! It is not my intent to disappoint you with my words and actions. I love you!"

And a message to my boys: "Your mom is human, too. Sometimes I don't make the best decision. As an adult, it is my responsibility to consider the risks and make decisions accordingly, being prepared to accept both the positive and the negative consequences. I love you most."

Finally, to my readers: the sum of one decision does not have the power to derail your life forever. You might fall, but once you are back on the ground with your feet underneath you, a new climb can begin. It's your choice whether that climb will be for good or for evil. We all share a responsibility to lead with empathy, respect, and kindness as we navigate the beautiful and dark surprises of our own lives, most of which are not caused by another human being, but by circumstances entirely out of our control. We must make the best decisions we can with the information we have at the time, in order to fulfill this human responsibility: to love.

That gummy in Denver was my second experience with marijuana. Only this time, I was no longer the high-performing executive woman needing a mental break. I was a cancer patient fueled by anxiety and insomnia. The sleep I experienced under the fog of a drug was just what I needed that night in Denver. "Cuff me and take me to jail," I thought. I was already in a prison barred by cancer.

Before heading back home, I took a direct flight from Denver to Pensacola, Florida, where I would rendezvous with three more of my best girlfriends, who were on standby to pick me up from the airport. As I arrived, I couldn't wait to tell Jeannette, Nicole, and Amy about my crime. We were all excited for a beach trip. A trip we had made together several times over the previous years.

It would be our last beach trip together before I returned home to share the news with my oncologist. The news that I would agree to chemotherapy.

I tucked the three remaining gummies from my legal purchase of marijuana-infused candy into my carry-on bag and hopped into a rideshare for the Denver International Airport. Nervous, I imagined that an airport police dog would sniff out my crime before I could even commit it. Transporting three little weed gummies across state lines and into a state where it was not legal would surely land me in a real prison.

Truth be told, prison almost sounded much better than what I was going home to. The gummies made it, undetected, and I enjoyed them while lying on the white sandy beaches of Alabama's beautiful Gulf Coast under a blue, sunny sky with my girlfriends by my side. They enjoyed fruity frozen beverages while I relaxed after indulging in a fruity-tasting weed gummy. Our day on the beach was filled with conversation and lots of laughter.

Arriving home from the combined off-site and girls' beach trip, my port was inserted into my body. On Friday, August 18, 2017, the anesthesiologist sent me to the twilight zone. When I woke up, I had a new incision. The incisions from my double mastectomy had healed nicely, and over time, they would fade and become less noticeable. This new incision would eventually become a new scar as well. A scar that sits proudly on the top of my right breast. Today, the dash tattoo on my chest has a healthy pinkish tone—another dash tattoo to remind me to live my life to the glory of God. God had marked me, and I belonged to Him. This I knew with more conviction than I had ever felt since accepting Him into my life at age thirteen.

The skin above my right breast lifted to show the outline of a small device that would transport poison from a plastic bag into my bloodstream. The first round of chemo was scheduled for August 24, 2017. Two days prior, my hairstylist, Jana Hill, who also served as my best friend, cut and lightened my hair to a brownish-blond color.

By September, my hair began to fall out. Visiting Jana one last time, we chose purple to match the company's brand and the career I loved so much. She dyed my hair purple and shaved a cute design in the back, where it was shorter, to achieve the elegant shape of a cute pixie. My hair faded to a beautiful lilac color just before it was gone.

Rather than have clumps of hair falling out, I elected to shave it and hosted a party to celebrate the occasion. Still, more hard work lay ahead. It was hard work for my career. It was hard work for my life. If I didn't undergo chemo, then my risk of recurrence and my risk of dying from this terrible disease would be elevated. I had to do everything in my power to beat it, even if that meant my focus, productivity, and work performance suffered in the process.

My colleagues had been supportive and encouraging. They had my back and knew that, given time, I would be back. I would go back to being the high-performing, high-achieving peer they were accustomed to working with. Along with our inclusive team, I helped achieve some significant goals in a remarkably short period. What I didn't know was that there was an unspoken deadline ahead. A deadline for when I would be expected to put my hard work back in the more appropriate place: my career and workplace. I'm not sure if others on my team were aware of this deadline. As for me, I was caught flat-footed on the day I learned about it.

# Chapter 14

# Chemobrain

The shave party wasn't for me. It was for my boys. They had managed through the surgery well, but these little boys did not want me to lose my hair. To them, that meant I was sick. A visible and public display of sickness. Up to this point, mommy just had booboos, and they had to be careful around her for a few short weeks. Losing my hair announced to the public that I was not okay. That their mommy was sick and that the type of sickness she had killed people. Even at their young age, they had the awareness to know that cancer was not a good thing.

My parents were taking care of me. Mom had moved in for the two weeks that the medical drains were present and dangling from the side of my body. Once the drains were removed and she knew I could maneuver my body safely on my own, she no longer stayed overnight. Arriving early in the morning, she would walk in the door to begin her motherly responsibilities. On the weeks when the boys were with me, Mom would get them ready for school, feed them breakfast, and transport them to school. While Jason was kind enough to extend their stay with him when I needed it, I didn't want to lose precious time with my boys, even if I didn't feel well or have the energy to care for them properly. My mom would be there to fill in the gaps. A husband wasn't something I had to fill in the gaps. I had my mom. She was my caregiver.

Returning from school drop-off, she would put in more work: cleaning my house, doing my laundry, fixing my breakfast and lunch, and mothering me. My dad was the handyman. He would arrive on demand if Mom reported a leaky faucet, a broken door handle, or something the boys had damaged that needed repair. With two young boys in the house, there was always something broken. Daddy, with his tools in hand, would go about his assignments. Mom would be sure to say "thank you" if I were asleep and unable to express my appreciation directly.

Just as my parents were doing, I had to take care of my boys. The care they needed wasn't just the regular motherly duties. They needed the same soft quilt my mother had draped over my shoulders. But I still needed the warm blanket, too. Drawing the boys closer, I made room for them. The quilt corners, which had been dragging on the floor, rested on the shoulders of all three of us. We were together in the safety of our family, my parents and their grandparents. We were together in the safety and comfort of their childhood home. A home I was fighting to keep by continuing to get up every day. On days my immune system was not compromised by chemotherapy, I went into the office and did my job to the best of my abilities at that time. Typically, for a week following treatment, my immune system would be weakened, and I elected to work from my home office rather than go into public spaces. I was careful to communicate with my boss and my team about why I was working from home but still available during those weeks, just as if I were in the office. Thankfully, I had a career that provided that level of flexibility.

The shave party I planned when my purple short hair faded to a beautiful lilac was for my boys. I planned and prepared every detail myself, just for them. I put in the hard work just for them. We had a bouncy house for the kids, donated by a friend (thank you, Gary!). A photo booth was available to capture the beautiful faces of all my friends and family in attendance. Our house was full. Friends and family spilled out into the back-yard after a champagne toast. Then, on my back porch, on the concrete my ex-husband had poured years before our marriage ended, the vibrating sound of hair clippers buzzed in my ear, and the joyful sound of kids playing in the background filled the air. The remaining hair on my head hit the hard surface. The juxtaposition was a blend of happiness and deep, deep sadness.

Just four rounds of chemotherapy. That was it. I felt lucky in comparison to others sitting in the treatment chairs around me in Clearview Cancer Institute's infusion room. My mom accom-panied me to each session. Once the bag of poison was empty, the clock started ticking. I would be energized for a few hours as the adrenaline and steroids moved through my body. Then, I would long for my bed and sleep for hours.

Mom made sure that I had a nutritious meal after each ses-sion. Water was essential to help my body move the poison through my system and flush the excess. Over the course of three months and four rounds, I gained two pounds. The visible side effects of chemo seemed to pass me by. Nausea never came. Fatigue came and went. No complications other than con-stipation. That was it. I was constipated. My family would joke, "You are full of shit."

"Nothing a little Metamucil couldn't fix," my mom suggested. Mixing the powdered fiber with orange juice became my new regular breakfast drink. Delicious! However, something just didn't seem right, and I couldn't put my finger on it. Yet, it was palpable, just like the breast lump had been. I could feel something, and it wasn't the Metamucil working inside my body. Something was unsettling in my mind. It was like an illusion, and I was wandering in the desert, alone.

At first, I thought it was just stress-induced forgetfulness. After all, I had a lot on my mind. Chemo was winding down, and I had a future to plan. The boys would ask about some minor thing, and my blank stare would prompt them to say, "Mom, we just talked about this," but my brain would not respond to the query.

Reminiscing about past adventures and activities with my family around the Sunday lunch table, I would pretend, contributing very little to the conversation, only to laugh at the right moment so as not to draw attention to myself. But I could not conjure up the memories. They eluded me, and it was frustrating.

The day I was prepared to share my concerns with my boss, we were already scheduled to have coffee together. One-on-one meetings were a common practice in our workplace. There was no cause for alarm; this was just a routine one-on-one. He wanted to catch up and see how I was doing. My body had tolerated chemotherapy just fine, and I was now settled into a new post-chemo, long-term treatment plan designed for the biology of my cancer: a daily pill, Tamoxifen, and a visit to my oncologist every three months for bloodwork. In reality, while my body had handled chemo just fine, my brain had not.

No one knew that I was shattering on the inside because I didn't tell anyone. I can't speak to my boss's perspective or what he was thinking. That's his perspective to share, and I would read his book if he were to write one. All I can confirm is that he validated what I suspected: my cognitive functioning had declined. I had chemobrain. It was not early-onset dementia. Chemobrain, also known as chemotherapy-related cognitive impairment (CICI) or cancer-related cognitive impairment, refers to cognitive difficulties experienced by some cancer patients during or after cancer treatment. These difficulties can include problems with memory, attention, concentration, and thinking speed.

During our coffee shop conversation, I couldn't blame him for the abrupt feedback. The coffee meeting my boss had scheduled wasn't just to check on me. It was to discuss my performance. It was a performance review disguised as a wellness check. Leading up to this meeting, I had volunteered to take on another research project. It was just another day at work. I was no stranger to leading projects or being a collaborative team member.

My work product had always been satisfactory, and at times, even exceptional. Some projects required tweaking or collaboration to build upon specific details, but I had never been scolded for delivering less than acceptable work. Yet this particular work product was labeled mediocre at best. Truth be told, it was terrible. Was he extending an olive branch, giving me another opportunity to prove myself? To prove my worth? To prove that I still belonged on his team? To confirm that I was the same Sonia who could deliver the same level of performance my colleagues had come to expect?

The blow came with such force that I was sure my body lay tattered on the ground, coffee shop bystanders left as witnesses. "We can no longer justify your salary and title," he said. The evidence behind his conclusion was the work product I had submitted. To make matters worse, he said my colleagues had also expressed concern. It wasn't just my boss; it was the people I had worked alongside for nearly eight years, people who had never before questioned my performance. Did my colleagues know the truth, too? That chemo was over, and so was my career.

The Lord surely had His hands around my mouth, keeping it closed, preventing me from screaming, "I QUIT!" and storming out the door. Instead, I told my boss that my long-term treatment plan had just begun, and I needed insurance. He agreed to give me a few days to process this news and assured me that it was not his intention to remove me from the team; together, we would find a solution. The solution was wrapped in the ugly package of a salary reduction and title demotion. After all, the company could no longer justify my salary and title given my poor performance. Appreciative of the gift of time, I knew more hard work lay ahead to figure out how I would keep a steady paycheck and insurance while searching for a new job. I couldn't quit. Not now.

The olive branch of a reduction in pay and a title demotion would buy me some time. For now, I had to come up with a plan. All my crisis planning experience had been gained from the businesses I worked for, and I had never applied it to a personal crisis. Especially not a personal crisis caused by cancer. The crisis communications I had been trained to create in college, along with my on-the-job experience, now had to be adapted for personal use. A crisis communications plan that I had created for this workplace following the deadly tornadoes in April 2011 would now serve as the framework that I would use to develop an exit plan. One that would allow me to quit my job responsibly.

As I processed the emotions and the brutal reality, I concluded that leaving this workplace would be career suicide. But I wasn't sure I could stay. Even still, the banter in my head continued with questions: "Who would hire someone who still bore the visible signs of sickness? Who would look at my recent health crisis and assume I would likely miss work?" My hair had just started to come back in. I was still working full-time and rarely missed a day, regardless of how I felt. That was how I was raised, and it was part of the recipe my grandfathers had taught me and my daddy had enforced with great discipline.

To make matters worse, if I didn't have income, the boys and I would have to move in with my parents. No income meant I couldn't afford a house on my own. The comment I heard in my early twenties resurfaced in my mind: "I would live in a house with dirt floors if it meant my family was there with me." The house would have to go on the market. The boys and I would have to pack up and move in with my parents. Their childhood home, the familiar, comfortable, steady home that Jason and I had agreed to keep for them after the divorce, would be gone. It would be another blow to my young boys.

Now, I love my parents, but I wasn't so sure we all needed to live under the same roof together. I needed a personalized crisis plan, so I set to work creating one.

After divorce and now cancer, I wasn't so sure the three of us could take another blow, at least not this soon. Losing their childhood home was not an option. Losing my job and career in the process was not an option. If I were forced out of my career, by cancer or by my boss, I knew my parents would welcome us under their roof. But I needed a plan that would prevent losing my house in the process. Just like Aunt Gail had done with Uncle Carl, keeping the boys' lives as stable as possible was a responsibility I had as their mother.

I confess that it was silly, in hindsight. It was ridiculous for me to think that I could do it. That I could continue working and productively contribute to our team. Anger and sadness faded as embarrassment set in. Cancer, this new character in my life, was stronger than me. Trying to denounce its presence, to rebuke its secret takeover, this was not about martyrdom; this was about motherhood. I wasn't voluntarily suffering. I wasn't brave like a lioness teaching her young how to hunt in the wild. This was survival. This was the human version of an isolated wildebeest fighting off a large predator to protect its young. Cancer was on the hunt, and its tactics of nausea, pain, and fatigue could not penetrate my defenses. So instead, to force me into submission, it attacked my brain.

The decline in my cognitive function had gone unnoticed. Slowly, it became more challenging to speak coherent sentences. The words were there, but my brain couldn't keep up with processing thoughts, connecting emotions, and forming coherent sentences. All of these once naturally occurring functions, processes my brain had performed with lightning speed, now lagged. "Early onset dementia" sat in the search bar, as if my computer were just as confused as I was. I couldn't help but think this was how my Uncle Carl had felt all his life: frustration with his cognitive ability, knowing he was different due to a medical condition. A medical condition he had zero control over. The recognizable signs of chemobrain came too late for me to save my career from demise.

I began to wonder if I had made a terrible mistake. In an aggressive attempt to keep my boys' lives as normal as possible, I had failed. They were left out in the open, unprotected, because their mom was weak. At this point, I had come too far to elect the Family Medical Leave Act (FMLA) benefit. My job was already in jeopardy. If I took FMLA, then the trick of eliminating my position or forcing me into an even lower salary and another title demotion would undoubtedly be the punishment cancer would bestow upon its combative victim.

What I needed was insurance, a routine paycheck, and normalcy. That's what my boys needed, too. My boys remained on my insurance following the divorce. During the weeks they were with me, they relied on my paycheck. Following the divorce and learning to live in two separate homes, normalcy was already on shaky ground.

All the feelings I had towards something so microscopic that it took electromagnetic radiation to even be seen by the human eye had to be muted. This was no time for emotion. Over the next few days, I thought about the money my parents had invested in my college education. They had worked hard to cover my tuition and provide me with spending money while I worked as a Resident Assistant, which helped offset my housing and meal plan costs. I thought about the time and money I had invested in going back to school for my Master's in Business Administration, only to add another year of studying to achieve my Accreditation in Public Relations.

I thought about my failed marriage and how I had been so focused on my career that I neglected a key relationship with the man I needed at this very moment. I thought about my boys and the decisions I had to make to ensure I would be their mom for many, many more years to come. Acceptance of this uncomfortable position didn't seem possible. Honestly, I had never felt this uncomfortable in my own skin.

The conversation with my boss at the coffee shop was over. Facing a salary cut and title demotion, my spirit felt as if it had levitated into the air, as though I had just taken my last breath. Still, I had to remind myself to breathe: "Breathe in...one, two, three, four. Out...one, two, three, four." Every eye in that coffee shop was on me, witnessing my career imploding into oblivion.

As that fatal coffee shop conversation came to an end, rather than shouting, "I QUIT," I stood and walked out the door. Around the corner on Jefferson Street in downtown Huntsville, just outside one of two downtown bars people my age would frequent, tears leaped from my eyes. I couldn't draw air in. I was having a panic attack, and with shaky hands, I called my mom.

"MOM," I cried in a hysterical plea for help, not even sure words were coming out of my mouth. After providing her with a synopsis of the meeting, I continued. "I can't quit. Not now." Fourteen years of investing in a career I loved, and the hard work represented in the long list of highlights and successes, felt wasted.

I lost my marriage. I couldn't lose my career, too. It was my life, and I wanted to give my boys a good life in their childhood home. It was how I would continue to keep health insurance. It was how I would continue to financially support my boys and myself. There was no other choice but to stay. Wiping my tears, I stood up straight and lifted my head. My mom's words, her comforting voice, grounded me. Then, I walked back to my office, where my colleagues—the very ones I had just been told were concerned about my performance and behavior—sat at their respective desks. No one knew about the conversation that had just transpired, and I never spoke a word of it to anyone.

When my boss and I met for a follow-up conversation to discuss my reduced salary and lower-level title, what we didn't discuss was my secret plan to defeat cancer and reclaim my career.

# Chapter 15

# Do Nothing

On the day I realized that I needed a crisis plan for my career and life, a former colleague came to mind. I had met her while working at Crestwood. She was a community volunteer who had retired from a decorated career in television news management.

The coffee mug was warm in the palms of my hand, and I hoped she wouldn't notice my unmanicured fingernails, bitten down to the quick from the high level of anxiety I was experiencing. Before we started our conversation, I glanced over my shoulder. My eyes were fixed on the table. It was the same table where, just a few short days earlier, I had sat as the realization that my career was over took hold. It was there that my disappointed boss informed me of my poor performance. It was where I almost blurted out, "I QUIT."

No longer needing a reminder to breathe, I broke the ice. "I need to quit my job," I said calmly. Linda's face was a mix of confusion and curiosity as I continued with the talking points I had prepared for this coffee conversation. She sat quietly and listened. Once I had made my case, she began with her thoughtful, probing questions. Then, she spoke two powerful words: "Do nothing." Two words spoken by a well-respected leader in our community. "For one year, do nothing." She continued to explain, and it all made sense. I would not quit and abandon my career. I would not leave and put my children in jeopardy of losing their childhood home. I would not stop, and I would not go without a paycheck or health insurance. I would slow down and continue to struggle for one entire year.

Linda advised that once that year was over, I would then be free to decide to leave the workplace if I still felt it was necessary. She believed that both my colleagues and I needed time. She equally believed that time would resolve my chemobrain. I would rebound into the high-performing professional that my boss, colleagues, and even I knew me to be. It was permission to slow down and do nothing. To avoid taking emotional actions, such as quitting a job without a backup plan. A backup plan that would guarantee income, health insurance, and normalcy for me and my boys.

With the wisdom only lived experiences could provide, my coffee guest continued to articulate her assessment of my current situation. She explained that everyone close to me was processing my cancer diagnosis in their own way, including my colleagues and boss. It wasn't fair to think this was only about me. Cancer affects everyone in your life, and it's an emotionally challenging experience. I realized I needed to be empathetic to the position I had put them all in, too.

Following her advice, I agreed to do nothing for one year. Over the next twelve months, I planned to be better prepared to make a decision. Now was not the time to make this life-altering decision. I would leave once I found a replacement job, rebuilt my emergency savings fund, and completely healed from chemobrain. I had one year to stand still and do nothing.

As Linda concluded her advice, she instructed me, "Do not volunteer for projects you are not ready for." She continued, knowing that I was single at the time, "Do not date. You have no room for distraction. Just do your job, and do it well." I committed myself to the discipline of doing nothing but hard work.

The self-talk became hostile. A salary cut and title demotion were what I deserved for my poor performance on a project that I had volunteered to take on. A pay cut and a new, lower-level title were my punishment. Cancer was not to blame. Chemobrain wasn't to blame. I was to blame, and so was my performance. I should have been stronger, more focused, more polished. My performance should have continued to be satisfactory, if not exceptional, as I battled through cancer treatment. As I fought to keep my boys' childhood home. Our home.

It was tough at first to go into the office every day with my new, lower-level title. Learning from my first boss, Lori, I was extremely discreet with the details that had led to my new title and role within the company. I told my colleagues it had all been my choice to take a step back and focus on my recovery. No one knew that I had help in making that decision, or at least they didn't hear it from me.

I felt like a baby calf I had witnessed from my childhood, learning how to walk on its new, wobbly legs now that it was no longer in the safe incubated womb of its mother. Slowly, week after week, and unknowingly to anyone else in the office, my legs became stronger. I settled into my new role, trying to make myself as small as I possibly could.

Occasionally, my big and bold personality would spill over, only to be met with a Slack message or comment reminding me to retreat back inside, where it was safe. I was thankful to have only been demoted, not realizing that my demotion had become someone else's wishful promotion.

The clock started ticking, and I secretly worked on my "do nothing for one year" crisis plan after hours in the safety of my home, alone. In twelve months, another deadline would arrive. This time, I would be prepared. Rather than shouting the words "I QUIT," I would be prepared to calmly say, "I resign," just as I had done at Disney after 9/11.

A little over six months had passed since our first difficult conversation, when my boss asked to meet again. Only this time, it wasn't over coffee. Reflecting on the level of performance from the previous months, I had no reason for concern. My performance hadn't come into question since I bombed the research project. With urgency in his voice, he explained the situation. "I need your help. Do you think you are ready?" It wasn't my performance this time; it was an opportunity to prove myself, to prove my worth, to prove cancer wrong. Linda's advice was still fresh in my mind. She had told me not to volunteer for any projects unless I was sure my performance could deliver and meet expectations. I replied to my boss, "Yes, I can do it," and I believed it.

As I navigated my role in human resources, the sting of the salary cut and title demotion had subsided. The majority of my team was focused on a strategic project, putting in considerable effort to meet the deadline. The deadline was upon us, and we were way behind. It was not the fault of our team; the timeline was aggressive. It was a deadline that everyone was aware of and one we were working together as a team to meet.

They worked away behind their computers, focused on completing the assignment to create the next iteration of our service delivery. I was charged with buying them some time. Side-by-side with my boss and another colleague, Joy Moore, we set up mission control in our boardroom, and for two weeks, we worked hard. Joy had been one of the very first individuals hired under my new role as Director of Human Resources, a step down from a Vice President title that came with a 10% reduction in my salary.

As I scrolled through the numerous applications in our applicant tracking system, Joy's resume caught my attention. On paper, she had the experience and had articulated that she had the skills we were looking for in a candidate. I coordinated every detail of her interview experience. Channeling my Disney training and the teachings of the orthodontist, I planned every detail to curate an excellent experience for a candidate we really wanted on our team. On the day of her in-person interview, I wore a cute new outfit I had purchased recently: army green, taper-legged, cargo-style dress slacks, and a navy-and-cream vertical striped blouse. To round out the look, I added a pop of color with orange-red kitten heels—a simple dash of spice. Not to mention that my hair was now growing back, and I was rocking the sexy Demi Moore look she debuted in *G.I. Jane*.

Joy and I immediately clicked, and she would become a dear friend in the office. What was even better was that this new badass woman on my team knew nothing of my transgressions or of the conversation I had with my boss that had led to a salary cut and title demotion. It was a fresh start with a new colleague, and we became fast friends.

She would tell me, "Sonia, you were the first person I met, and you just had a look about you. When I met you, I knew I wanted to work with you." After all, she didn't know my deep, dark past or how I had failed miserably to keep up the pace and performance during my cancer battle. She didn't know that I had something to prove to myself. She also didn't realize that I was under a personal deadline, and I only had five more months to go.

Now on an urgent assignment, this was my chance to prove to my boss, my colleagues, and myself that I was back on track. The high-performing professional was back. Joy, my boss, and I would leave the office around midnight, only to return at five a.m. We organized numerous spreadsheets, and there were innumerable numbers for my brain to process. But my brain was doing it. The veil of chemobrain had lifted, and I had been given the opportunity to prove it. I wanted to hug my boss's neck. I couldn't believe it. I didn't quit. He didn't fire me. He had given me space to heal. I also didn't ask for a bonus, a raise, or a new elevated title. I was happy with where I was in life and impressed that two professionals had come together after a difficult conversation, put a plan in place, and been patient with one another in the process. My boss was an incredible leader; he cast the vision for me to translate into an operational plan. We made a great team. My career was back on track.

While I sat in the boardroom night after night, my youngest son was embarking on a significant life transition into kindergarten. I had made sure to handle every precious detail, and my mom was helping me get all the pieces in place. He had a brand new first-day-of-school outfit and a new backpack neatly filled with school supplies. My baby was going to kindergarten.

As I continued to report to work every day and do my job well, I secretly planned for the day when I would resign. I would resign on my terms, not on cancer's terms. Over five months, from double mastectomy to the last round of chemo, I watched as my healthy emergency fund shrank. Seven thousand dollars in combined co-pays, medical supplies, and therapeutic massage fees were paid out of pocket. As I worked through my personal budget, I realized I needed to rebuild my emergency fund. I had to replace the $7,000 and contribute even more. My boys and I would need the safety net. We would need financial security.

Cancer was an unexpected threat to my budget. I had to right-size my own personal finances. Fortunately, this was at a time when minimalism was becoming mainstream. Not only did I need to claw back lifestyle creep, but I also needed to account for expense exposure. Financial discipline was complex for me, but I did stick to the emergency fund rule and tried to keep the credit card balances at a manageable level. That would be priority number one: financial health. Paycheck after paycheck, I tucked money away, and I continued to plan in secret.

Our team was nearing completion of the strategic project and preparing it for implementation. The next task assigned to me was one I was familiar with. It was another urgent assignment, and one in my wheelhouse: a "voice of the customer" tour. I had done it. After the first urgent assignment, I had proven myself worthy of my career after all. This assignment involved the key responsibilities of my former role, minus the title and salary that once came with it.

I was comfortable with our customers, having nurtured relationships with almost all of them during my tenure, until the dreadful demotion. No one else on the team had better relationships with our customers than I did. A colleague joined me, and we set off, touring the Southeast and visiting each customer one by one. It was invigorating. I was back. My career wasn't over. Maybe I should abandon my "do nothing for one year" plan. The salary cut and title demotion weren't retribution; they had been a safety net. Still, I never broached the subject when in conversation with my boss. We never discussed a bonus, a salary increase, or reinstating my old title, despite my rebound into the high-performing executive leader I had always been.

Fresh off the customer tour, I settled back into the human resources department. The job was done. My team had delivered, and our customers were happy. As I settled back into my HR duties, another candidate came highly recommended for an open Vice President position —a role I should have asked to interview for myself. But that request was never made. This individual would assume the responsibilities I once held as Vice President before my demotion, along with a slew of others that I had no experience with, such as business operations, which were far beyond my limited experience in Human Resources and customer service. Carefully preparing all the details for the candidate's interview, I was asked to participate, given my historical customer knowledge.

Sitting around the table in easy conversation, he answered our questions to our liking. He, I'll call him Sergeant here, was hired, and I would now report to him. At first, Sergeant was kind and curious. During our walking one-on-one meetings, he would inquire about our customers and my history with them. Eager to help and be useful, I openly shared my historical knowledge. This cadence continued, and time was running out. Only three months remained in my twelve-month plan. "But I can learn from him; he's mentoring me," I told myself. I should stay and learn more about business operations. Knowledge I both wanted and needed. This information would be necessary to help me advance my career once my one-year timeline expires. He, too, had been carefully placed in my path as someone I could learn from.

It was another routine weekly one-on-one with Sergeant. Our relationship had been productive, and I was learning a great deal from him. Expecting to discuss progress on current projects, this one-on-one started differently. It was my performance, again. But this time, it was a different gentleman, a new person who had not observed my terrible fall from grace, telling me I had failed, and he was concerned.

Sergeant informed me that a customer had complained, and the complaint was specifically about me. Not afraid of constructive criticism, and with skin made thicker over the last year thanks to cancer, I inquired, "Tell me more." Some points were valid, while others did not sit well with me; the little twinge in my stomach gave him away. Ending the conversation, he had one more thing to say. "You know you can leave." The implication was clear: he would gladly accept my resignation. He was proud of his performance, sitting chesty in his chair. I matched his confidence, but rather than engage, I remained docile, because that was the one thing I did know. But it was my secret to keep. If cancer or my previous boss hadn't forced me out, Sergeant certainly wasn't going to have the satisfaction.

As I exited the meeting room, where Sergeant extended a gracious invitation to resign, I sang to myself under my breath the lyrics from a P!nk song I was obsessed with. Interestingly, it was the same song I played in my head when I went skydiving earlier that year with my girlfriends, "I Am Here" by P!nk. The lyrics go, "I've already seen the bottom, so there's nothing to fear." P!nk, thank you so much for that song. You are an incredible artist. I'm equally impressed with your ability to navigate a professional world where you were told you weren't feminine enough and were too brazen to make it in the entertainment industry. Like my Great-Uncle Carl, music was my escape, too. Music helped me connect my thoughts to the corresponding emotions, enabling me to process them in a healthy manner.

I continued to ponder why he would invite me to self-terminate over a single infraction. My performance had not been addressed since my previous boss allowed me to prove myself to him and my colleagues. My performance was satisfactory. If there had been a problem with my performance, someone would have told me, and I would have been given the chance to correct my mistakes.

Seeking feedback from my colleague and friend, Joy, I asked her about the specific customer complaint that had been shared with me. She assured me that, while the customer's voice was indeed valid, it was not mine alone to carry. After all, we had collaborated on the solution we would present to this customer to resolve a problem they were experiencing. If our solution was not appropriate, did not meet their expectations, and they complained, then she should be reprimanded as well. She felt that something had been lost in translation and that we could recover from this slight.

People made honest mistakes in business, I was sure of it. These same people were given an opportunity through coaching and mentoring to self-correct. I was in human resources and had been studying best practices regarding performance reviews and the various types of individuals that comprised a team. In the books I was reading, I had learned that some human resource professionals establish a grading rubric.

It was a simple rubric. On a team, you had A players, B players, and C players. C players needed to be moved out of the organization, and the author carefully described humane and legal ways to do it. B players required coaching to help them further develop their knowledge, skills, and abilities. The author, again, provided tips and strategies. Lastly, A players were the ones you wanted to retain and grow.

After successfully completing two urgent assignments, I was surely back in the A-player category. At the very least, a B+ player. So, why hadn't I been offered coaching or mentoring by the new person I now reported to? I had three more months to prepare. Leaving the paid workforce was not the plan, but leaving this organization was expected to happen at the end of the year. If only I were brave enough to do it.

# Chapter 16

# Italy

Soon after my conversation with Sergeant, I hopped on an airplane at Huntsville International Airport and flew to Italy on a solo trip. This trip had been planned for over a year to commemorate the day I rang the bell, signifying that cancer was over and that I had been victorious on the battlefield. My own personal version of *Eat, Pray, Love*, although not as lengthy as Elizabeth Gilbert's quest for self, would involve spending seven days alone in Rome and Naples, savoring pasta and wine, and meandering through the streets.

I landed in Rome early on October 6, 2018. It was a Saturday. As I checked into the hotel I had booked for my first night, the Alimandi Vaticano Hotel in Rome, the line for tickets into Vatican City was already wrapped around the street corner. I had not proactively booked any excursions, choosing instead to avoid being tied to a schedule and to allow for spontaneous activities.

The hotel concierge was gracious as he informed me that my plan to tour the Vatican would not be possible without purchasing a ticket in advance. But he could not shake me. Polite and jovial, I made a request that put his concierge skills to the test. "Is there a restaurant nearby where I can grab some lunch? I'm starving." He made a recommendation, and his hand gestures made perfect sense as he mapped out the path I would need to take. As I thanked him, I added another request. "Can you secure me a private, English-speaking tour guide so I can have a personal experience touring the Vatican?"

The hotel concierge was flabbergasted by my insane request, especially after he had just told me that I needed to remove a Vatican tour from my itinerary. According to him, it was not going to happen.

I walked to the recommended lunch spot and enjoyed my very first plate of homemade Italian pasta during my trip, all by myself. During lunch, I Googled and searched for alternative excursions since the Vatican tour was out. Satisfied with a full belly and lifted spirits from a half-carafe of Italian wine, I slowly walked back to the hotel to freshen up before hitting the streets of Rome. As soon as I walked into the hotel, the concierge's face lit up. He couldn't believe he had managed to secure me a private, English-speaking tour guide. I had thirty minutes to get ready before the guide arrived to escort me across the street for a private tour of the Vatican. Both of our jaws dropped, and I tipped him well for a job well done.

What happened next left me in awe. I had actually pulled off a week-long *Eat, Pray, Love* adventure. When the tour guide arrived, I knew the money I had just spent would not be wasted. Here stood this tall, dark, and handsome Italian man—and he was all mine for the next three hours.

Get your mind out of the gutter. This was not a *Fifty Shades of Grey* sequel, although my mind did entertain the thought. As we walked, he talked. His dreamy accent had me in a trance, and for three hours, I floated alongside this sexy man. I don't remember anything he said about the historic art or the significance of the property we were touring. I didn't care.

After the tour, I purchased a souvenir book that provided specific details about the art and property that this man had spent hours telling me about. My head was so lost in paradise with the handsome Italian that I hadn't realized I had purchased the Italian version rather than the English one. The details of my tour continued to elude me.

The day after my date with the dreamy Italian man, I rose early, ready to start my day of adventure. Unsure what would be on the docket, I was greeted in the lobby by the hotel concierge, the same one who had pulled a rabbit out of his hat the day before. "Good morning! I'm trying to determine what I should do today. Do you have any suggestions?" I asked. His face lit up again as he informed me that on Sundays, the Pope gives his blessing in St. Peter's Square at Vatican City. After slipping him another tip for his kindness, I walked the short distance to St. Peter's Square, where thousands of people had gathered to receive the Pope's blessing.

As Pope Francis appeared at the window high above the square, the crowd fell silent. Even though there were thousands of people, you could hear a pin drop. In Latin, the Pope began to speak his blessing. When he prayed, everyone in the square prayed together, each in their own language. It was one of the most breathtaking experiences I had ever had. Here I was, on a celebratory solo trip to Italy following breast cancer, and I felt like the only person in that square being blessed by the Holy Father. And, I'm not even Catholic. I'm a Southern Baptist to my core.

Satisfied that I had enjoyed the sights of Vatican City, I grabbed my luggage, which the utilitarian hotel concierge had handled, requested a rideshare, and headed to my next hotel in the heart of Rome. Hotel Ralais Orso would be my home for two nights, providing me with quick access to all the sites of historic Rome, Italy.

With nothing on my agenda, I walked, deep in thought about my plan, poking holes in the SWOT (Strengths, Weaknesses, Opportunities, Threats) analysis I had completed as it all came together. The only weakness identified was whether I would be brave enough to resign from my position in two short months. Two threats still loomed, leaving my plan full of risk. I did not have a backup job that would provide a routine paycheck and access to health insurance. There was still more hard work to do. Hard work that only I could do to prepare for the day that I would accept Sergeant's invitation to tender my resignation.

On Tuesday, October 9, 2018, I departed Rome and headed for Naples by train. Arriving later in the evening, I checked into my hotel, Hotel San Francesco a Monte Napoli, which sat high on a hill overlooking the city and the Gulf of Naples. This hotel, a former monastery, was stunning. Making my way to the rooftop restaurant, I dined alone as I continued to work through my plan in my mind.

With my belly full of yet another pasta-filled plate, I took my refilled glass of wine in hand and prepared to retire to my room. At the table next to mine sat two women: one older and one younger. I thought, "Oh, how lovely, a mother-and-daughter duo. I wish I had brought my mom with me." We made eye contact and exchanged a warm hello, immediately recognizing each other's accents. They invited me to join them for a conversation.

They were visiting from Seattle, Washington. I shared that I was on a solo trip and that I lived in Huntsville, Alabama.

Confirming that they were a mother-daughter duo, they kindly asked what I had planned for the following day. "I think I'm going to take the train to Pompeii," I replied. I had not disclosed the purpose of my solo trip, careful to be discreet with personal information and not overshare with strangers I had just met in Naples, Italy. The mother's face lit up. "You should join us! We're going to Pompeii tomorrow, and I've already booked a private tour guide. He will be at our hotel at 8 a.m. Meet us in the lobby so you don't have to go alone. Oh, and I'll cover the cost of the tour guide if you cover the cost of the rideshare and train tickets to get there."

Her invitation sounded reasonable, and they appeared to be good people. I agreed to the terms of our arrangement and retired to my room, where I finished my glass of wine before drifting off to sleep like a baby.

The next morning, the day of the Pompeii tour, I rose early for coffee. When I met my new friends in the lobby of the hotel, I had no idea what I had just gotten myself into. The private tour guide was already giving his introductory speech when I approached. We introduced ourselves, and he explained his credentials. This tour guide was more than qualified to take us on a private tour of Pompeii because he was a modern-day Indiana Jones who had actually excavated parts of the historic site. I could not believe what my ears were hearing. The Pompeii tour was phenomenal and perfectly matched my experience in St. Peter's Square, where I received a blessing from Pope Francis, as well as my dreamy exchange with a private Italian tour guide in Vatican City.

One year after my fourth and final round of chemotherapy, I spent a week alone in Italy and met so many wonderful people. It was the trip of a lifetime, and I was thankful that I had invested in both the trip and the time I needed to do deep work. When I returned home, I was ready to resign my position and move on with my career, following the salary cut and title demotion.

Back home, my youngest son, Max, had been in kindergarten for three months, and it had been a tough three months for him. As he left the safety of his grandparents' care to enter an unfamiliar world, his behavior wasn't always perfect. My mom was our eyes and ears when it came to our family's well-being, always observing behavior. She was constantly monitoring me as well as my boys, searching for signs of distress and areas where she could apply her nurturing wisdom. The same went for my daddy and every other safe adult in Max's life, and in ours.

The caller from Max's school didn't provide specifics, only requesting that I come pick Max up immediately. Upon arrival, the Vice Principal shared details of what had transpired a few days earlier, explaining that another mother had expressed concerns. To protect the privacy of the children involved, I will not give specifics. After all, I was once the kid who swung a purse full of rocks over my head on the school bus in a threatening manner. I knew firsthand what elementary students were capable of if push came to shove. My little boy was struggling to adjust to this new life as a student, surrounded by all these new people. He was also struggling to process life under two separate roofs, and with a mom who had lost her hair during chemotherapy because she had cancer. And cancer kills.

It was October, and my time was running out. I had less than three months to secure a job, and now I needed a position that would allow me more time at home with my children. Max especially required me to be present, to help him navigate this significant life change for such a little human. Divorce, cancer, and now kindergarten, Max was communicating through his behavior that he was struggling, too. He didn't yet have the words or the awareness to express it effectively, which was typical for a child of his age.

With a new level of urgency, I changed the keywords of my job search from leadership positions to entry-level roles. They would be less demanding, allowing me to redirect my focus from my career to my boys. I consoled myself by thinking it would only be for a short time. "Take a W-2 job and focus on your boys," I told myself repeatedly. My career would have to wait.

By now, my emergency fund was healthy. I had the financial runway needed for a career transition, knowing I would likely be without a paycheck for a few weeks as I made the switch. I still didn't have a backup job, so I added a few more weeks of expenses to my transition budget. I had enough money saved to float me for six months. To avoid exhausting my funds, I planned not to take that much time. At most, it would be a month.

A month I could spend focused on my boys. Surely, I would be back in a job and receiving a routine paycheck within that time. I just had to have insurance to cover my long-term cancer treatment, which consisted of a daily pill and an injection every three months. This treatment was designed to reduce my risk of recurrence. It was my lifeline to more years with my boys.

Sitting on the exam table, my oncologist reviewed my blood work. Everything looked good. He was pleased with the treatment plan. As usual, he turned to me and asked how I was doing. "Doctor, I'm planning to leave my job. I need to take a step back, but I may have a short break in insurance coverage. Can we take that into consideration when scheduling my next appointment?" Our doctor-patient relationship had solidified over nineteen months. We spoke candidly about my life and how I was adjusting to this new long-term treatment plan. He knew how important my career was to me as well. He didn't give me any advice, only encouraging words. "Good for you."

What he said next reminded me of a key ingredient in the recipe my great-grandparents had set in motion for our family. Although my immediate family structure differed from theirs, with a divorce on my resume, our family was close and in a good place. No stranger to hard work, I had nailed that part of the recipe, too. My relationship with God was still estranged, yet He continued to guide and provide for me.

"Alabama has a Medicaid program for patients just like you." He knew the toils of cancer and what it did to the body and brain. I wasn't telling him anything he hadn't heard before, and he had access to resources for situations like mine. "I will send a referral to social services. Expect a call from a social worker to discuss the specifics." I would have insurance, even if I were without a job for a short period.

After consulting with my parents, I reviewed my secret plan that I had been working on. "I plan to resign from my position on December 1." I intended to leave at the end of December 2018. Providing notice at the beginning of the month would give my team four weeks to transition my responsibilities. As I explained the details of my plan to my parents, the money part didn't worry them. Our family took care of its own, and they would step in where needed. I assured them that my emergency fund was healthy and that I had sufficient savings to cover my living expenses.

"But, what about insurance?" my mom questioned. I knew Mom would be nervous about insurance. It was her nature to be concerned, and she certainly didn't want me to miss any treatments. She had witnessed firsthand all the hard work that went into ensuring I reduced my risk of recurrence as aggressively as possible. She carried flashbacks from surgery, stripping my drains, chemotherapy, and all the emotions that came along with being a caregiver to a cancer patient, a cancer patient who was her daughter.

I continued with the final detail of my plan, which involved the Alabama Breast and Cervical Cancer Early Detection Program. "I qualify for Medicaid. The social worker at Clearview Cancer Institute confirmed it."

Both of my parents gave their blessings, not that they thought I needed it, and supported my plan to resign. Surprisingly, through this conversation with my parents, the three of us decided I would not be in a hurry to reenter the paid workforce. I would pause my career. A career pause was just what I needed. It would give me time to fully recover from the emotional toll of cancer, focus on getting my body and brain stronger, and spend more time being present with my boys.

I was still undecided about whether I would actually leave. With the help of Sergeant and his invitation for me to resign, plus Max's less-than-desirable behavior at school, all the pieces were in place for me to take responsible action and resign from my career. I didn't have to abandon my career. Neither Sergeant, my previous boss, nor cancer had taken it from me. I paused my career for my boys, a decision I could make alone. It was an opportunity that only I could work hard to transform into a healthy and happy reality. On December 18, 2018, I worked my last day on the job. I didn't have another job to walk into; what I had instead was my boys' childhood home.

The hard work put into planning a career transition had paid off. Not only had my year of laboring and planning enabled me to pay bills and purchase necessary items, but I had also drawn on my trusted network to overcome the barrier of health insurance. The fruits of my labor were delivered to me in time spent with my boys—just the three of us.

I took six whole months off, only taking on small consulting projects to supplement my income. Two organizations trusted me to deliver on special projects that required extra short-term help. The leaders of those two organizations have no idea how the work I completed for them would impact me. Not only was it extra money, but it was fulfilling work with two incredible organizations. Those two organizations, to this day, I cherish and support with my time and, when available, with donations. Contributions that help further their work in supporting cancer patients and empowering badass professional women. My friendships with the organizations' top leaders, both women ahead of me in their experience, proved that women truly need one another.

# Chapter 17

# Indeed

During my first career pause, from January to June 2019, I made it a habit to check job postings at least once a week. Pulling up Indeed on my computer's internet search bar, I would browse leadership job postings. Eventually, I came across an Executive Director role with a nonprofit organization. Curious, I read through the job description.

Volunteer work with several nonprofits and service on the boards of NAPRCA and Leadership Greater Huntsville were the extent of my nonprofit experience. On the surface, the opportunity with BIO Alabama aligned perfectly with the goals that my Executive Coach, Linda DeLuca, had helped me develop. Linda, a different Linda from "do nothing" Linda, and I began working together when I left the paid workforce to take a career pause. I aspired to land a role in healthcare or biotechnology. Public Relations and marketing were my strengths, and cancer had ignited a new interest to learn as much as I could about cancer research and cancer patient support services.

Texting a friend who worked at HudsonAlpha Institute for Biotechnology, I asked if she would consider meeting me for lunch. Our conversation started as usual, with the usual mom talk about our kids and their activities. When she asked what I had been up to, I told her about my career pause and how I was preparing to re-enter the paid workforce. I didn't have to mention the position that I had recently reviewed. She interrupted, "I know the perfect role. You have to apply."

Following my friend's cheerful advice, I applied for the job. During the interview, the individual leading the conversation hesitated before telling me that, unfortunately, the organization likely wouldn't meet my salary expectations and that insurance would not be part of the total compensation package.

This statewide professional nonprofit organization, an affiliate of the international biotech community, the Biotechnology Innovation Organization, struggled to get its revenue flywheel turning. The Board had planned and prepared by building up enough revenue in the coffers to hire the organization's first full-time Executive Director. I responded, "I am not a scientist and I know nothing about biotechnology, but I know sales and marketing." That was exactly what this organization needed.

Confident that I could get the revenue flywheel turning, we agreed on a salary that the organization could afford. It was well below the Medicaid threshold of household earnings, which meant I could stay on Medicaid until I was able to generate enough revenue to dictate a salary increase. Once that time came, we could reevaluate the total compensation package and even include health insurance.

I began my tenure with BIO Alabama by embarking on a statewide tour to meet with each of the thirty board members. Every conversation was fascinating to me. Some even took me through their labs and explained their cutting-edge research. It was all so intriguing. After my Board tour concluded, I prepared a strategic plan to share at my first Board meeting, gathering feedback before finalizing and implementing it.

The first goal, established in collaboration with the thirty-person Board, was straightforward. As a professional organization, our main revenue stream was membership. Increasing membership, which in turn increased our recurring revenue to a certain level, was the first goal. I knew that to increase membership, organizations and individuals needed to be aware of BIO Alabama's existence, so we included a goal to raise awareness, primarily through social media. This was going to be fun because I would be able to put the foundations of my career and my strengths to work. All of my experience leading up to this point fits perfectly in this role. I would ideate, design, and create all the social media assets without needing expensive consultants for part-time help. I was an expert in designing low-cost public relations campaigns with maximum impact.

Progress was slow, which was par for the course in nonprofit work, where more and more responsibilities were piled on one person due to limited resources. However, I was able to manage all the administrative tasks and strategic planning effectively, and my brain was handling the workload just fine. We were able to hire a part-time bookkeeper, who dealt with the tasks that I had zero interest in doing—reconciling bank accounts, preparing financial statements, and, of course, paying bills. The momentum was beginning to pick up.

HudsonAlpha was gracious enough to provide a desk where I could work and be near some of the organization's members located in Huntsville, Alabama. A friend from Huntsville, Loren Traylor Gidson, who had relocated to Birmingham, Alabama, let me crash in her spare bedroom every other week, since I had agreed to spend a certain number of days in Birmingham to be near the thriving biotech ecosystem bolstered by the University of Alabama at Birmingham.

The organization I was working for didn't have the funds to pay a large Executive Director's salary, and it certainly didn't have the resources for expensive hotels or rentals. Every other week, I would arrive at Loren's apartment, enter the door code, and settle into the bedroom she had made available for me. In the evenings, on the rare nights we were both in the apartment together, we would talk about life, love, family, and our careers. She was good medicine for a soul who needed the company of someone who understood the surprises life can deliver. Loren never made me feel as though I was imposing on her personal space. She opened her home to me at a time when I needed it most. My career was back, and I was ready to prove it. Thank you, Loren, for your Southern hospitality.

In addition to Loren, when I traveled to Mobile to engage with the emerging biotechnology community in the southern part of our state, I would stay at my dad's first cousin's house on Lafayette Street. It was a darling Creole-style house painted a light pink with a gabled roof. Jasyn Fowler and his husband, Jamie Avera, called it the "dollhouse." It was haunted, and they had stories to prove it. While I never encountered a ghost while staying in the dollhouse, I was aware that spirits were present, and I kept my eyes peeled for an apparition to appear right before my eyes. I also knew that if a ghost had appeared, I would surely die of a heart attack right there in a pink, life-size dollhouse.

The nights I spent in Mobile with Jasyn and Jamie were enjoyable. We would either cook dinner or head to a local restaurant and talk for hours about family, especially Jasyn's grandmother and my great-grandmother, Mamie. Jasyn was fascinated by our ancestry. Over the years, he had collected all the details of our family's Irish heritage, along with photographs that helped him map out the family tree in images. Jasyn and Jamie visited Ireland often and had even found our family's cemetery across the pond, thousands of miles away. Ireland would be added to my travel list.

Jasyn took after our grandmother, Mamie, and our Aunt Gail. He is a talented costumier who makes elaborate gowns and tableau designs for the annual Mobile Mardi Gras balls. Each year, friends and friends of friends contacted Jasyn with their dreams of a beautiful dress, and Jasyn would go to work, hand-stitching every bead, sequin, and piece of fabric. If his docket were full, Jasyn would enlist Aunt Gail to help bring the dreams to life for his clients. Back home in Hollytree, Alabama, Aunt Gail would spend hours behind her sewing machine, and then ship the final pieces of art to Mobile for Jasyn to hand-deliver. Jamie is a talented real estate photographer who brings majestic beach properties along the beautiful Alabama coast and Florida panhandle to life. They, too, fluffed the red carpet for me with Southern hospitality on full display. The gift of a big, beautiful family and the recipe we all follow: family, hard work, and faith in God.

"Sonia, only essential workers will be allowed access to the building," a friend at HudsonAlpha informed me. Safer-at-home orders were issued in 2020 due to the COVID-19 pandemic. My company email had been eerily quiet leading up to the safer-at-home requirements. As the pandemic paralyzed our country, biotech researchers and scientists were considered essential as they scrambled to develop a successful vaccine and educate the public on proven safety measures. Medical masks were required in public spaces if you had to go out. Still, everyone was encouraged to shelter in place while a highly contagious enemy plagued our communities.

On lockdown, I began to wonder if the sales flywheel for BIO Alabama would ever start turning. After all, how was I going to grow a nonprofit that no one knew about during a time when I couldn't leave my house to share the good word, especially when budgets were being slashed while nonessential workers were banned from working altogether? Individuals and organizations had closed their pocketbooks while sheltering in place.

Since my email was quiet and my phone wasn't ringing, I took the time to double down on the social media plan my Board had approved. Every day, new content filled my inbox from the Google alerts I had set up. I shared and reshared every mention of any Alabama biotech company involved in pandemic relief and recovery efforts. The only problem was that we didn't have a large following on our social media platforms. Would the posts I created and shared even reach our target audience? Each week, I made a note of the number of followers on each platform. We were less concerned about engagement; our goal was to gain followers, regardless of whether they commented, liked, or shared. Once we had the followers, I could focus on engagement.

Armed with a nonprofit board consisting of thirty members geographically dispersed throughout Alabama, our Board members were the organization's greatest asset. A thirty-member Board was not ideal for a busy Executive Director. Still, our large, remote Board was engaged and activated for impact.

I began sharing routine social media guides, ensuring that I sent photographs, links, and even copy to each Board member. Politely asking and encouraging them, or someone on their team, to post the supplied content on their personal and organizational Facebook, Instagram, and LinkedIn accounts. I was spoon-feeding our public relations tactics to each Board member, making it as easy as possible for them to take action. After all, our Board was stacked with high-performing, high-demand executives with large networks that our organization desperately needed to reach.

The day finally came. A few weeks into the safer-at-home orders, my phone rang. "Hello, Sonia, this is..." the voice began. "My organization has been supporting essential biotech companies, and we would like to do more." The revenue flywheel began to turn slowly. Phone call after phone call, email inquiry after email inquiry, our organizational membership started to grow amid a pandemic, despite tightened corporate and individual purse strings. Our revenue was increasing, and our Board was energized. During one of the most challenging periods for most businesses, this small, previously unknown nonprofit finally came to the attention of its target audience, elected officials, and influencers.

In time, we adjusted our strategic plan as goals were accomplished. The Board determined it was time to host a statewide conference. We had the financial means to pull it off thanks to the revenue generated through new professional memberships. The Board commissioned me to begin initial research.

Reporting back, I felt confident that we could secure sponsorships and that people would attend. The only problem was that, while safer-at-home restrictions had now been lifted, large in-person events, such as conferences, were still banned. If an organization hosted a public event, it would likely be roasted on social media. If we were to host a conference to showcase the incredible work of our Alabama biotech community and avoid negative comments on social media, we would have to do it remotely. I had no clue how to pull that off. I had never planned an in-person event at this level, much less a remote event at this scale. It seemed impossible.

Several Board members volunteered to be on the planning committee. As the brainstorming began, we discussed ideas, resources, and actions. A handful of membership organizations offered expert resources, secured speakers, and promoted the event. The traditional conference swag bag was not necessary since it was a remote conference. However, the Board entertained my idea of shipping swag boxes to a shortlist of VIPs, influencers, and supporters to garner some pre-conference excitement and set the tone for the caliber of the event our organization would host.

Our shortlist of swag box recipients continued to expand as Board members added the names of key individuals who deserved a box filled with logoed items and a personalized note. If it weren't for budget limitations, we would have kept adding names. The list was finalized at one hundred recipients. I transformed my home office, which was actually my dining room, into an assembly line that would have Amazon executives on the edge of their seats and taking notes. I was alone, surrounded by boxes of coffee mugs, notepads, and ink pens. With only a few short days to pack the swag boxes and ship them in time to arrive two weeks ahead of the conference, I fired up a single-person assembly line and worked alone at night.

First, I cut the customized tape branded with our logo that I had designed and ordered from Sticker Mule. Next, I configured the flat, pre-cut cardboard boxes from U-Line, stacked in the corner. As I folded the bottom lip of each box, a custom piece of tape was placed to seal the bottom tightly. Next, a large box of white crinkled paper, another U-Line item delivered to my doorstep, sat nearby, and I scooped up two handfuls and dropped them into one box after the other. Wrapping coffee mugs in bubble wrap, they went in first, followed by the remaining items. During the workday, I wrote handwritten notes on branded note cards, each with a personalized message for the recipient. The final step was another strip of branded tape across the top to seal the box closed.

Mailing labels were completed and affixed with the recipient's name and address neatly centered on the top of each box. One by one, they were loaded into my SUV for transportation to the post office. I had already briefed my Board on the anticipated and ideal level of impact. Once the boxes were shipped, I waited. The first message regarding the swag box appeared in my inbox, then another. It was the signal that our public relations campaign to promote our conference was working. Recipients were emailing to thank us for the box and to confirm their registration.

This small nonprofit, largely unknown to many and barely able to afford an Executive Director, was poised to host a large and ambitious remote conference. The event would span three days in October 2020, following a period when the world had been closed for business. Links to the Zoom meetings were shared in the online agenda, and the attendee count started to increase in the virtual meeting room. Square-framed faces of panelists and individual keynotes appeared on computer screens around the state and the Southeast. Individuals tuned in to hear details about how the biotechnology ecosystem in Alabama had been thriving in the wake of the pandemic. Planning, preparing, and hosting a successful remote conference for a little-known nonprofit remains one of my many career highlights.

Already dreaming about what we would do next year for our conference, which would hopefully be in person, the thought of leaving my position as Executive Director hadn't crossed my mind. The undeniable strategic impact of a well-crafted long-term public relations campaign, coupled with the resourcefulness and frugality of an expert public relations practitioner, allowed the Board to increase my salary. However, it was still below the Medicaid annual household earnings cap. I was making it just fine on a small income. With a modest mortgage and an eight-year-old vehicle fully paid off, my living expenses were low. I was in no rush to secure a larger salary. With new organizational goals in place, we will reevaluate my compensation soon.

# Chapter 18

# Invitation

It wasn't a coffee shop. This time, we met at Ruth's Chris for dinner. My former boss, who had previously devastated me with a salary reduction and a title demotion, unbeknownst to me, was about to offer me an opportunity to reclaim my career at an organization I held in high regard. He had something he wanted to discuss with me. No longer my boss, we had remained friends and stayed in touch. Plus, he no longer had the authority to critique my performance or lack thereof. This conversation was not about my performance or my well-being. I never burned a bridge in our small town. I never spoke of our history and the tough decisions we had made as professionals. After all, it was my fault that my performance had slipped, and I had no desire to admit that I was the problem, with cancer only partly to blame.

Still high from the successful remote statewide biotechnology conference, I shared the details of that career highlight. With a break in the conversation, I was not expecting his invitation. Even after the tough decision he delivered to me in that coffee shop three years ago, we both valued our friendship over our business decisions. We had stayed in touch, and our limited interactions had been positive.

"I want you to come back as CEO," he began. As he continued to talk through his plan, I quickly replayed the bright spots and the dark moments of my previous tenure under his leadership. He was a visionary. I was not. He wanted to scar the Earth. I did not. That's why we made a great team. He cast the vision, and I operationalized it for the six years of our professional relationship—until cancer benched me.

Dinner ended, and he agreed to give me a few days. The next day, I called my mom to schedule dinner. "I have something I want to talk to you and Daddy about." By now, both my parents were well aware of my struggle with chemobrain, and they had helped me navigate my first pause until I returned to the paid workforce. "It will be demanding," I debated. "I can't do this alone. I will need your help." Single for five years now, our co-parenting reality was firm, and the boys were healthy and happy. I continued to poke holes in his invitation.

The Executive Director role I currently held was incredibly fulfilling. Indirectly, I felt like I was making an impact on cancer research and services for cancer patients, while exploring other exciting biotech topics, such as AgTech, rare diseases, and pharmaceuticals. But this was an invitation that few people would ever receive in their lifetime. This was an invitation to be the Chief Executive Officer of a small- to medium-sized business. A highly regarded and successful company founded in Huntsville over a decade ago. It was my opportunity to prove to myself that cancer had not stifled my career.

It is not my intent to minimize the position I held at a statewide nonprofit. That position placed me in rooms and exposed me to people I otherwise never would have met. It challenged me in new ways, allowing me to develop new knowledge, skills, and abilities. However, this invitation took me a step further in my quest to become an executive leader. An effective executive leader who had gleaned lessons from my early mistakes as a young manager. It was also redemption for a past career I believed had crashed and burned due to a medical crisis. This invitation was proof that I was worthy of being on his team, worthy to lead his organization and his people.

It was during the two weeks in mission control, when we worked around the clock to give our team the time they needed to complete a strategic project, that earned me this invitation. Or maybe I just had what it took to chase my dreams and achieve my personal goals, just like my dad had taught me through his actions and words. I, too, was accustomed to setting goals. Once I completed one, I would set another. Daddy always told my sister and me, "If you are in the right, things will work out as they should." I was beginning to believe him.

There were two more people I needed to talk to. Around the dinner table at a restaurant, of course, because I wasn't much of a cook. The boys' dad was the chef in our family. During the weeks the boys were with me, we would often eat out.

I sat with my two boys to explain the decision their mother needed to make. Consumed by the meal before them, I was not sure they were listening, so I continued with the details. "It would mean I would have less time at home with you. Is that okay?" Accustomed to spending quality time with their grandparents, my boys loved having more time with their mom. My boys also didn't worry about how I spent my days when they were at school. Their wants were more basic. My boys wanted quality time with me, their mother.

Continuing to learn the art of setting boundaries—not only to give my boys the time they desired and deserved, but to be fully present during that time—I agreed to interview for the Chief Executive Officer position, a position I had been invited to take on given my historical performance and ability to add value to an organization's bottom line. My dad's wisdom chimed in the background, "Sonia, if it's meant to be, then it will be." My parents knew my work ethic. They had observed it over twenty-plus years by now as I navigated high school, college, and my early career. My parents believed in me and trusted me to make the best decision for me and my boys. I got the job—another dream job on my resume.

It was January 2021, and the world was still waking up from the pandemic. The first year as Chief Executive Officer was a lonely experience. My eyes were wide open to the challenges that lay ahead as a new CEO in a familiar business, with a familiar team. A small number of individuals on the team, the team I would lead, had witnessed my failures as a young manager. Trust had to be reestablished. I needed them more than they needed me. The first year was about establishing a new kind of trust within the organization. My daily rituals and routines consisted of one-on-one conversations to capture the voice of the individual contributors who made up my team, a deep review of what had transpired throughout the pandemic, and deep thinking about our future together as a team.

My escape was CrossFit, a training program of varied, functional movements performed during high-intensity workouts, with nutrition counseling and community support built in. I joined RocketCity CrossFit, and for that first year, I was as disciplined at the gym as I was in building trust with my colleagues. For a year, I did nothing but work and work out. By now, Major was well into his middle school football career, and he would occasionally join me in the gym for a workout.

A few solo and friend trips were sprinkled in to give me the mental and emotional break required of executive leaders. That year, I traveled to Key West with a dear high school friend, still recovering from divorce and co-parenting his pre-teen daughter. It was a nice escape for both of us. We caught up on life and reminisced about our high school days. He would have been an excellent life partner, but I was in no position to take on a long-distance relationship or any relationship. This particular friend had built an incredible engineering career in Atlanta, Georgia. We still keep in touch from time to time. He will always be a great friend whom I can call if needed.

As is often the case for an executive leader, there was a mix of easy and tough decisions to make. The most challenging choices had me in tears on the phone with the person who had delivered the invitation, my former boss. He took on the mentor role well, coaching me through one tough decision after another. I am so grateful for his patience and guidance during this time. My career wasn't over due to cancer. My job was just getting started, and the energy I felt was contagious within my team.

# Chapter 19

# Momentum

Moving into year two in my role as Chief Executive Officer, my team and I began to see the fruits of our labor. We had achieved our first big goal within eighteen months. When I started my CEO tour of duty, the company was in the red, and our Board had commissioned the team to work toward achieving four concrete financial goals. Each one was audacious in its own right, but the Board understood the fourth and final goad to be the toughest to get across the finish line. Bound by confidentiality, the details of those goals will not be discussed in this book. As the reader, you have the creative space to fill in those gaps using details from the big goals you have achieved in your own career.

The momentum was palpable, and everyone on the team was ready to tackle the next big goal—goal number two. We didn't waste time with unproductive meetings. We didn't pontificate on useless topics. And we certainly didn't spend money on team-building activities or social events. Instead, we scheduled a monthly all-hands meeting and used that time to celebrate our wins and collaborate on solving problems. As CEO of a small team, my primary responsibility was resource allocation, as we were operating under a dual strategy: extreme expense reduction coupled with aggressive growth.

The weekly cadence of one-on-ones was reduced to just a handful with my leadership team. I never prepared an agenda or talking points for the thirty-minute conversations I had with each leader individually, week after week. Deep in the day-to-day happenings and key performance indicators, I let each leader set their own agenda and talking points.

In some sessions, all we talked about was family. Catching up on their kids' latest dramatic tantrums or new hobbies, we spoke as if we were sitting around the dinner table together. We talked as if we were family. Other sessions focused on a roadblock they or one of their direct reports had encountered. In some sessions, I was left to carry the conversation, and I made a conscious effort to coach and mentor rather than command and control.

Failures occurred in tandem with our successes. By year three, we knocked down three of our goals and celebrated with a team outing. The team voted that bowling would be fun, and it was enjoyable indeed.

We bowled, and then those who were free of kids or home responsibilities for the evening dined together. As a leader and a mother, I fully understood the delicate balance between a demanding career and home life, and I never made after-hours events mandatory. Through empathy, I tried to meet my team members where they were in their lives, and I trusted them to make the best decisions for themselves and their families without fear of retaliation.

It was now the beginning of year four, three years under my belt as Chief Executive Officer. Three years of hard work had paid off. With three audacious goals achieved, we set out to tackle the fourth and final goal. Under orders to keep expenses as low as possible, I had balanced the demands of executive leadership with those of a tactical contributor up to this point—all without an executive assistant. We had hired a young lady, a talented professional with ambitious career goals, to lighten my load. However, she was quickly taken on by others for high-impact projects. I was happy to see her grow. Therefore, I gladly relieved her of administrative duties so she could support the rest of the team, who all benefited from the extra help.

After my first year, I voluntarily took a pay cut to preserve the salaries of our individual contributors and help us achieve our first two significant goals. It was a temporary pay cut, and I had previously survived a less dramatic salary reduction at the same company, as well as living well below the Medicaid annual household earnings threshold for eighteen months following my first career pause. It was that experience I drew from when I had a difficult financial conversation with my leadership team.

My entire leadership team agreed to follow my lead. Crystal, Steve, and Jennifer were so brave and committed to doing what was right for our team, organization, customers, and shareholders. Within a year of taking a pay cut, every one of us was back at the level of pay we once held. Phasing in increases over time; my salary was the last to rebound to its original amount within one year of the voluntary cut. On top of all that, I did not receive any performance bonuses, although I did benefit from distributions as an equity stakeholder in the company.

The distributions were from my old equity stake from my previous tenure, not from any new equity resulting from the employee incentive stock options portion of my executive compensation package. Still, I never asked for more money. As part of planning a bonus for our entire team in year four of my tenure, I was included in the bonus approved by my Board. It was the only bonus I received in four years, and I had never asked for one. I was taught that hard work pays off, and it did.

Every one of my team members had their lane, and I trusted them to execute. I equally trusted them to come to me when they hit a wall. When they did, we would huddle up to collaborate on solving the problem. This was what leadership was all about for me: collaborating in a psychologically safe environment with peers you trust. It was a fun, energizing, and engaging experience, and our entire team participated. I thought I was getting the hang of it, but another life surprise lay ahead, undetected.

Together, we solved problem after problem. Problems were often presented to us by our customers. We were always solving problems for the very people responsible for our paychecks. Like before, I held key relationships with our customers. With too many relationships for one person to manage effectively, I began grooming every team member so they, too, could foster key relationships with the individuals they directly served, and they did. Some were better than others, but everyone was putting in the hard work as I continued to coach and mentor those who lagged. My sister, Amanda, was also on the team in a full-time capacity by now, based on her performance and ability to add value to our company's bottom line.

It wasn't that the individuals lagging were failures. They just needed a little more care and attention to develop new knowledge, skills, and abilities. They showed up for coaching. They showed up for constructive feedback. Armed with encouraging words and practical advice, they forged ahead while I quietly observed their progress and behavior. Just as a mother does with her children, I monitored my team for signs of distress to intervene appropriately when needed.

Our team refrained from engaging in unproductive Slack chatter. Everyone was encouraged to pick up the phone and call colleagues directly instead, fostering connection and collaboration. Voice-to-voice conversations were much more effective for solving problems, and they also fostered relationships between our team members, since we operated in a 100% remote work environment. Most of these huddles were on demand, without needing a formal calendar invitation.

My calendar had once been full of stakeholder meetings, customer tours, and one-on-ones. By the end of my tenure, an empty calendar signaled to me that I had done a great job coaching and mentoring my team. Data points associated with activity level were not added to our already comprehensive list of key performance indicators. In fact, I had never been in an organization where activity level was a key indicator. If I had monitored Slack activity by individual contributors, I likely would have coached them to reduce their activity. Time on Slack meant time away from their key responsibility—our customers.

Our leadership team modeled this behavior for all individual contributors, limiting unproductive Slack chatter, preferring to jump on on-demand phone calls instead. Our conversations were always professional, focused, and impactful, with a few jokes and lighthearted banter added for entertainment. My leadership team kept me informed of any situation or action that might prompt a stakeholder to contact me, making sure to provide key details, seek my guidance, and plan appropriately to reduce any dissatisfaction.

Year four came into focus, and all the pieces fell into place. The final strategic piece was a hired gun. Ellie Kovacs and I had previously worked together for eight years at this same company. We were familiar with each other's strengths and weaknesses. Very different in style, she was gifted with skills and knowledge I did not possess. Vice versa, I was equipped with skills and knowledge she did not have. By the time I left for my first pause, her career was taking off. Her career was a rocket ship blasting off just as mine had been. She left the same company under similar conditions, minus the chemobrain or medical crisis, thank goodness. That's her story to tell, and I hope she does one day.

Ellie and I were kindred spirits, both strong-willed, high-performing, professional women and equally strong-willed, high-performing, nurturing mothers. The balance was exhausting, but we supported each other. Flexible with our calendars, we easily shifted meetings when a sick child needed attention from mom or a special school event came up. We never had to explain ourselves to each other. Mutual respect, both as professionals and as mothers, brought us closer together. We were a unified duo, each other's right hand, and we were getting things done. Our success was demonstrated by our company's financial performance and the positive feedback from our Board.

Ellie left me in awe of what she accomplished in such a short time. She was disciplined with her focus and protective of her time. With each objective, she implemented a new set of strategic analytics and processes, driven by an intrinsic desire to be a great executive leader of people. The people directly reporting to Ellie appreciated the professional camaraderie between a leader and an individual contributor. How did I know? They told me, and I personally observed interactions that confirmed their claims. The company's financials further proved that Ellie was a great choice to be my successor one day.

Professional and focused, Ellie and I had already eliminated any distractions that might get in the way of achieving the fourth strategic goal. The final goal was in our sights. There was no extra time or space for water cooler chatter, interpersonal conflict, or idle hands. Each team member contributed to the fourth strategic goal, and I was their protector, ensuring their time and focus were maintained.

Things started to boil as we prepared for a crucial meeting. The original plan was for the meeting to be held at our office in Huntsville, Alabama, and we were assured this wouldn't be a problem. Leading up to that decision, Ellie and I had expressed the challenges of travel we faced due to our responsibilities as mothers. As a single mom, securing a babysitter for a two-night stay in New York would be tough. Meanwhile, as a co-parenting mom, I did my best to avoid traveling during the weeks my boys were with me, given our already limited time together due to our co-parenting arrangement. Our request to hold the meeting at our office seemed reasonable, and it was agreed that the meeting would be held in Huntsville. We extended our gratitude to all those involved in planning and attending the meeting. We knew that meant others would have to travel, be away from the people they loved most, and we deeply appreciated their sacrifice.

A day or two later, we were informed that one of the young men we were meeting with would not be able to make the trip to Huntsville. He was a key participant in this meeting, and his wife was very pregnant. It wasn't an ideal time for him to be out of town. As mothers, Ellie and I empathized with his situation. The end of a pregnancy could be an uncomfortable time for a mother-to-be, and the birth of a child was special—something not to be missed. We happily conceded, made arrangements for our kids, and booked our flights. I offered to help Ellie secure a babysitter, while my mom happily agreed to keep an eye on my children. We had a plan. A plan we both contributed to and supported each other throughout. Together, we began to see a new path of leadership, one where mothers could shine.

I flew out early in the morning. I wanted time to get my bearings in New York City while finalizing my preparations for our essential meeting, which would clinch our fourth and final goal. Ellie couldn't fly out of Huntsville International Airport until the afternoon due to her daughter's babysitter's schedule. We agreed to meet up for dinner that night in the city to conduct a pre-mortem on the big meeting scheduled for the next morning. It was a Thursday, and we rose early, each getting ready over a warm cup of coffee in our individual hotel rooms. Meeting in the lobby, we walked out onto Park Avenue in New York City for our meeting. The crucial meeting.

It was in my nature to connect with people on a personal level, observing conversations and filing away details that I could reference later. While plating my lunch, I learned that one of the meeting attendees—one of the individuals we needed to impress—was in the throes of a personal cancer battle: his wife's breast cancer fight. It's a fraternal community of cancer patients, survivors, and their caregivers. We shared a brief conversation, and I transitioned into presentation mode.

Rapid-fire questions poured in for hours, and when the meeting finally concluded, Ellie and I were exhausted. Introverts by nature, the hours of extroversion led us straight back to our hotel rooms for some much-needed alone time. Time for personal reflection before meeting up with the individuals from our meeting for a business dinner. We went through a retrospective exercise and concluded that there were areas where we could have performed better, but overall, we were pleased with our effort.

We were also grateful and comforted by the fact that the external team supporting us agreed to manage the action items from the meeting until we returned to Huntsville. Boarding my flight the next day, I tried to relax and give my body a chance to fight the seasonal cold I had developed before leaving for this work trip. The uncomfortable symptoms of sinus pressure, headache, and a sore throat were escalating quickly. My body had been under intense stress, whether positive or negative, from the rigorous preparation and activities leading up to this significant meeting. After cancer, I became very attuned to my body, and I knew I needed some rest.

By now, my voice was weak, my head was pounding, and I feared a sinus infection was on the horizon. Some sinus infections I could manage with over-the-counter medicine and still trudge through work without much rest. This particular cold and sinus infection drained me. When I got home, I immediately went to bed, trusting the external project team to handle the behind-the-scenes work on the action items from the crucial meeting. I would review everything after some much-needed rest.

I slept for about two hours. When I woke up, my phone indicated that I had missed several calls. I had intentionally silenced my phone—as a healthy boundary for peaceful rest—and I had a slew of unread text messages referencing important emails that needed my immediate attention. The caller and sender of these messages was my former boss. This individual had invited me back to take on the role of CEO, and he was calling me constantly.

Reaching for the pack of over-the-counter sinus medicine, I popped open a Monster energy drink and swallowed the pills. At my computer, I went through the emails one by one, only to realize that the hard work put into building our team up to this point was about to come crashing down around me. Even worse, the pace and stress from the months leading up to this point were now straining my ability to communicate effectively with my children and with a new, very important man in my life. I was dating again, and it was a serious relationship.

Not realizing the stress and high activity level had also taken a toll on some of the people I loved the most, a career that arguably led to my divorce was now upending a new relationship. I was engaged to be married. While a date had not been set, I was doing my best to keep all distractions at bay; I couldn't wait to begin a new chapter with this new man in my life.

The individual to whom I almost screamed, "I QUIT," in the coffee shop, and the very same individual who had invited me to come back to this company, had once again inserted himself. He didn't trust Ellie or me to do our jobs: the jobs we were hired to do and the very work required to accomplish the fourth goal. I was shattering on the inside, and no one knew it.

This was not my first experience with this feeling, and I felt confident that I had developed coping mechanisms to prevent a dramatic outcome. I certainly wasn't thinking, based on the positive feedback, that my performance was in question again. Yet, I was struggling, and these were new struggles for which I did not have the benefit of lived experiences to draw wisdom from.

He didn't tell us directly that his trust had faded. After all, I had been unreachable for hours, and that was simply unacceptable. What was worse, Ellie, too, had taken some time with her daughter once she returned home. She had also been unavailable for a few hours. Both of our careers were now on the line. Only I had an escape route. Ellie was winding down her first year, and the plan was for her to transition into my role at the end of my four-year commitment. When I returned as Chief Executive Officer, I made a promise to myself to stay for four years, and we had a succession plan in place. However, that plan would end up in someone else's hands, and we had failed to recognize the signs.

I was caught flat-footed again by my inability to connect the dots of posturing and business politics. With the birth of a child imminent, a follow-up meeting to the crucial meeting was scheduled for a Sunday morning, just three days after the high-stakes meeting, and the same Sunday of a major life event for my family. Ellie and I still had a chance to get this final goal across the finish line, and this meeting was it. We spent our Saturday, already drained from being away from our children on business travel, preparing for another pivotal meeting. This meeting would close the fourth goal, marking it a success.

# Chapter 20

# Sunday

It was the Saturday after our trip to New York, where Ellie and I had our crucial meeting. I still wasn't feeling great, but I managed to rally. This time, I took the over-the-counter medication for my sinus infection with water instead of a Monster energy drink.

Our follow-up meeting would take place the next morning, a Sunday. I complied by accepting the calendar invite. Only Ellie and the external project team were aware of the special day on my calendar, penciled in for that particular Sunday. It was a milestone celebration for my parents, a day that meant the world to our family.

As we made concessions for a young professional whose wife was about to have a baby, not once but twice, no one seemed to care about two mothers trying their damnedest to be great executive leaders and mothers simultaneously. I was equally trying to be a great daughter. Comments were starting to circulate from just one individual, suggesting we didn't have what it took to do the job. Accepting a Sunday morning video call was one way of proving that we had what it took to be effective executive leaders.

Ellie and I were not strangers to long work days and weekend grinds. That was part of being high-performing and effective executive leaders. We were not afraid of hard work; we had grown wiser in establishing healthy boundaries to protect our emotional, mental, and physical health. Like most high-performing executive leaders, we took care of ourselves so we could show up at our best for our team, customers, and stakeholders. We had no idea that others interpreted our boundaries as laziness, which led to the implication that we were not suited to be executive leaders.

"I'm so sorry. I'm gonna need your help Sunday morning," I explained to my sister. Careful not to divulge any details of the meeting so as to protect her from questions or inquiries from colleagues. If she didn't have the knowledge, she couldn't communicate it to anyone else—not that she would. However, this was our boundary, a boundary established by two sisters who worked at the same company. One sister was an individual contributor who reported to a manager within the department she was assigned. The other sister was the Chief Executive Officer on a mission to prove that cancer had not taken her career from her.

It was my parents' fiftieth wedding anniversary, and our church had planned a surprise reception. My parents had indicated early on that they would rather take a trip instead of spending money on a reception. My sister and I gifted them seed money to book their Alaskan cruise. They would spend their golden 50th wedding anniversary exploring Alaska. It was a bucket list item for them. Dad was now seventy, and Mom was sixty-eight. They needed to pack their travel in while they still could.

Mom often reminisced about her memories of traveling with her parents. Her father had passed away in 2020, just before the pandemic. Before his health declined, he and Granny Evelyn, along with friends or family, would pack up for routine road trips. Granddaddy Wayne loved to drive across the country, taking in the sights of fields and the natural landscape.

"Laptop, check. Headset, check. Charger, check." As I packed up my home office, I talked to myself while running through the checklist. The boys and I got in the car and headed to our church early on that Sunday morning. Somehow, I managed to get all the decorations to the fellowship hall the day before, while also working on action items for the Sunday morning video call. But there was still a lot of work to be done, and I now questioned why I had even volunteered to handle the decorations.

It was my parents' 50th wedding anniversary reception, and I wanted it to be special. More importantly, I wanted to actively participate in planning and preparing for such a wonderful celebration for my parents. I wanted to contribute to the hard work our church family was putting in to surprise their Pastor and his wife. Not only was I a daughter, but I was also the preacher's daughter.

The sacrifice, discipline, and love my parents had provided had paid off, as evidenced by my accomplishments. This was an experience I would never have again. It was also an experience I would never have in my lifetime, even though I was engaged to be married. My new love and I would have to live until he was ninety-seven and I was ninety-four if we were going to celebrate fifty years of marriage. We were healthy, minus my cancer diagnosis, but I wasn't so sure we would live that long. The memories would need to be bold to sustain me long after my parents were gone, too. It was an important day not only for my parents but also for me. Just one day, that's all I needed and wanted. This fact did not diminish my commitment to doing my job well.

Through the threshold, I started barking orders. So much needed to be done before my Zoom call. I kept checking the clock to make sure I stopped exactly thirty minutes ahead, which would give me time to polish up my face, adjust my hair, and conduct one final review of the purpose for this meeting. After all, a disheveled look was not ideal for a high-performing executive woman, especially when this meeting had the power to clinch the fourth and final goal.

"Excuse me," I shouted to get the attention of family and friends as they scrambled to finish the last details for the celebration. "I'm about to jump on a video call, and I need it to be as quiet as possible in here." Sitting down, I put on my gaming headset, chosen for its superior sound quality, and adjusted the microphone. With a deep breath, I launched the Zoom meeting on my computer.

When the call ended, I bolted out the door and hurried across the street to our church's sanctuary. The church house was packed. Friends and family had gathered in the Mt. Nebo Baptist Church sanctuary to celebrate my parents. My Great-Aunt Gladys was stalling. It was time for me to unveil the secret celebration we had planned. I stepped up to the pulpit and delivered the speech I had prepared for my parents and for the congregation they shepherd to hear.

It's hard to keep secrets from my mom. I had requested several items from her. "Mom, can I borrow your wedding dress?" I had to come up with excuses for needing all the trinkets from their wedding day, safely hidden in her cedar chest. She was suspicious that something was being planned, if all the plants I had purchased as decorations and stored in my dining room hadn't already given it away.

Mom knew she was always welcome in my house. The only boundary we had set was that she would send a heads-up text. Our relationship had grown so close that I was even comfortable talking about my sex life with her. "Mom, I'm a single woman with needs. I don't want you to walk into a situation that will embarrass us both." She understood the assignment and the boundary. Now she always sends me a text before coming to my house. I love her for respecting my boundaries.

My dad was utterly overwhelmed with surprise. The celebration had begun, and my parents were beaming with happiness. That afternoon, our entire family watched as Mom and Dad caught up with old friends, hugged countless necks, and told story after story. I had done it. I had been present for this special day. I had contributed in a way I knew I would cherish for so many years to come. Yet, the guilt was percolating, and that little ball of anxiety was bubbling in my stomach. Our final goal, the goal I thought was within our reach, would not be achieved. We would learn this news when the new work week began on the following Monday.

Victory vanished after checking off each milestone our team had accomplished up to this point. I pondered whether I should deploy the parachute built into my plan. Almost four years ago, when I accepted the role as Chief Executive Officer, I had set a self-imposed limit: I would give it four years. Having survived cancer, time was of the essence. Pressure from fear of recur-

rence, fear of disability, and fear of death had ignited my wanderlust.

In four years, I would be ready to experience something new
and pursue the next step in my career. If I could not deliver the
desired results, I would step aside for someone else to complete
the job. With the help of my Board Chairman, we identified Ellie
as the person who would succeed me at the end of my four-year
term. Throughout all the meetings and preparations to achieve
our final goal, it was determined that I should plan to stay at
least twelve to twenty-four months after the four-year mark. It
was the expectation of the individuals we had met with in New
York, and I was pleased to continue the work, because it signified we had achieved all four goals commissioned by our Board.
It also meant my career was advancing to the next stage.

Our team was solid. Individual contributors were growing and
expanding their knowledge, skills, and abilities. I loved my team
and enjoyed leading them. My primary role had shifted from
project lead to coach and mentor. It was this very hesitation to
leave that sounded alarm bells. I wasn't sure I was ready to give
up before accomplishing the final goal. Speaking individually to
my colleagues, I expressed my desire to continue our work. We
had come so far, and our accomplishments were proof that we
could forge ahead successfully together.

At this juncture, I had been working with an Executive Coach
on and off for six years. Unsure if I needed an executive coach or
a therapist at the outset of our relationship, I expressed to Linda
that I aspired to be a great people leader, following in my dad's
footsteps. I wanted to grow through real-world leadership experiences, and given my early missteps as a young manager, Linda

guided me in establishing leadership principles to research and develop.

Empathy was key. I, too, am an empath just like my Granny Evelyn. She set the example of how to treat people, regardless of whether they were experiencing good times or bad. Her way of showing empathy came through covered dishes, homemade German chocolate cakes, and time. Granny Evelyn, along with my grandfather, would often visit neighbors who were sick or carve out time for funeral home visits to comfort grieving friends. These characteristics were not limited to just her and my grandfather. My parents and my Granddaddy Carl and Granny Ruth were precisely the same. Empathy had been demonstrated to me all my life.

Cancer uncovered my deep empathetic nature, and Linda helped me frame it productively. She provided the dots for me to connect in my own way to develop this essential leadership quality. In addition to being an empathetic leader, I aspired to be a respectful leader. My lived experiences up to that point had shaped this desire. When people face an existential crisis, whether related to health, family, or finances, they often already feel demoralized. As a leader, I wanted to be a bright spot: firm, but respectful. To round out the key traits of my leadership style, I added "kind" to the short list of three words.

Reflecting on what my high school coaches did for me as a student-athlete, I recognized it was a healthy mix of tough love, discipline, and kindness. They were quick to call attention to improvements that needed to be made to excel on the basketball court. Still, they also consistently delivered the news in a way that developed the athlete mentally, emotionally, and physically. That was the work of a coach. If anyone lagged on the line when the whistle blew, each athlete knew another endurance drill would be added. Everyone was expected to hustle.

Once we had identified my leadership principles, we needed to address the blind spots revealed by individuals who worked closely with me. Direct, unfiltered feedback from trusted peers helped me identify areas for improvement in my work habits—a mix of good and some less-than-desirable qualities. It came down to emotional intelligence, and we put a lot of work into labeling emotions, discussing tactics to keep emotions in check, and role-playing to practice responses and reactions to situations that would move the anxiety from my stomach to my throat and out of my mouth before I could stop myself. Emotional control was a new muscle I needed to develop, and one essential for an executive leader.

Continuing in this role and revising our strategic plan to set us up for another opportunity to tackle the fourth goal was something I believed I could do, and I knew it based on my historical performance. But I wasn't so sure I would be given the opportunity. I was prepared just in case. Another career pause had been planned and prepared. The crisis plan sat safely on the shelf. It was a proven strategy that already helped me transition into my first career pause six years earlier. It included a healthy emergency fund, the ability to minimize financial exposure and risk, and health insurance.

A proven personal plan, similar to the many business plans I had successfully implemented before. Lived experiences and the benefit of wisdom told me I could decide to stay or leave. I would be fine. My boys would be fine. And my team would be fine under the leadership of Ellie. It was a decision only I could make. It was not someone else's decision. The hard work had already been done.

# Chapter 21

# Voice

Before the climax of my beloved career, he and I met again. This time in my office. It was another meeting with my former boss, the same person who had invited me to take the position I now held. By then, our relationship had evolved, and I was more comfortable speaking my truth. A healthy, candid business debate unfolded. We were respectful, giving each other the space to talk and listening carefully in return.

The weather was beautiful, unseasonably warm for the time of year. By now, it was November 2024. We set off on a walk down Meridian Street for a one-on-one, turning left onto Pratt Avenue. The conversation was productive. We candidly discussed the transgressions of the weeks leading up to this particular conversation. He made me feel as though he wanted me to continue, that I deserved this position, and that I could move forward in developing a new strategy to achieve our fourth goal. We had been very successful, and he congratulated me on achieving three out of the four goals. After all, they were ambitious goals that had a positive impact on all stakeholders.

After this conversation, my energy level began to tick up following the heartbreak of missing the final milestone in my four years as CEO. I had every reason to trust him. He could have fired me after chemobrain paralyzed my professional abilities, but he didn't. Instead, he made space for me to heal, even though a salary cut and title demotion were part of our mutually agreed-upon plan. He was a visionary leader, and our organization was an exceptional place to work. We agreed that I would stay and help develop and implement our new strategy for the new year. It was a decision I felt great about.

Unexpectedly, his demeanor shifted. It was subtle at first, but it evolved into passive-aggressive remarks and then quickly accelerated into hostility. These emotions were all directed at me, and he blamed my performance. I collected the feedback and pondered the criticism, trying to identify when and where the transgressions had occurred under my leadership.

I had conversations with colleagues to fact-check statements he made. Still, I was left confused by the mixed messages I had received. Every one of our Board members had told me, both collectively and individually, that they were proud and pleased with our progress and the successes we had enjoyed together as a team. Ellie was an equal recipient of the accolades, and rightfully so. She had earned every positive comment, and so had I. Our hard work had paid off, even if the fourth and final big goal was not accomplished. It was a goal that most businesses would never have the opportunity even to consider.

Sitting in a different coffee shop one month later, the familiar buzz of conversation and the scent of roasted coffee beans filled the air. I took a deep breath. I had called this meeting to discuss my performance. I had requested a meeting with Mentor, a character introduced in chapter 11. Ellie was in attendance as well. I wanted a witness for this particular conversation.

I was unsure of where this confidence came from, as I'm pretty docile until I'm backed into a corner and have to scratch and claw my way out. Cancer brought that characteristic out in me. The grit and toughness developed in my childhood served me well, and I kept the proverbial purse of rocks on standby, never intending actually to use it for its intended purpose. The dread of this conversation boiled in the pit of my stomach because I knew the decision I had to make.

I didn't go into specifics regarding the fatal research project I had submitted while fighting back the symptoms of chemobrain. The self-control I had somehow maintained through that experience, even though I knew my career was over, remained with me in this moment, too. The salary cut and title demotion from seven years ago were also not included on the list of talking points. All I had to explain was that my former boss's feedback, the very same inviter who had asked me back, contradicted what more people had already told me than just him. It was positive feedback that even the person sitting across the table from us during this conversation had given when our fourth goal vanished into thin air. However, my performance had come into question again by the same person from so many years ago. I needed to know the truth, and I had to use my voice for myself. I needed to know if this was about me—or him.

The conversation was over. I was proud of how I controlled all the emotions raging in my body. Mentor rose and walked out of the coffee shop. My colleague, Ellie, was by my side. I had to use my voice. I had to fight for myself, just like I had coached my sister to do when she was placed on administrative leave. Just like I had done while recovering from a double mastectomy, four rounds of chemotherapy, and months of chemobrain. Here I was following my own advice, and I wasn't afraid. I wasn't alone. Ellie was by my side. My dad's wisdom buzzed in my mind: "If you are in the right, then things will work out as they should." My daddy had learned the recipe, and he knew it well. I couldn't help but think he had heard those wise words many times from his own father. Only this time, I truly believed him.

There was no drama, no words wielded like tiny knives, and there was no fanfare. My career was over, and the next day, I would tender my resignation from the position I had been invited to take, resigning from my beloved career as an executive leader. The hard work had been done. I didn't need permission from anyone else. Rather than doing nothing, this time I had to take action and use my voice to speak my truth.

Walking into the office that morning, Ellie and I had a meeting with my former boss to discuss our research assignment for the next iteration of our strategic plan. A normal, healthy business debate ensued as Ellie and I defended our research and position. As the meeting drew to an end, he dismissed Ellie. That was my invitation to stay. "Don't cry. Don't cry," buzzed in my head. "Breathe in...one, two, three, four. Breathe out...one, two, three, four," I coached myself, trying to slow my heart down and keep the flush from exposing the truth. I wasn't going to quit. Today, I would resign.

He was more direct this time. No small talk. No wellness check disguised as a performance review. Before I could offer up my resignation, he said, "Sonia, I am offering you severance. Effective immediately, you are released from your duties." After dismissing me from my responsibilities, he continued. "You mismanaged the company." Severance was a generous act of kindness, an olive branch of goodwill. My career could now be summed up in one word: mismanagement. My voice cracked when I asked him to explain. As he stumbled to find the right words, he finally said, "You hired your sister. That's nepotism, and it's unethical." Tears swelled in my eyes. There was nothing more to say. I had mismanaged by engaging in nepotism. My sister, earning an entry-level salary as a customer service representative and recruiter, had been cast as the demise of my career. I hadn't realized she was so powerful.

There it was, my voice. A voice I had been trying out for over two decades of an incredible twenty-year career. A voice that brought me here. My once submissive demeanor and rigid sense of propriety had evolved. But in that moment, I had nothing more to say. I didn't defend myself. Sometimes silence is the most potent form of communication. Signifying the meeting was over, he said, "I will send your severance agreement to your personal email address. Take your time to review and let me know if you have any questions." It was over, my beloved career.

We walked out together. Standing in the parking lot, we turned to face each other. "This is business," he said. And we hugged. The hysterical tears never came. I didn't call my mom immediately. I got in my car and drove home to the house that was my boys' childhood home. I was relieved. For weeks, I had been poring over my personal finances, devising a plan for my second pause—the escape route I had preemptively built when I accepted the Chief Executive Officer position. Had I known all along that I would need an escape hatch? Or was a higher power making room for something bigger?

Pausing my career for a second time, I knew it wasn't career suicide. My lived experiences had taught me that I could always make money. Now it was time to pause again, and this time, it would be for one year.

I called my oncologist, and a referral was made to social services. I was still undergoing long-term cancer treatment, and I still had two more years to go. The effort to reduce my risk of recurrence had already been ongoing for eight years, and I had come too far to stop now. Sure, I was tired of the three-month cadence of blood work and injections, the daily cadence of medications, and the relentless symptoms of medically induced perimenopause that never seemed to ease. But my resolve was stronger than my fatigue. I had come so far to ensure I would remain Major and Max's mommy, and cancer would not defeat me. I could apply for Medicaid. Clearview Cancer Institute confirmed, once again, through the Alabama Breast and Cervical Cancer Prevention Program nurse manager, that I qualified. I would have health insurance.

# Part III: Faith in God

The final section of my book highlights the beautiful surprises woven into the hard work. Here, I honor some special people, places, and moments that were perfectly placed along my path up to this point in my life. Some of the characters remain active and present in my story, while others have stepped away. All are surprises for you, the reader. Surprises that only God could have dreamed up and delivered. This section is written as a series of short stories with characters mentioned in the previous two sections, family and hard work, as well as new characters who hold a special place in my life.

# Chapter 22

# Maria

*The following story begins when I first cut my hair in preparation for chemotherapy in August 2017, and introduces you, the reader, to a very special woman in my life.*

"Why did you cut your hair? Do you have cancer?" The rapid-fire questions came from the most intimidating interrogator, a seven-year-old boy. Unsatisfied with my response, he shifted his weight, looked at me, and stated, "But you're not old."

It was typical seven-year-old banter around a topic his little mind associated with death. As I began my well-curated response, designed to keep the subject light for the kids, Sam's next question leaped from his mouth. The words were like daggers aimed straight at my heart. "Who's going to be Major and Max's mommy?"

Sam was one of my bonus neighborhood kids. During the summer, he and the rest of the neighborhood kids would raid my refrigerator for a cold fruit juice. The open pantry door was an indicator that the kids had found their favorite snacks, which I tried to keep stocked. I loved having a house full of kids, and I kept the refrigerator and pantry stocked just for moments like this.

In all fairness, Sam's grandfather, Larry, was fighting a hard battle with cancer. He would later lose that battle. From time to time, Larry and I would see each other at Clearview Cancer Institute. When it came time to host my head-shaving party, he was on the invitation list. We took a picture together, our eyes locked on one another as if he were telepathically communicating a deep secret to me. He was dying. He knew he was dying, and so did the people who loved him most. The very same people he loved the most.

"I am!" I barked back at Sam. And just like that, the conversation was over. The kids scattered off to their next adventure. As for me, I took the opportunity to have a little talk with Jesus. "Please don't make me a liar. Please let me be Major and Max's mommy for a very long time. PLEASE, LET MY BABIES HAVE A MOMMY!"

This last statement hung in the air as a reminder that cancer does and can end in a horrific truth: death. Unbeknownst to me, in just five short months, the question of whether Major and Max would have a mommy would shift to whether their mommy would have a career. Would their mommy have a paycheck, health insurance, and still keep them in their childhood home? The weight of these questions was unbearable. It was so much to process, and my brain was at the height of its struggle with chemobrain.

Divine intervention was the only explanation. Divorced, it wasn't lost on me that my ex-husband, Jason, would find love again. I wanted him to be happy. The boys needed a happy father. The prayer was simple. I prayed for a great woman who would love my boys as if they were her own. After all, I wasn't sure if I would always be here to be Major and Max's mommy.

This prayer only intensified as each milestone of cancer treatment passed. It was dramatic, I know. My cancer diagnosis was textbook, and there was no cause for concern. My prognosis was a positive one. Still, in the back of my mind, there was always a lingering "what if."

While scrolling through Facebook one day, I came across the picture Jason had posted. Curious, I sent him a text. "Are you and Maria dating?" As soon as I pressed send, I regretted it and wanted the earth to swallow me. I had overstepped. It was none of my business. I had relinquished my authority to know the details of Jason's life years ago. I had no right to ask, nor to share my opinion.

Jason, being the man he is and continues to be, responded to my text, "Yes, I was going to tell you." My heart skipped a beat. I knew Jason had great taste in women; I mean, he did marry me. However, the dread of who his next love would be hung over me like a rain cloud that wouldn't go away. I often wondered who this woman would be when he eventually fell in love again. Would her principles and values align with mine? Did she love Jesus? Would she love my boys? Would she be a healthy and happy influence on my boys? As the questions came, my prayers continued. "Please let her love my boys as much as she loves Jesus."

Maria was no stranger to my boys. In fact, she had been their Sunday School teacher at Mt. Nebo Baptist Church for a few years until a life surprise required time and space for her to heal. She loved my boys, and my boys loved her. Maria and I had known each other for a few years before she started dating Jason. Sure, it was tough to see another woman step into a motherly role in my children's lives. Jason and Maria's relationship caused a twinge of jealousy that would last a few months until I found myself in her shoes as a bonus mom myself.

But Sam's interrogation from a few years ago echoed through the noise. The "who's going to be Major and Max's mommy" question haunted me, recalling the prayer from that very day, which ended with the words, "Please ensure Major and Max have a mommy." It's as if God placed a backup mom directly in their path.

Now, Maria is my co-mom. She's no backup. She's the real deal. The jealousy I once felt dissipated. It's tough to be a mom, but being a bonus mom was even harder. I now have the life experience to engage with Maria in deep empathy fully. Aware of the bystanders watching and waiting for drama to erupt between us, the drama never came. Maria is an equal co-parenting partner. We meet up for coffee or margaritas, not as often as we'd like, to talk about life, our careers, and, most importantly, our boys.

She placed a beautiful word art above the front door of their new home, a home she shares with Jason and our boys. It reads "Just Me, You, and the Boys." I'm not sure if it ever crossed her mind to add "…. and Mom." Knowing her, if I had suggested it, she would have grabbed a Sharpie and written it herself.

I love that piece of art. It's a symbol of her undeniable love for a man and two children who are not biologically hers, but whom she treats as if she had labored hours for each one. To be clear, I didn't labor for hours either. As both of my pregnancies drew nearer to the forty-week mark, I made it clear that an epidural would be a part of the birth plan. My obstetrician and I joked that I wouldn't get a trophy if I had natural births. I opted for the pain-free plan.

Aside from a kidney stone, my pregnancy with Major was magical. I savored every moment in awe of my body as it grew a little human inside. With Max, my pregnancy was more complicated, and I boldly declared he would be the last baby I would have in my womb. I was diagnosed with gestational diabetes and developed a daily routine of checking my blood sugar to ensure my levels stayed within the appropriate range for the second half of my pregnancy with Max.

On the day he was born, Jason and I were so excited to meet our second son. I couldn't wait to begin skin-on-skin contact immediately, just as I had done with his big brother.

When Max arrived, there was no loud cry. A slimy baby was not placed on my bare chest, ready to bond with his mother and begin the natural nudging a newborn does to make its way toward its mom's breast for nutrition. The delivery nurse took Max and placed him in a medical basin. He was blue and not breathing. The medical team, calm and working in silence, barely made a commotion. In a short few minutes, they placed my baby on my chest. "The cord was wrapped around his neck. We got him out just in time. He's fine, just needed a little help to get his lungs firing." Yet another divine intervention.

Having worked at the hospital where I delivered both my babies, I was good friends with the nursery nurse manager, Judy. During my first pregnancy, I worked at Crestwood as part of the Marketing and Public Relations department. By the time my second pregnancy came around, I had already advanced in my career.

Recalling a day when the nursery manager was sad, an emotion she rarely put on display, Judy told me that she had lost a baby earlier that day. An umbilical cord injury had resulted in a stillbirth. She was heartbroken, and the story she shared broke my heart as well.

I knew the risks of pregnancy and labor. I had also heard heartbreaking stories from friends and family who had experienced such devastating loss. My baby boy was healthy. The medical team did not cause alarm. As I labored, they realized Max was in distress, and they did their job well. This information about a distressed baby was not communicated to his parents due to the risk that his mother might panic and be unable to deliver him in time. The medical team's discretion was necessary. This experience cemented the decision I had declared during pregnancy: I would not have any more children. It was too scary, too risky.

Fast forward four years, and I was reminded of my decision not to have any more children. Jason and I had been divorced for nearly two years, but I asked the question anyway. As I consulted with a radiation oncologist a few weeks after my breast cancer diagnosis, I felt more comfortable talking to a female doctor about the topic. I asked, "Um, I'm thirty-six and single. What if I meet someone and we want to have a baby together? Will I even have that option?" My mom was sitting next to me, and I'm sure her jaw dropped. She knew I had passionately declared there would be no more babies for me after Max.

The doctor told me my options. I could harvest eggs before treatment, or I could wait until my long-term treatment was over. By then, my body would be exposed to medications and chemicals that would put me into a high-risk category, not to mention my age. At thirty-six and given the biology of my cancer, I was sure to be on tamoxifen and in a state of medical menopause until my mid-forties. I appreciated her candor when she concluded with, "You may need to remove the consideration of a baby from your mind."

I didn't want to have another baby, but being told I wouldn't be able to and that the choice would no longer be mine only made me want one. I'm thankful for the two healthy pregnancies I experienced and the two healthy boys I already have, because I know there are many women who long to have just one healthy pregnancy and one healthy baby. I had two. The desire for another baby passed with time. After all, I had my career, and once cancer was behind me, it would take off.

I told myself that once I started dating, I would likely meet and fall in love with a man who had children. If God wanted me to have more children, it would be through that path. I thought about being a bonus mom and how I would navigate building a relationship with a child or children who were not my own biologically. I just knew I would be a great bonus mom. After all, I had a great teacher, Maria.

With another brief conversation with Jesus, I began a quiet prayer. "Lord, thank you so much for sending Maria to us. If it is Your will, I promise to be a great bonus mom who loves children who are not biologically mine as if I had given birth to them. Please let me love them as much as I love you."

A house full of kids was still possible. That fact satisfied my desire to have another baby. If I were blessed with a bonus mom experience, I knew I would put in the hard work required to be a great one, and my family would grow as a result. God had answered my prayer, and my boys now have two moms as a result. I had no reason not to believe in Him. After all, He had answered so many of my prayers, most of them in times of significant distress, that I believed in Him with all my heart.

# Chapter 23

# Book

*The following story begins in January 2019, as I embarked on my first career pause. This story concludes at the beginning of my second career pause in January 2025.*

It was January 2019, and I was settling into my first career pause after the "do nothing for one year" advice had run its course. The twelve months of planning had served their purpose, and I voluntarily left the paid workforce on December 18, 2018. It was the most terrifying decision, beyond cancer treatment decisions, that I had made in my short thirty-eight years of life. Never would I have imagined that I would find myself in such an unfamiliar and extremely uncomfortable position: unemployed.

After building a career I loved through a lot of hard work, from my first dream job out of college to a fulfilling managerial role, I had put myself on the fast track to executive leadership. Cancer, however, derailed that plan.

As I grieved the loss of my career, I tried to fill my time and space with friends and family. One day in particular, a friend invited me to join him on a short trip to Scottsboro, Alabama. Scottsboro was just a forty-five-minute drive from my house, and we were headed there to browse treasures at the world-renowned thrift store, Unclaimed Baggage.

With a healthy emergency fund and health insurance, I was strictly managing my budget since I didn't have new income coming in every two weeks. Tagging along, not expecting to spend any money, I explored the book section while my friend shopped. The bright yellow cover of a book caught my eye, and I pulled it from the shelf.

Reading the title, I looked around, intent on catching the person who had placed it there for me to find. I was ready to demand that they hand over the tiny, clear earpiece they were surely using to communicate the findings of their secret investigation. I flashed back to the earpieces used in the daily powdered soap anthrax scares at Disney when I was a scared college student. Only now, I was in a thrift store, unemployed, and a scared mother of two. Certainly, someone was watching me because I was the threat.

Flipping the book open to skim the summary on the inside flap, I closed it and looked back at the title: *Work, Pause, Thrive: How to Pause for Parenthood Without Killing Your Career*, written by Lisen Stromberg. I tucked the book under my arm. With the little stash of cash in my purse, I paid for the book, eager to get home and begin reading.

After reading this book for the first time, I felt a sense of relief. The author perfectly captured the fear and anxiety of a career pause. On my second read, I sat down with a pencil and highlighter to take notes and highlight key points. I was terrified to pause my career after cancer, after a year of doing nothing. Fearful that I would not reenter the paid workforce at the level

I had been when I left, this book seemed to appear out of thin air. It was precisely the information I needed as I began planning for my return to the paid workforce.

As I started applying for jobs, I reminded myself to manage my expectations, given that I had been off for three months. According to my plan, now was the time to begin networking and submitting applications if I wanted new income coming in by June 2019.

Writing every day or even every week was not a habit; however, I did develop the habit of carrying a notebook and pencil with me wherever I went. Writing by hand helped me retain information more effectively than typing notes on my phone. The chemobrain I had experienced in the months surrounding my salary cut and title demotion had improved, but my memory still struggled to recall details. A pencil and a notebook became tools to help me heal my brain after it had been poisoned. It's a practice I continue to this day.

Rather than forget, I write everything down. Post-it notes and notepads are a staple in my life. Since my brain was poisoned and deprived of hormones, it aged rapidly, making it unable to perform at an optimal level—a necessary result, given the alternative: a recurrence of cancer. Slowly, over time, I've had to adopt tools and allocate more time for my brain to deliver satisfactory outputs.

My mom is still serving as my scribe, with friendly reminders. "Sonia, remember you volunteered to bring sourdough bread and tea to the church lunch." Other reminders come in the form of text messages, usually with an image of a vital school announcement she saw on Facebook. "Sonia, put this on your calendar. It's about the boys' back-to-school orientations." Mom has always been fully aware of my limitations, and she's always been there to help fill the gaps. A caregiver by trade, even though she never earned a dime for her work.

I like to think that my great-grandparents and grandparents are watching from Heaven, pleased with my handling of their recipe. The measuring stick I used, title and salary, indicated that I, too, was pleased with my hard work in my career. Unsure whether my hard work as a mother was paying off, I informed my boys over dinner at a nearby restaurant that I had left my job, having been offered severance and asked to leave. As of January 2025, severance propelled me into my second career pause. I continued to explain my intentions for resigning and the reasons behind them. Each goal I achieved as Chief Executive Officer, along with the one fatal missed accomplishment, was shared in detail with my boys, now sixteen and twelve. I unpacked the process I had used to plan and prepare for a second career pause, assuring them that their mom was prepared and that we would be okay.

As I wrapped up a conversation that I figured was boring to a teenager and a pre-teen, my sixteen-year-old son responded with a statement that had my jaw on the floor by the time he finished his sentence. Major said, "Mom, we're proud of you."

Now, what happened next could only be explained by the same divine control I had felt when I wanted to scream "I QUIT" to my boss that day in the coffee shop back in 2017. Only this time, the emotion was pure joy, and I didn't want to quit. I never wanted to resign from being the mother of these two boys. I wanted to leap in the air and shout, "MY KIDS ARE PROUD OF ME," pulling them in for a group hug as we danced around the restaurant. But I played it cool. He was a teenager, after all, and this moment required a nonchalant "thank you" rather than a grand display of affection.

The hard work of a mother has no actual measuring stick, but in that moment, I knew I had been successful. It motivated me to plan for my next career move. The title would be "stay-at-home mom" for at least one year, caring for two boys in their formative years, and there was no amount of money that could measure this hard work. On my second pause, I would be a full-time stay-at-home mom, just like my mother had been throughout my childhood.

To keep my brain engaged, I set a goal to write a book while on my second career pause. The process of writing this book required me to set new, healthy boundaries with my family, especially my boys and my mom, who had grown accustomed to my on-demand attention. At first, it felt hurtful to ask the three people I loved the most to give me uninterrupted time and space. I explained to them that my brain required complete focus to capture the words for this book.

Trusting the process, I established boundaries that would support my brain as I put in the hard work. I'm genuinely in awe of what my brain was able to accomplish. Even if feelings were hurt in the process, I stayed true to the new coping mechanisms I had developed through life's beautiful and dark surprises that strengthened my emotional and mental ceiling. This book was all for me. It was proof that my career was not over and proof that my brain could handle a heavy load. Furthermore, it was proof that I had mastered the recipe and was ready for something much bigger.

The book found in Unclaimed Baggage cost less than $5. It was a welcome surprise that provided me with words of encouragement as I traversed not one, but two career pauses. It felt perfectly placed on my path, arriving with perfect timing. So perfect, it could only be divine intervention.

# Chapter 24

# Divine Intervention

*The following story unfolds over a short period in 2021, beginning at the end of June and continuing through the end of December. It was my first year as Chief Executive Officer, and my career had taken off following my first career pause.*

I hadn't dated anyone seriously since my divorce and my cancer diagnosis. Dating wasn't a priority. When I saved up extra money, my boys and I would travel whenever possible. It was our hobby, a shared hobby. Avid race fans, we tried to attend at least one race—F1, IndyCar, or NASCAR—each year.

We went on a long weekend trip to New York City for Max's birthday, a Thanksgiving trip to Charleston, South Caroline, and routine day trips to nearby attractions. One of their favorite attractions to visit in North Alabama was the U.S. Space and Rocket Center. We visited Civil War memorials, as they were both fascinated by the history of war and weaponry. We loved traveling together and also enjoyed browsing through the photographs we had taken to capture the moments. They proved the trips had been fun and would leave us with memories to sustain us for a lifetime. Then, together, we would plan our next trip.

As my oldest son began transitioning into his formative years, a period of life when time with friends became increasingly important, our travel schedule naturally started to decline. It was good timing, as I had just accepted a new position as Chief Executive Officer. I wanted one entire year with as few distractions as possible so I could focus on my career and being a damned good leader of the people under my care in my new role.

On one Saturday, my parents were at church hosting Vacation Bible School for the children in our church community. This was something they had done my entire life. Daddy wasn't feeling well and lay down on a church pew. One of the deacons of the church, Doyle, later drove him home so my mom could continue working at VBS. Doyle returned to the church and kept calling to check on my dad since he was home alone. His final call prompted him to suggest that my mom leave, pick up my dad, and take him to the emergency room. Mom arrived home, got Daddy in the car, and then drove him to Crestwood. He was lucid but in a lot of pain as she went.

Earlier that same week, my dad's doctor determined he had a blockage in his colon rather than a suspected kidney stone. Daddy had experienced a total of 50 kidney stones in his life to date. Confident that with plenty of fluids, the blockage would resolve itself, as most do, he was still instructed to get to the ER if the pain intensified.

As soon as Mom got Dad in the door of the ER, he passed out and was quickly wheeled into a room where the nurses and technicians began their assessment. Surgery was scheduled first thing the following morning to clear the blockage. His efforts to clear the blockage by drinking plenty of water had not been practical in this case.

A routine surgical procedure for this type of condition, with the risks appropriately discussed, the medical team encouraged my mom to go home. Although safer-at-home orders had been lifted for over a year, a new surge of COVID-19 was emerging. It was safest to spend as little time as possible in the hospital if you weren't a patient under the care of a medical professional. Plus, my dad was stable, sedated, and in good hands. He was at Crestwood, a familiar place to my parents, given my eight-year career at the hospital.

The nurse assured my mom, "We will call you in the morning when he is being prepped for surgery." The call would be her signal to return to the hospital. She would get a night of rest at home in her own bed, alone.

I was still asleep when my phone rang early in the morning. Since I rarely kept my ringer on at night, I had set it to full volume before I went to sleep, just in case my mom called with an update. It was my mom calling. She was back at the hospital.

Expecting an update on the surgery time and my orders on when to arrive at the hospital, my ears were met instead with a hysterical voice. I didn't even hear what she said. The sound of her voice was enough. "MOM, NO! NO!" I cried.

She told me to go to the hospital as soon as possible. The boys were still asleep, so I called Jason. "I've got to get to the hospital. That's all I know. The boys are still sleeping. Can you come and get them?" He agreed. Jason had been kept informed about Daddy's condition. After all, my parents still treated him as if he were their son-in-law. Jason, in return, continued to treat my parents as if they were still his in-laws. He held my parents in high regard, and they equally respected him as the father of their grandchildren.

The prognosis was grim. My mom, receiving the call, arrived at the hospital in the morning. Dad was being prepped for surgery. However, the medical team took him back to the operating room before Mom was able to see him and kiss him goodbye. They were ahead of schedule, and Mom, disappointed that she didn't get to see her love before surgery, understood the tight schedule of a caregiver in a hospital.

When she arrived at the hospital, she was politely ushered to a private consultation room where the doctor would provide an update following surgery. She had no reason for concern. The nurses had provided an update on Daddy's condition. He, too, had rested well the night before and was still in stable condition, prepared for a routine surgery to clear his colon of a blockage.

When the doctor opened the door to the small consultation room where my mom sat, he said, "You should call your family. I'm not sure your husband will make it through the day."

It still breaks my heart to think about it. Alone, she heard the most terrifying news. Her husband, my daddy, may not make it. It took me back to the day I was alone, hearing the ominous words: "It looks suspicious." My heart shattered because I knew the type of pain and emotion that rushed through my mom's body alone.

Unbeknownst to the doctor, when you told someone in our family to "call the family" because someone we loved may not make it, a mix of blood relatives and church relatives would descend on a hospital like a legion of angels. Within hours on this particular Sunday, Mt. Nebo Baptist Church would be filled with our church family, all praying for my dad and their pastor. There was no preacher behind the pulpit sharing the gospel. There were only parishioners in the pews being led in prayer by the deacons.

The third-floor intensive care unit waiting room at Crestwood, with a new variant of COVID-19 on the rise, was packed so full that people spilled into the hallways. Our family, friends, and Daddy's young adult Sunday School class came to comfort my mom, sister, and me during one of our greatest times of need.

As soon as I saw the hospital security guard, respecting his authority and the message he was about to deliver to this rowdy crowd of people loitering in the hospital halls, I bolted for the elevator ahead of his chastising, knowing he would soon request that we move the party outside for everyone's safety. Hospital leadership had started implementing its level one COVID-19 safety protocol. Everyone in this party for my daddy, who lay behind a locked door in the intensive care unit, complied respectfully with the security guard because he was absolutely right.

Once on the elevator, I was alone. I had beaten the mob as they were being evacuated from the hospital. Now, on the first floor, I walked into a small room. This was a room I had walked by hundreds of times during my tenure at Crestwood, and yet I realized I had never seen anyone sitting in this comfortable place of refuge. I had only entered it because it was a quiet place and perfect for organizing a media interview with a medical professional, as media relations was a key responsibility of my job during my years at the hospital.

The chapel, located inside the hospital, sat empty. It was my place of refuge, a backup Mt. Nebo Baptist Church, where I took a seat and shed tears and snot. I prayed diligently and faithfully for my family. Daddy had told us many times not to be sad. When his time came, we should celebrate because he had lived a great life. He spoke those words often to comfort his family. But he also trusted that his family would be just fine. The dash on his tombstone would be proof that he followed the recipe perfectly: family, hard work, and faith in God.

Daddy did survive, but he had a long road to recovery. Thirteen feet of his colon had to be removed over five days and three surgeries. His incision was left open, which was the proper procedure for this condition, a severe colon blockage. When a part of the colon is removed, there's always the chance that more may die, and dead tissue must be removed to prevent infection and foster proper recovery. In the surgical intensive care unit waiting room at Crestwood, we sat and waited for five days, unsure if my daddy would leave the hospital alive.

The final surgery had been scheduled. Together, my mom, sister, and a handful of family members sat in the tiny waiting room. One particular family member was my Uncle Larry, Daddy's big brother and best friend. A built-in lifelong companion, his parents had gifted him. With him was his wife of nearly fifty years, my Aunt Maggie.

Uncle Larry was a quiet yet revered man, faithful in prayer. Up until this point, I didn't recall him and me ever engaging in a deep conversation. While Mom, Amanda, and Aunt Maggie took their turn visiting Dad in his ICU room, I was left alone in the waiting room with Uncle Larry. His quiet voice began a one-sided conversation as I watched tears well up in this grown man's eyes. His voice began to shake, and I comforted him during his time of heartache and fear that he might lose his baby brother.

Once Mom, Amanda, and Aunt Maggie returned from their short visit, I called my mom and sister out into the hallway for a conversation all my own. I instructed them never to leave me alone with Uncle Larry in a situation like this again. It wasn't that I didn't love my Uncle Larry, but I too was terrified and felt myself hitting an emotional ceiling. Once Daddy was fully recovered, we would share this story with him and his brother later. As the story unfolded, laughter erupted. Our family's humor, our go-to coping mechanism, helped me process Uncle Larry's grief healthily and productively.

On the day of Daddy's final surgery, a hospital employee greeted us and informed my mom, sister, and me that we should proceed to the private consultation room across the hall from the surgery department. Uncle Larry and Aunt Maggie were present on this day, too. They stayed behind in the waiting room as Mom, Amanda, and I made our way to the consultation room.

Filing into the small room, which was about the size of a closet, we avoided eye contact with each other and were careful not to utter a sound, waiting in silence. All three of us were praying our own silent prayers. As I mentioned earlier, Daddy had the habit of telling us that death was of no concern to him, and when he did die, he wanted us to be happy and joyful. He had lived a great life for God, put in the hard work, and had a beautiful family he loved. When it was his time, it would be cause for celebration. Still, his wife and daughters were selfish humans, and we wanted him to be here for many, many more years.

The doctor had done well to manage our expectations. We waited for the news that would shatter our world. But that news never came. Daddy had made it through his third and final surgery. The surgeon was able to suture his belly closed. As the doctor opened the door to the consultation room where we stood apart from one another, we waited for him to say he was gone. He began his update with a gleeful tone. "Surgery went well. We were able to close him up. I've got to be honest with you, I didn't think he would make it through this final surgery."

The surgeon had done his job well. The medical team had appropriately communicated the risks, and we had done our part in a risk assessment. For four nights, my mom went home alone. It was her preference, giving herself time and space. To fill the empty house, she pulled out old photo albums, carefully organized with mostly pictures she had taken. She also had a collection of photographs from my Granddaddy Carl and Granny Ruth's house.

One photograph after another was neatly tucked into a folder. My mom, alone, did the hard work of preparing for her true love's funeral. Each picture had to be just right as she flipped through the pages of album after album. Now we laugh and tease Daddy, saying he was the only person we knew who got to preview his life in photographs on display for mourners. These photographs were meant to be shared at his funeral because none of us expected him to walk out of the hospital alive.

As the doctor continued to explain the prognosis and next steps, our spirits lifted. The doctor exited the room, leaving the three people who loved my daddy the most together. Finally making eye contact, still with no words spoken, my mom brought her two daughters together, and we hugged each other tighter than we had ever hugged before. Together, we rushed back to tell my Uncle Larry and Aunt Maggie the incredible news, and I was saved from another emotional standoff with my Uncle Larry.

Daddy was still a very sick man. For eleven days, a machine breathed for him. After spending thirteen days in the intensive care unit, he was well enough to move into a regular hospital room. By then, the hospital had implemented its level one COVID-19 lockdown protocol, and visitors were limited. My mom went back and forth to the hospital to be with Daddy. Amanda and I limited our visits to minimize the risk of intro-ducing foreign germs into Daddy's safe, sterile hospital environ-ment, as well as to respect the incredible life-saving work of medical professionals. Instead, together we poured our time and attention into our mom—the ultimate caregiver, and our care-giver.

Amanda and I took turns bringing her food, decorating her parked car in the hospital parking lot with cards and flowers her grandchildren had made for her, and coordinating dinners with friends to keep her distracted. While Mom spent her days with Daddy in the hospital, Amanda and I worked to care for her, just like she had always done for us.

Finally, my dad was moved out of the ICU and into a regular hospital room. The boys and I had plans to meet Mom for dinner and catch up on Daddy's condition. They had spent the day at their Nana and Papa's house in Gurley, Alabama.

Excited to visit their Gramma, we pulled out onto Highway 72 and headed west toward Huntsville. The car came out of nowhere and smashed into the driver's side just behind my door. I don't remember the 360-degree turn my white, one-year-old Lexus GX made in the middle of a busy highway. Knocked out for a few seconds from the driver-side airbag, I came to. We were sitting still in the driveway of the Chevron gas station. My car had been hit with such force that it spun and stopped an estimated twenty feet from where it had been on the road.

I heard Major's voice from the back seat, "Mom, are you okay?" Fuzzy, my brain finally made sense of what had just happened. Major was fine, and I looked over at Max, who was sitting in the passenger seat. He was scared. "Get out of the car, boys, and walk as far away as you can. Watch for other vehicles as you exit," I commanded. A first responder was already at my door.

We were okay. No one was hurt in either vehicle. The innovative safety features of modern cars helped limit the physical damage to my body. The boys' Nana, Jason's mom, arrived on the scene first, followed by my sister and brother-in-law, Scott. My sister made her way to me as I still sat in the car, while the first responders carefully assessed the situation. "Don't tell Mom," I told my sister. "She doesn't need anything else on her plate right now."

Major was standing nearby and confessed that he had already told Gramma we wouldn't be meeting her for dinner. He had explained to her that we had just been in a car wreck and that our car would only be leaving on the back of a tow truck. He comforted my mom, his grandmother, by assuring her that we were all okay and that she did not need to worry. Even as a young boy, he observed the way the adults in his life treated one another, and he understood the recipe. At that moment, a thirteen-year-old boy took on the role of a man to protect his family from heartache.

By now, the adrenaline had tightened my body, and I was shaking. Still in shock, the paramedics placed me in the ambulance to assess me. "Ms. Robinson, do you need to go to the hospital?" I honestly wasn't sure. There was no blood, but my chest was so tight. I rubbed my left breast to ensure the medical-grade balloon was still in its correct position. It felt as though my breast implant, the new balloon placed after a double mastectomy, had been ripped from its enclosure and shoved under my armpit by the seat belt—a safety device that prevented life-threatening injuries and saved my life, as my car was struck by another vehicle that had lost control after its brakes went out. The driver and passenger of the other vehicle were okay, and they were more concerned about me as I heard them calling out, "Is she okay? Is she okay?"

My head was fuzzy, and I couldn't focus. "You have a concussion," the paramedic declared. "Ms. Robinson, do you want to go to the hospital?" My sister was just outside the ambulance, and we made eye contact. I wasn't sure I should go. I would have no one with me. I would have no one to sit with me there because my mom was with our dad. Amanda and Scott were going to stay behind to handle the tow truck arrangements. Nana had taken the boys with her and would drop them off at their dad's house.

I elected to go to the hospital. Since my emergency contact, my mom, was already unavailable, I requested that the ambulance take me to Crestwood. "I have to go to Crestwood. Can you please take me there? My mom is already there." I started to cry. The emotion of everything hit me. The realization, a sad re-alization, that I had no one to call. I had no one who would rush in panic to the hospital to be with me. My mom, my emergency contact, was right where she was supposed to be: with the love of her life. She was comforting and nurturing her true love.

That night, lying on an emergency room gurney, the nurse gave me a muscle relaxer, and my body began to calm from the trauma of the car accident. My head was still fuzzy, and I was unable to open my eyes. Lying in a hospital bed with the lights low, my mom had taken time away from my daddy to sit by my side. I declared, "Mom, it's time. It's time for me to find an emer-gency contact, because look at us. You've been at the hospital for weeks with Daddy. I had to request to come to Crestwood because you were already here." The laughter was more subtle because it hurt to move my body.

# Chapter 25

# Emergency Contact

*T*he following story is a continuation of the previous chapter and shares details of my declaration to start dating again.

It became another joke between my mom, sister, and me that I needed an emergency contact. Daddy had been in the hospital for weeks, and Mom, who was my emergency contact, was out of commission caring for the love of her life. She had no time or energy to come to my rescue if I had an emergency. My car crash was a sign, a divine intervention, so I decided that I would try to find a new emergency contact. After all, the experience my family just had was proof I needed one, and I needed one now.

Just like that, I decided that at the start of the new year, I would start dating to secure an emergency contact. One year into my role as CEO, our team was on the verge of achieving our first audacious goal. Trust had been built, and my team was beginning to thrive. I had one more tough decision to make under the careful mentorship of the gentleman who had invited me back to the company where I had spent eight years before leaving due to cancer. His mentorship was much needed and appreciated because I was organizing a reduction-in-force, and it broke my heart. It was necessary if our business was to survive the post-pandemic rebuild.

Gleaning from the lessons taught by Linda, my executive coach, I consulted with her on the best approach. A situation of this caliber required the highest level of empathy, respect, and kindness. Once the reduction in force was successfully implemented and once the stress of the negative profit and loss statement was behind me, I would have the emotional and mental bandwidth to open my mind to the possibility of true love. I would begin dating again. I would wait until the first of the year, and then I might give Bumble another try since it worked for me once before. I didn't know Bumble wouldn't be necessary. On December 30, 2021, I went on a date, and we didn't meet on a dating app.

While Daddy was in the hospital, it wasn't unusual for old friends and acquaintances to send me direct messages on Facebook Messenger to check in on Daddy's progress. Every message was sure to include phrases like "I'm thinking about y'all" and "let me know if you need anything." Our friends, family, and my parents' neighbors were so gracious with their time and energy. Neighbors kept my parents' yard mowed. Friends and family delivered food and sweet treats. Some even handed Mom a wad of cash during their visits.

Mom was uncomfortable taking cash from people. She and Dad were financially healthy and had great insurance, a benefit of retiring from a government municipality many years prior. Daddy had a traditional retirement plan, common for his generation, in which a portion of his salary was deferred into a mandatory retirement fund, and health insurance was part of the total post-retirement compensation plan.

I encouraged her by saying, "Mom, people want to help, and sometimes the only way they know how to help is by giving you money. Take the money so they can receive a blessing. Let them help." She took the money and later confessed to me that she had donated all of it to other people in need. To Mom's family and friends who slipped in some extra cash, thank you! Mom, on your behalf, donated over $500 to other people. That is who my mom is: a caregiver to all.

A direct message from a guy, an acquaintance, didn't stand out among the string of notes I was reading. I knew him, and he knew me and my family, too. Early in our marriage, Jason and I had a pontoon boat. We loved spending time at Tims Ford Lake in Tennessee. That was our shared hobby, and it was so much fun. It's now a hobby he shares with Maria and our boys. The boys love it, and Jason loves trying to toss them from the tube, grinning ear to ear as they glide across the water, laughing the whole way.

At the time, this particular man and his wife also had a boat. They would occasionally join the group of boats parked in our self-declared cove, Owl Hollow. Or, as we country folk like to say, "Ooooowl Holler." I remember hopping on his boat along with some other friends to be entertained by grown men trying to wake surf. Their dad bods were on full display for bystanders. Bystanders, not concerned with their 'dad bods,' were full of laughter, more concerned about the cold drink in their hands and the warm sun on their faces. Me included.

By now, Amanda, Scott, and I had established the habit of updating Daddy on everyone who had been asking about him and praying for him. Daddy was home, and one evening at my parents' house, I gave my update on who had reached out. "You may not know him, Daddy," I said, but I still wanted to be sure he knew about everyone who was thinking of and praying for him and his family.

My brother-in-law, Scott, spoke up. "Yeah, you know him." Then, Scott asked if I knew that he and his wife had divorced a few years ago. I did not. Keeping up with the life surprises of others was not in my nature. After all, I had my own life surprises to navigate, so I wasn't overly concerned with other people's painful pile of memories.

As Scott continued to talk about a different topic, I recalled the lake days on this guy's boat. He was cute, even with a dad bod. I had a mom bod that would match his dad bod perfectly. I remember him being funny and kind. It was then that I remembered that I needed an emergency contact.

# Chapter 26

# Quest for Love

*The following story covers my quest for love from the moment I chose to reenter the dating world after cancer in October 2018. The story will take you, the reader, through the very beginning of a beautiful fairy tale—a romance that truly began in December 2023, when I boldly declared that I would start dating again at the start of the new year.*

At the first anniversary of my last chemotherapy session, after pouring all my love into the one person guaranteed to be with me my entire life, myself, I was ready to give my love away. I loved myself so much, and I felt stronger emotionally and mentally than I ever had. My recent experiences—cancer, a salary reduction, a title demotion, and the hostile behavior of a supervisor—felt like a pile of shit. Shit is gross, and it needs to be cleaned up. Only I could do the hard work of cleaning it up. It was my responsibility; no one else could save me.

As my hair grew back following four rounds of chemo, every few weeks I would visit my friend, the one who gently shaved my head as chemo took my hair. She shaped the new growth into a cute pixie. No longer bearing the markers of a cancer patient, I told my girlfriends, Jeannette, Nicole, and Amy, "I think I will start dating again." They erupted in unison, "YES!"

We chose Bumble as the app that would announce my availability to the online dating world. With their careful guidance, we selected the photos and crafted the summary. He and I never would have met if it weren't for a dating app. Our paths never would have crossed. I walked into the coffee shop, the same coffee shop where I fought back the words "I QUIT," because my friends had insisted that I meet this new guy in a familiar and busy place, on the slight chance that I would be kidnapped.

His profile picture was on my phone screen as I scanned the crowd. This tall, dark, and very handsome man stood at attention. Our eyes met, and we both smiled. Unsure of how the first meeting with an online stranger was supposed to go, I extended my hand, inviting a handshake. He said, "Come here and give me a hug."

We began seeing each other regularly. Both of us were coming off a challenging year. I was recovering from cancer, and he was recovering from a divorce. He had just relocated to Huntsville to be close to his children, and he was a fantastic and present father to two older children. One was in college and the other in high school. I met his children only once, and in passing, we exchanged a "hello, it's nice to meet you." Together, this Bumble guy and I agreed this would be a fun and adventurous courtship. After all, we were both in need of some good fun and adventure. We weren't exclusive, but we were safe, mindful, and respectful of our bodies and emotions.

For over two years, we kept things simple, but our conversations were far from superficial. We talked about our lived experiences openly and honestly. We talked about the brutal battle against our emotions. Unbeknownst to each other, we were healing in the process.

As I re-entered the paid workforce following my first career pause and began traveling more, distance naturally grew between us. He was dating someone else, and it became more serious—someone he would fall in love with and eventually marry. We lost touch, but I still think of him and the love he gave me. In turn, I think about the love I gave him.

In my quest for love, I found a friend who would also learn the curves of my body and the imperfect lines of my scars. He made me feel like a woman, in every sense of the word. It makes me smile. We weren't going to be each other's true love or lifelong love. He and I were just two people placed in each other's path at the right time for the right duration. He, too, was a faithful man and a flawed protagonist in his own story. I wish he would write a book. I would definitely read it.

Fast forward to the time I realized I needed an emergency contact. I re-engaged on Facebook Messenger and reread the message from an acquaintance checking in on my dad. This new guy and I had exchanged quick direct messages back and forth for nearly four months until he asked if I wanted to meet up. "We should meet for coffee or a beer," he suggested. A potential suitor as an emergency contact, I thought—the emergency contact I desperately needed. I agreed to meet.

He extended a peculiar invitation to meet over coffee or beer. The Bumble guy suggested we meet for coffee. That short courtship was fun and full of adventure. This new guy might add to the fun and adventure. I suggested we meet for a beer. After all, we both had demanding days at work, and carving out time for a coffee date would turn into a game of calendar Tetris more complicated than anything I'd ever played. I didn't have an executive assistant managing my business life, much less my dating life. Meeting for a beer would be easier and put this new plan in motion much sooner than waiting for coffee ever could.

We set a date, time, and location. On December 30, 2021, I walked into Greenbus Brewery, located on Eustis Avenue in downtown Huntsville, to meet a potential new emergency contact. My life would never be the same.

Taking our time, we began hanging out as often as our busy schedules permitted, with or without our children. A bike enthusiast, he was eager for me to ride with him as he got his exercise in, and I could get a workout in, too. I was no longer working out with regularity, as the demands of work and raising two boys limited my free time for a sweat session. Going to the gym had been replaced with walks and home workouts because I loved to move my body healthily and productively, even with a busy schedule.

Cycling is a time-consuming sport and hobby. If I were riding regularly, we could ride together and spend more time together. After spending a year dedicated to a disciplined CrossFit regimen, I was in shape. I could ride long distances, just not at the speed of veteran cyclists. It was a physical struggle. I made a concerted effort to adopt a new hobby and spend quality time with the new guy I was falling madly in love with. Perhaps it was a test to see if I was the one—a test of endurance and a foreshadowing of a life surprise.

Nine months into our courtship, he invited me to join him on the annual Spring City Cycling Club "All-You-Can-Eat Century" ride. With no clue what I was getting myself into, not even knowing that a century in biking terms meant one hundred miles, I thought to myself, "What have I done?" Encouragingly, he said I could choose when to turn, and assured me that if I needed an escape hatch, he would support my decision.

There was a thirty-mile loop and a sixty-mile loop, an escape route for a weak and weary cyclist, which I was sure to be. We had clocked miles together, but not thirty and certainly not sixty. Not overly confident in my own ability to bike double-digit miles, I opted for the thirty-mile loop, and he supported my decision. It was settled: I would exit early, leaving him to ride the one-hundred-mile loop alone. Well, not technically alone, be-cause the group he was riding with could maintain the required watts. For the remainder of this story, I will refer to this new guy as "Love."

A small group of us, including Love's son, who was also a great cyclist, planned to ride together. When the thirty-mile marker came into sight, I planned to turn and finish the ride alone. Love and his son shared the hobby of cycling, and I loved that they spent quality time together.

Each member of the group checked on me and provided en-couraging words, as well as jokes, as we rode. The weather was beautiful and not too hot for a September day in North Al-abama. I was having a great time, and pedaling circles for miles didn't seem so harsh. Thirty miles felt easy.

"Hey Sonia, you still thinking about the thirty-mile loop?" Firm in my decision, I hollered back, "Yep!" When laughter erupted, someone shouted, "You missed the thirty-mile turn back there."

This test, a test of endurance, would take me to the sixty-mile turn. I wasn't sure I would make it through the day. The emotional, mental, and physical labor silenced me. I was reaching a new ceiling in my emotional, cognitive, and physical abilities.

Focused, I would not miss that turn. I couldn't miss that turn, so I fell silent. Silence was my go-to coping mechanism since my brain had been tattered by chemo, daily medicine, and years of medical menopause. Five years in a constant state of perimenopause meant enduring hot flashes, night sweats, mood swings, weight gain, and fatigue. Sexy, I know, and this new guy was here for it.

My brain required silence to focus and process difficult things. The miles were adding up, and I wasn't so sure I would be able to make it back alone. With thirty miles in, I took the sixty-mile turn to begin my thirty-mile journey back. "I'll stop at the second-to-last nutrition tent and wait on y'all." That was my safety net, giving me time to rest and leaving about fifteen miles of biking to go.

Exchanging goodbyes and good lucks, I made the turn that saved me from the one-hundred-mile loop. The lonely miles ahead made space for deep thinking. This, I realized, was why people fall in love with cycling. This was why Love always wanted to be on his bike. It's just you, your mind, and your body doing all the hard work. Alone, I could go at my own pace and stop to rest along the way without disturbing another cyclist's attempt to fulfill their ideal ride based on their own pace and limits.

I, too, slowed the pace so I wouldn't struggle for the fifteen miles that would deliver me from this hell. At times, I paused along the way. At times, I sped along, especially when the dog, I was sure was rabid and demon-possessed, bolted down a hill from its resting place. "Not today, Satan. Not today," I thought, and my legs kicked into high gear. I'm not sure where the strength and energy came from, but I survived a near-death dog attack, and I was sure of it.

With plenty of time to rest, I parked my bike at the second-to-last nutrition site, where new friends I had made through this new adventure offered me pickles, homemade fried pies, cookies, and some much-needed encouragement to finish this torturous activity. Sharing my story of the near-fatal dog attack, these new friends and I filled the open air with conversation and laughter.

I sat eating junk food to replenish the calories I had burned. With plenty of new friends to keep me company, I sat and waited for the man I was sure I would spend the rest of my life with to arrive. As he and the others pulled into the nutrition stop, I was so happy to be reunited with Love. We finished the ride together. As I struggled, he would fall back beside me and make some jokes or hazing comments. He wanted me to finish the ride. He was so happy that I was there with him, spending my time engaged in his favorite hobby.

He was also beaming with pride that I had not only biked thirty miles, but I had biked sixty. An accomplishment that he never missed an opportunity to brag about when we were in the company of other cyclists. It was the longest time I had ever spent in the saddle of a machine powered by my body. It felt amazing and equally exhausting. However, I was also proud of the hard work. Love was a great coach and mentor as we biked together, both as individuals and as lovers.

After that sixty-mile ride, we continued to ride together. I was trying so hard to fall in love with this hobby the way Love had, but biking wasn't for me. In one last attempt, he adjusted his electronic bicycle, which he hardly ever used, so it fit me. The All-You-Can-Eat was coming up again, and I planned to bike all one hundred miles on an e-bike with my true love.

I could keep up with him thanks to the power boost from a battery pack that rested beneath my body. It was terrible. Only a few miles in, I regretted my decision and had just under one hundred miles to go before I could escape. Recalling the mantra, "The definition of insanity is doing the same thing over and over and expecting different results," I realized a new emotional, mental, and physical ceiling would be met that day, and I quit. However, first, I rode the hundred miles on an e-bike. To be clear, when I set a goal and commit to accomplishing something, I don't stop short of success. That's who I was, and I knew it with a deep conviction, proven by my past life performances.

The ride started in the middle of pouring rain, and even on an e-bike, I couldn't maintain my watts at the preferred level. Love would race ahead only to slow down, giving me time to catch up. On challenging climbs, my power boost kicked into high gear, and I would run ahead of him, only to catch his hazing jabs as he inevitably came racing past me again on the straight, flat road. To a cyclist, this was frustrating. Together, we would never form the two-person peloton required to preserve energy as cyclists forged ahead. This kind man never vented frustration toward me. He was just happy I had given him my time and supported him by pursuing an interest in his passion: cycling.

After that ride, I felt defeated and confessed to him that I was done with cycling. We had tried to create a shared hobby to spend more time together, but it just wasn't working for me. Instead, we agreed that I would go anywhere and everywhere with him for rides and races, serving as his pit crew when needed. Another mutually agreed-upon boundary in our relationship, and one that allowed us to keep spending quality time together, lost in conversation. Mature love, true love, had finally found a home in my heart.

I equally had a demanding hobby: travel. Early in our relationship, I flew to Orlando to spend half of spring break with him and his children. My boys were spending their spring break with their dad, so I had the extra time. I remember the second night of this Disney spring break trip as vividly as if I were still lying there in the wet bed.

Disney is expensive, and Love insisted that I room with him and his kiddos. He planned to sleep in the bed with his son, while I slept in the other full-size bed with his daughter. The sleeping arrangement saved me hundreds of dollars on a hotel room of my own. It seemed reasonable, even though some bystanders might pop out with a box of popcorn and others might interject with their opinions. We were careful with our closeness and display of affection in front of little eyes. Love had a daughter, a little girl who already had me wrapped around her little fingers. He was raising her to be an independent and strong woman who would stand her ground in the face of adversity. This little girl had a big and bold personality. We were drawn to each other like moths to a flame. I was going to be her bonus mom, and I believed it.

The first morning I was there, we rose early for the chosen park rope drop. Disney's attention to detail was remarkable. Each night, crews carefully washed and cleaned every surface, scraped away every rogue piece of gum from the painted concrete, and prepared for the next day. In the morning, eager guests gathered behind a rope, waiting in anticipation for it to drop so they could begin their day in the most magical place on Earth.

The words leaped from my mouth before I knew what I had done: "I'll fix her hair." After all, I had seen the work of a single father when it came to hairstyling. If I were here and going to Disney with this new guy and his children, then his daughter's hair needed to show the world that she was cared for and that I knew what I was doing.

I sat quietly watching YouTube videos on how to braid hair. It took me several tries, while this little girl sat patiently, happy to spend time with her new friend. The braid looked awful, and this little girl's fine hair sprang loose from the uneven rope I had created in my first-ever attempt at braiding. After all, I was the mother of two boys, and those types of shills had never been required of me. Walking out the door to make the rope drop, I snagged one of the hats her dad had brought for her. Perfect. She could wear a hat, and no one would ever know I had failed my first test as a self-declared bonus mom.

Calling my sister to share the somewhat embarrassing failure, I told her what I had done and how I regretted never offering to fix Anna's, my niece's, dark, thick, and long hair on the mornings she spent the nights with me. I would always tell Amanda and Anna that the one rule when Anna stayed overnight at my house was that she was responsible for her own hair. They should plan accordingly before dropping her off for a slumber party with her Big Nonny and her two boy cousins.

Oh, wait, the wet bed. Yes, I left that cliffhanger unresolved a little too long. After our first very long day, hopping from one Disney park to another, we made it back to our shared hotel room. I was exhausted, convinced that Love and his son treated a Disney vacation like an Olympic sport—with them as the gold medalists. We found this sweet little girl passed out in a deep sleep in the stroller, her oversized body spilling out of it.

I gently changed her clothes from sweaty, smelly athletic shorts and shirt to soft, clean pajamas as she slept through the entire wardrobe change. I didn't have the heart to wake her up to use the bathroom one last time before bedtime, as I always did when my boys were her age. A small bladder, holding the contents of Disney-induced hydration, exploded in our warm and dry bed that night.

At first, I thought I was dreaming, and once I snapped awake, I wondered if perhaps I was the one who had wet the bed. It had been a very long time since I did something like that. As I continued my investigation of this mysterious liquid, it finally dawned on me, and I said quietly to myself, "I should have woken her up." It was both the responsible and the motherly thing to do. I was being punished for my inability to be a great bonus mom.

As I lifted my wet body from the damp bed, I tiptoed over to where Love lay sleeping with his son. Gently shaking him awake, I whispered, "I need your help." Together, we cleaned up the mess, trying to get the wet bedclothes off without disturbing

Sleeping Beauty as we changed her clothes so she would be dry. We laughed under our breath as we worked.

It was redemption that I could do this bonus mom thing and do it well. I just needed the strong arms of a man who would learn my curves and my scars intimately to help me. We would make a great team as parents to four children. I believed it at that moment, and we had only been dating for three short months. In my quest for love, it seemed to appear out of nowhere, like divine intervention itself.

# Chapter 27

# Romance

*The following story reveals true love. A love that everyone hopes to experience in their lifetime, even if for only a short period. It's the kind of love that provides photographs and memories to sustain us.*

New York would be our first solo trip together. It was a dry run to see just how healthy Love and I would be as travel partners, just the two of us. My version of the All-You-Can-Eat bike ride. It was a make-or-break trip.

With Hamilton tickets I had purchased before the pandemic closed the world down, originally intending to take a solo trip or bring the boys back to New York, the Broadway show was the only thing on our agenda. We walked the streets of the city, popping into bars along the way. As we walked hand in hand, conversation and laughter filled the space between us.

We stumbled upon a large, docked sailboat that had been converted into a restaurant. It was packed, and we didn't have reservations. Bummed, we exited the ship, only for the hostess to call after us, "We had a cancellation. Please, come back. We have a table for two just for you." At lunch, we ordered a dozen raw oysters as an appetizer. We settled in to enjoy our meal together.

Observing how we each preferred to doctor the slimy mollusk, he glanced up to stare deep into my eyes, then grabbed his phone and snapped a picture of me. He wanted to capture a moment he was spending with a beautiful woman, so he turned his phone around to show me the image. "You have something on your nose."

Laughing as my heart sped up when he poked fun at me. That picture would be printed and framed as a gift to him for our very first Christmas together. A reminder for us both not to take life too seriously and to have fun in the process. A reminder that we were madly in love with each other. I believed it. I loved this man and his children.

As our New York trip came to a close, we rented bikes and cruised through Central Park. I had been thinking all along that I had found my forever travel companion. Another travel test was administered in December 2023 when we took all four of our kids, ranging in age from seven to seventeen, to Universal Studios and Disney. We aced the test. The kids had a great time, and we all bonded as a unit. A new family in bloom, my expanding family with a man and his children who were not biologically mine. I would be a bonus mom, and I made sure to work hard at being a great one, just like Maria had taught me.

Boston was on the docket for my forty-third birthday trip. Unknowingly, the London and Paris trip we had planned for the summer of 2024 would be our last trip together. It would be the trip where he proposed at the Eiffel Tower, and I said, "Yes."

Confessing months before our London and Paris trip, I shared that I romanticized about Love proposing at the Eiffel Tower. We laughed as we dreamed about our new life together. Love and I had been talking about the next step for months. The Eiffel Tower proposal was far-fetched. It was the kind of proposal only meant for the movies. It wasn't something that happened in real life, and certainly not in mine. After all, the series of events from the past few years had been packed with plot twists that only Saturday Night Live writers could bring to life with the help of talented comedians.

Continuing to excel in my role as an executive leader, the final piece was in place: a lover. I had successfully rebounded my career after a pause following cancer. I had followed the guidance from the divine book *Work, Pause, Thrive*. I didn't have any reason for concern. My Board members, who held the authority to fire me without cause because I lived in an "at will" state, Alabama, were supportive.

I had no concerns over my performance; the feedback I was getting was all "atta boys" and "keep up the great work." So I did. I did my job well. Even better, I now had a man with strong arms who intimately knew my curves and also knew my scars in ways no other man ever had. He was the one. He was my forever love. After setting a three-date rule but never actually communicating it, we made love for the first time.

Hey now, I was a Christian and raised with Southern Baptist principles, but I was also a woman in her prime with needs. That night, as he kissed me, I whispered, "You are dangerous." Love had waited patiently, planning to make his move. He knew precisely when to take me into his arms. It was magical.

Another one of my romantic thoughts was, "Let's create a RomCom scene in Publix," I would say when I knew he was on his way to the grocery store at the same time I was planning to go. The scene would unfold with him bumping into my cart (or "buggy," as I called it), and the sparks would fly. Our little romantic comedy. Our love story. The wild imagination of my youth remained intact after all these years.

We wouldn't play out a romantic comedy scene; instead, we would push our individual carts as we shopped for dinner items to prepare separately for our own children. Together, we gave each other the time and space we needed with our own children. It was a mutually agreed-upon, healthy, and happy boundary. One designed to protect the emotional and mental integrity of not just ourselves, but also of our four children. Parenting, and parenting well, were essential to both of us. Love and I had failed in previous marriages, but we would not fail as parents.

We discussed blending our families, the challenges, and the joy of having a house full of four kids. It seemed possible with him. My disappointment in not being able to have another baby of my own had been replaced by embracing bonus mom life. I wanted to focus almost exclusively on the blending process as a mother. My career was at a pivotal point, and my team had one more big goal to accomplish. That goal and my team were top priorities. Once that goal was achieved, I would have the capacity to focus on blending and building our new family. Again, we agreed on a mutual boundary.

By now, wisdom from lived experiences had provided me with a painful understanding of my own limitations. I had previous experiences hitting my own emotional and mental ceiling over and over again. With each impact, the ceiling did rise a little higher, giving me time and space to recover from the trauma. My lived experiences had been hard ones, and I developed new ways of coping with heightened emotions as well as demanding mental tasks. Linda, my executive coach, had trained me well. The emotional control muscle I flexed daily in the role of CEO, as well as the tasks of an executive leader, had become essential. It had to be the strongest muscle developed to withstand the pressures, demands, scorekeeping bystanders, and the noise that comes along with being a damn good leader of people.

Together, we discussed that I would be entirely focused on work until the fourth and final audacious goal was achieved. This was an intentional effort to protect my emotional and mental bandwidth. We were in no rush to formalize our relationship. We loved each other and had the rest of our lives to be together. This man, Love, had been placed perfectly in my path at the right time—something this romantic could only describe as divine.

# Chapter 28

# YES!

*This is the story of when I said "YES!" to the love of my life on the Eiffel Tower in Paris, France. A made-for-television romantic exchange between two flawed lovers.*

With four children involved, Love and I both needed the proper headspace to expand our parenting responsibilities and merge our families together in the process. We wouldn't get married for another year or so. The engagement was the first step. He wanted my input on "THE" ring, and I wanted to leave room for him to add his own touch of style.

In and out of jewelry stores, I collected ideas and passed along details that drew my attention. Each jewelry store carefully observed and added notes to a secret binder just in case they were the chosen store where the ring might be purchased. It was so much fun, and we only visited one jewelry store together. I told him I would marry him with paper rings as Taylor Swift's song played in my mind: "I like shiny things, but I'd marry you with paper rings, Uh-huh, that's right, Darling, you're the one I want....."

With our London and Paris trip quickly approaching, I was distracted by wrapping up outstanding action items at work and packing for the trip. The thought of a proposal in Paris, on the Eiffel Tower, had long left my mind. I had forgotten my confession after he confessed that he preferred a quiet, intimate place alone to pop the question. Our small travel group, consisting of seven people in total, included me and my boys, as well as my adult niece, Anna, and adult nephew, Lane. Love and his teenage son also joined us on this dream trip. I was over the moon with excitement while equally nervous about the fourth and final big goal I was returning home to.

We were all thrilled about the trip. A printed copy of the carefully planned itinerary, prepared by me with input from each traveler, was inside my computer bag, along with my laptop, in case a work need arose while we were away. It was a demand and expectation of the job. Should something happen, I was the leader. I would step into any required action, regardless of whether I was on vacation or not.

My team and I frequently discussed fracture points and risks, conducting pre-mortems to develop action items designed to minimize risks while also preparing for action, driven by the sense of urgency inherent in our services and the audiences we served. Together, we created a short list of non-negotiables. I would help the team wrap their minds around what those non-negotiables should be, warning them, "When the microphone is in my face, because it will not be you in the hot seat, what will I be able to say with deep conviction around the job that we did as a team?"

This question and warning set the headspace needed to think through safety first and foremost. Our team agreed to three non-negotiables. All other decisions had guardrails, and the team understood the limits of what decisions were theirs to make independently and which required team consensus. Our entire team trusted the non-negotiables and guardrails. We trusted each other.

My team never reached out to me throughout my once-in-a-lifetime trip. The non-negotiables and guardrails worked exactly as intended. Our entire team had a mutual respect for one another, and we all agreed that vacations and time off must be protected. I led by example and refrained from reaching out to my colleagues when they were on vacation. The trust between these professionals under my care was palpable. It had been forged through mutual respect for one another as men, women, mothers, fathers, friends, colleagues, and flawed protagonists. Myself included.

As I sent the out-of-office reminder to the team, our general Slack channel fired up with messages: "Have fun! Don't worry about this place. We can't wait to see all of the pictures." Throughout the nine-day trip across two countries, I didn't worry. I didn't have any reason for concern. Our team was solid, with everyone having each other's backs, especially when it came to supporting the rest and restoration of a colleague. And especially when it came to the safety and well-being of our youngest customers, who were the primary recipients of our services.

The trip began with a mechanical issue. The plane parked on the tarmac at Huntsville International Airport was deemed unfit to fly. To be clear, this was not a reflection of my hometown airport, which I loved for its convenience and small-town charm, or a reflection of the airline itself. A plane grounded due to a mechanical problem was a standard operating occurrence, and

I would much rather the mechanical issue be identified on the ground rather than in the air.

The plane was grounded, and so were we. With no other flights out of HSV that would guarantee arrival in time for our next flight from Atlanta to Heathrow, I sprang into action. "Stay with our bags," I advised my fellow travelers. We were going to miss our Atlanta flight and would have been forced to delay our trip by one day if I hadn't taken action. My career had prepared me for a moment just like this. In business, there are always surprises that require improvisation, just like a grounded plane.

Quickly moving out of vacation mode and into CEO mode, I called the airline. The lady at the American Airlines counter suggested, with urgency, that I make the call right away because the phone queue would tick up rapidly and I could end up waiting on hold longer than my patience could withstand.

Dialing the customer service number, an agent picked up on the third ring. "Yes, we can update your flight out of Atlanta. Seven seats, right? Okay, let me confirm the details." Armed with new flights, the next problem arose. We only had four and a half hours to make it to the Atlanta airport. Otherwise, we would miss our new flight to Heathrow, and we would likely lose the money that we already spent to keep our travel agenda as planned.

Still on the phone with the customer service representative, I informed her that I would not hang up until I had confirmed our means of transportation to Atlanta and verified that we could make the new flight. "Grab our bags and follow me, please," I told the others frantically. Any attempt to save money vanished as I jogged to the rental car counter downstairs, near the luggage turnstiles. I continued to express my gratitude to this lifeline on the phone, our vacation's lifeline, as my breathing intensified. Not thinking to note the person's name, I wish I had written it down so I could write a note of thanks to this American Airlines angel.

With new flights confirmed, we piled into the biggest rental car available. After all, there were seven of us, and the luggage proved we were going to be away for a week, and five of us would be gone for an extra two days. The rental car company had a large SUV, and I snatched it up for a one-way trip. Love jumped behind the wheel. Looking at each other, we were unsure if we had enough time. As we replayed the clock in our heads, we both knew it was going to be tight. There was no easy route to Atlanta from Huntsville. Atlanta traffic could be a crap shoot, so I informed our passengers that we would only have time for one rapid stop at the midway point.

Proud of our team effort, we arrived at the Atlanta airport with just enough time to return the rental car, use the bathroom, and grab a quick snack. Excited by our vacation victory, we all boarded the plane bound for Heathrow. We had made it, and our packed agenda was intact.

For this trip, with seven people, we had discussed that each child traveling with us, even my adult niece and nephew, could choose an excursion that interested them. We would explore together, enjoying the vacation and observing each individual's joy in their chosen excursion. Taught by my mom's example, I made sure to capture candid and posed photographs to document our adventure. Photographs to help us recall memories well into our old age.

A party of seven was taking in all the sights and enjoying all the great food together. This was my family. We were missing one—the littlest, and Love's daughter—but we promised ourselves we would bring her when she was older. Another trip was planned for us to enjoy together in the future. We would return to the city of love with our daughter one day.

He had indicated that he wanted the proposal to be private, a special moment between only the two of us. That was a quality I loved so much about him. He was intentional with his time and his emotions. I was full of wanderlust, big and bold in just about everything I did, and he grounded me. Finally, I was tethered to the ground by strong arms, arms that intimately knew my curves. My scars did not bother him, and he was sensitive to the brutal battle I had fought. A battle against cancer. A struggle that I had won. "You are the strongest woman I know," he would often tell me.

Playful, charismatic, and a great storyteller—qualities that reminded me of my Granddaddy Carl—Love felt like home. My romanticized Eiffel Tower proposal, which I had confessed to him, was not private, and I respected his vision for the proposal. The thought was gone from my mind, distracted by our dream vacation.

After spending two days in London, we boarded a train for Paris. We were all excited to see the Eiffel Tower, but it was dark when we arrived. We stood in awe as its lights sparkled—the beautiful, magnificent structure in the city of love. Planning to return during daylight, we walked back to our hotel, exhausted. Each of us was saying goodnight. Max was with me in one hotel room. Major, Lane, and Anna were in one hotel room. Love and his son were in another room.

The next day, we rose early to catch the tour bus for Normandy, France. An item on the itinerary that everyone wanted to do. It was a wonderful day, and I was able to carve out a few minutes alone on Utah Beach to absorb the weight of its historical significance. It was a sobering and reflective few minutes with the sun on my face. The sun was beaming down on a French beach, and I was with six people I loved the most in the world, who loved me. The same sun had shone on me years earlier as I lay on a different beach, thousands of miles away, surrounded by my dearest girlfriends. High on a weed gummy, the sun on my face, I thought about my own sobering reality: chemotherapy.

I pause here to acknowledge that cancer and chemotherapy do not compare to the horrific battles of World War II. Thank you to all our service men, women, and their families, especially those who gave the greatest sacrifice, their lives. I'm so grateful for the opportunity to visit that hallowed ground in France.

The day after our Normandy trip, we boarded another train. This time, we were heading to Gevrey-Chambertin, a small French town, to witness Stage 7 of the Tour de France. The Tour de France was the chosen excursion for Love and his son. Later, we would all agree that it was the best day, though we were careful not to minimize the joy and meaning of our other fantastic excursions. Our travel group, my family, together in this little, charming French town, lounged around as the roar of the crowd indicated that another cyclist was approaching. It was relaxing and had a slower pace compared to what we had experienced thus far on our once-in-a-lifetime trip.

On our last day in Paris, we left our luggage in the lobby of the hotel and took off toward the Eiffel Tower. In daylight, it seemed larger and taller. We all went to the middle platform; some took the stairs, while I elected to take the elevator so I could observe firsthand the diagonal lift as the car tilted upward, carrying us to the middle platform. The upper platform was closed, thank goodness. My only skydiving experience, meant to commemorate the first anniversary of my chemo start date, revealed that heights were not my thing.

Snapping pictures and watching our kids take in the sights, Love and I were finally able to carve out a small space, just the two of us, to take in the view. We talked about all that had transpired on this trip thus far and stood in awe of the beauty around us. Turning away for a split second, I turned back and saw a little black box in his hand. "I guess I need to get down on one knee," he said. My romanticized confession collided with his private vision. It was magical. Only I hadn't stopped to think about whether he had asked my boys for my hand in marriage.

Surely he had asked the two loves of my life, the two men who had stood by me after breast cancer, a double mastectomy, four rounds of chemo, and a failed career, for my hand. In that moment, I realized we had never become lost in a deep conversation about my boys and me, together in the trenches of a cancer diagnosis. We had never discussed how fast my boys had to grow up. We had never discussed how a badass executive leader managed to keep her shit together to arrive at this moment on the Eiffel Tower with the love of her life.

Max was only four when he observed this odd exchange between his mom and Gramma as my mom stripped my medical drains. Major was the man of the house by the time he was eight. It wasn't Love's fault; I simply never brought it up, thinking everyone must have similar types of experiences with their children at that stage of life. After all, that was our reality, our narrative, and it was a lonely one. I, with the help of my parents, navigated breast cancer along with my boys.

For the remainder of our vacation, I felt as though I was floating in the clouds. My feet never touched the ground as the sun cast light onto a beautiful diamond that now rested perfectly on my left ring finger. I didn't notice the weight of the ring anchoring me to the Earth, a place where surprises lurked around every corner. He and I had experienced our share of surprises and knew they could pop up at any time.

Our party of seven, with me floating alongside them, walked to a charming French cafe. Breaking bread together, we shared our adventures and enjoyed a delicious meal. All agreed that this was the best meal yet, only second to the Five Guys Burger and Fries we had scarfed down on a different day.

When we arrived back in London, the party of seven on this once-in-a-lifetime trip made our way to our next hotel. After checking in, and with no time to settle in, we immediately went back downstairs to find some food. Between the hours and a missed train due to my inability to translate military time, it had been too long since we enjoyed our meal at the French cafe on the day we were engaged to be married. In my defense, I was still on cloud nine and not paying attention to the clock. Maybe, subconsciously, it was my way of squeezing in a few more hours in Paris, unaware of what awaited us back home. Still, no one complained about my shortcomings.

We eventually got on a train back to London. The kids were gracious and gave the newly engaged couple the master bedroom in our last hotel of the trip. Max and I had been rooming together the entire trip so far. That night, he shared the living room pullout couch with his cousin, Lane. The kids gifted us one night alone together. That night was perfect because we now held the title of Fiancé. Our commitment was now tattooed with the ring on my finger. And if one night of love, even with young ears just beyond a locked door, was our only indulgence, surely it was forgivable. Right? Our traditional values remained equally yoked in faith.

The next morning, we woke up happy. Kissing goodbye before he and his son headed to the airport. The five of us who remained headed to Silverstone for the F1 race. We said "I love you," and then went our separate ways. Major, Max, Lane, Anna, and I hopped in our rideshare to the train station. It was another whirlwind day for us. It was our first F1 experience, and we were amped up with excitement. The smiles on the boys' faces were all the proof I needed, along with the beautiful ring I couldn't take my eyes off of.

Anna tagged along, knowing her chosen excursion, shopping, was on the agenda for the next day. I had been saving for over a year, knowing that for Major's sixteenth birthday, I wanted to take my boys out of the country. Major wanted to go to a race, and the F1 race at Silverstone was our compromise. His mom's Sweet Sixteen birthday gift was a ticket in the cheapest seats available.

Planning for the London and Paris trip began a year in advance as I carefully put together a travel budget. Anna and Lane, to my surprise, asked if they could go, too. I added them to the budget and continued to save money. This would be Anna's high school graduation present from her Big Nonny, the name they gave me as their Aunt. She had just graduated from high school and would begin her collegiate softball career in the fall.

Because Big Nonny had to be fair in showering her love upon her niece and nephew, this would be Lane's belated graduation gift. Having graduated two years ahead of Anna, he was working and paying his way through engineering school. The gift of experience was my preferred gift over giving material items. The gift of intentional time spent together with my two boys and two additional adult kids, whom I treated as if they were my own—my sister's children.

Reflecting on the magical night we spent together following the most magical day, above the blue velvet headboard of the bed hung two pieces of art. Just above the bed where we made love, two framed anatomically correct hearts adorned in flowers. The art was beautiful. As I packed my suitcase for the journey home, I picked up my phone. Opening the camera app, I snapped a photo to preserve the memory. The memory of a night when Love and I both discovered new parts of each other, deeper parts with roots firmly binding us together. Unbreakable roots that would deliver nourishing hugs, kisses, and conversation to sustain us for the rest of our lives together.

Back home from our trip, as discussed and agreed upon, I refocused my attention on my career. The fourth and final goal my team and I were on a mission to achieve was squarely in our sights. Another powerful reason why I loved this man so much: he supported my career without question. As a small business owner himself, he understood the pressure and hard work involved in building a career to be proud of. As a provision for living a good life, he understood the hard work of building a meaningful career, and he told me he was always proud of me. His job was equally important to him. Often working ten- to twelve-hour days and putting in hours on weekends, he worked long and hard, just like my dad had.

If he expected a longer day than usual, I would plan and prepare dinner for us. Even after a long day of work, which was more physically demanding than my office job, he would insist that I sit while he cleaned the kitchen. That was our time to talk. I sat while he cleaned, both of us in deep conversation together in a kitchen where families were fed. It was a place I didn't think my Grandma Mamie had ever left. I was convinced the woman slept in the kitchen, and I was sure of it.

My parents have been my model for how two individuals can support each other as equal partners in a relationship, specifically in marriage. Dad worked physically demanding jobs as a day laborer and farmer. Mom was in the kitchen preparing meals, and we would all sit down and enjoy them together around the table. They understood the recipe and the ingredients required to build a family. Together with this new love, a mature love, we followed the recipe step by step.

With each two-week sprint, we had only a handful of days alone without the children. Careful not to display our sinful out-of-wedlock behavior, those few nights every two weeks were ours, and we used them to connect on a sensual level. Our mornings were spontaneous. Some mornings, we made love. On other mornings, I was up and out before Love, ready to greet a day filled with meetings and project work. On other mornings, I would sleep in while he rose early to prepare for his day.

Every morning we were together, I could count on one thing: a hot cup of coffee. A cup of coffee he would brew, fresh from his Keurig, and bring to me, whether I was still in bed or packing up to leave. This man brought me a cup of coffee every morning we were together, no matter what kind of morning it was.

We had both confessed our faith and been baptized under the covenants of Christian doctrine, and we wanted to be discreet in our sins, especially with younger children in the mix. A door could swing open, even if locked, at any time. These kids knew how to open a locked bedroom door. We rarely stayed over at each other's houses if our children were present. This was another quality I absolutely loved about this man. He loved his kids and didn't want to miss any precious time with them. We would hang out at each other's houses when our children were with us, cook dinner, and then kiss goodnight. This left us both time and space to focus on our children. A courtesy we extended equally to one another without question, our children came first and foremost. Together, Love and my first responsibility were to our children, and we held firmly to that shared value.

I will share a funny story about one night I stayed over with his children present, and I slept in the bed next to him. He had been in pain all evening, and the pain was only intensifying. Not wanting to go to the emergency room, I told him I would stay just in case he needed help with the kids in the morning. Later that night, it was decided that I would take him to the emergency room. He had appendicitis and required emergency surgery. As the nurse wheeled his hospital bed out to take him to the operating room, she escorted me to the consultation room. I knew the drill: someone would call me when surgery was done, and the doctor would meet me in the consultation room after surgery to give his report.

As I sat alone in the same consultation room where my sister, mom, and I had waited for the doctor to update us on Daddy, I waited. My phone never rang. The surgeon didn't open the door to the consultation room. There I sat with wild thoughts scrolling through my head, alone. When the door opened, all I received was an apology. "I am so sorry, the number we had for an emergency contact was not yours."

The hospital had called Love's ex-wife. When Love was being registered, he was in pain and perhaps not thinking straight, and he gave them his ex-wife's phone number as his emergency contact. Love's ex-wife was his emergency contact, not mine. We had only been dating for a short time. It was too soon to declare each other emergency contacts, so we laughed it off. However, I couldn't help but recall a comment once made to him during one of our deep conversations about life.

He loved his ex-wife, and he had wanted their marriage to work. It was not his choice to end a twenty-year marriage, but life is full of surprises. In another confession, I told him early in our courtship that my biggest fear was his ex-wife showing up on his doorstep asking to come home, to their home. Being the man he is and wanting his children raised in a home where both parents were under one roof, I was afraid he would welcome her back with open arms. It was silly of me to think this. She had remarried and was in love with another man. She wasn't coming back to this house, the one we would eventually talk about converting into our home together with four children.

The real and raw emotion of a woman in love, a flawed woman in love, is the only explanation for my wandering imagination. Life had already surprised me in significant ways, and I had become accustomed to conducting risk assessments on nearly every scenario.

We had both heard horror stories of divorce, second marriages, and blended families. Aware of the risk, we continued to discuss different scenarios and how we would, as a unit, navigate them, knowing our love was worth the risks. But first, before we could even think about blending, I had one more goal to accomplish: the final goal of my career. It was a goal I had been working on since I paused my career after cancer forced me to step away. The overwhelming desire to prove that cancer had not taken my career from me remained. Our team had one more big goal to achieve, and achieving this goal would be the proof I needed to satisfy this intrinsic need. I needed to prove myself.

It was my own expectations weighing me down. Some called it hubris, not understanding this fire that burned inside me. How could they? Cancer, or any health crisis, for that matter, changes you in ways that no one can understand unless they, too, have experienced it firsthand. This mission to achieve the fourth goal, this fight to prove cancer wrong, was what motivated me day in and day out to do my job well.

Often, this fire left me depleted and unable to be my ultimate self for those I loved most. One painful reminder came on Love's birthday. He called me that morning, and we had an ordinary conversation. After the call ended, I continued with my workday until my mom texted me, "Is it Love's birthday?" As soon as I read her text, my heart sank. I just talked to Love and hadn't wished him a happy birthday.

It sounds so silly now as I reflect back on it, but I was devastated and knew I was inching closer to a new ceiling for my emotional and mental capacity. If this were true love, everlasting love, how in the world could I forget to wish the man I love a happy birthday? Y'all, the pain and emotion were real. It hurt to think I forgot his birthday. But why?

# Chapter 29

# Love Lost

*This next story shares how our engagement ended abruptly. No fights. No angry tension or emotional outbursts between the two of us. Just like that, it was over, and I couldn't really tell anyone why. The fights, angry tension, and emotional outbursts were all happening inside me, in my own head. I was shattering on the inside, again, and no one knew it. I retreated into myself, like I always did, in silence.*

Up to this point, I had been feeling great. Healthy boundaries were in place, boundaries I learned to stand up for from previous experiences. With a clear headspace, I was more capable of identifying and naming emotions, just as my executive coach had taught me to do. Our team was making good progress toward our fourth and final goal. The feedback my colleague, Ellie, and I were receiving served as validation that we were progressing on the desired trajectory.

Challenges would arise, and our team would collaborate to problem-solve as they came our way. We remained fully aware that more hard work lay ahead. Together, Ellie and I remained focused. Our professional partnership was held together by the same desire to be badass executive women and nurturing mothers. We needed each other, and we were there for each other every step of the way. Both were equally motivated to achieve this final goal.

The morning we walked down Park Avenue to the crucial meeting in New York City, we paused to compliment each other on how beautiful and strong we each looked in our outfit. Ellie was in her teal green power dress. It hugged her curves and radiated a soft layer of confidence.

Attracted to tone-on-tone color patterns, I chose winter white slacks and a winter white button-up blouse with a tan blazer over my shoulders. The cheetah-print kitten heels I chose added a little spice, rounding out the look. Jokingly, we said to each other, "At least we look the part," as we power-walked the streets of New York.

Business success meant a lot of hard work, and we watched each other putting in the work. We knew hard work was a part of the recipe, and we mixed it in with a greater quantity than the other two ingredients because that was what this time called for—more hard work. The meeting we were about to walk into would be the tipping point. It would solidify my ability to look cancer in the eye and say, "You did not win." Cancer was a tough competitor. I was stronger. What I didn't know was that my career would be in jeopardy again, and cancer would be to blame.

Months after we ended our engagement, Love and I were still unable to discuss the circumstances that led to our breakup. It wasn't due to a lack of trying. We were both equally heartbroken. As I tried to heal, I picked up my journal and started writing a letter. "Dear..." and after a few sentences, my eyes blurred with tears until I could no longer see the page. This process repeated itself, and I never finished a single letter.

I simply couldn't put it into words, our reality—the end of a beautiful love story. The end of our love story. There wasn't anyone or anywhere to lay the blame. As I retreated inward, refusing to take his calls, he tried to reach me through my sister and mom, but I shut everyone out. This was hurt and heartbreak like I had never experienced.

Love and I were both shattered and trying our best to pick up our own pieces. Together, we had reached our own emotional and mental ceilings. We both punched the hardwood floors with our fists as our knees followed, crying and asking ourselves, "Why?" Neither of us knew the answer. We chalked it up to divine intervention, and we navigated our grief in solitude.

I cherished my career; it consumed my headspace leading up to this fatal point. It was also preventing me from showing up for the people I loved most. Physically, I was there, but emotionally and mentally, I was chipping away at this final goal. I was focused on the moment I would be able to say "I won. Bye, cancer." What I hadn't realized was the toil of dark surprises beginning to unfold—a series of losses lying directly ahead on my path toward true love.

Was this a pattern? Was I the problem? I had a divorce and a failed engagement on my resume, both of which stemmed from my intense desire to be successful, using title and salary as my measuring stick while weighing myself down with self-inflicted expectations. The evidence was strong. His ex-wife didn't show up at his door asking to be taken back. I didn't have to worry about that. It was me, and I slammed the door shut in his face.

Curious about my behavior, I asked a friend for her opinion. This friend, a therapist by trade, listened as I explained what had transpired over four short months following our magical engagement. "I just shut down and shut him out. Why would I do something like that to someone I loved?" I pleaded. She calmly responded, "You had reached a new emotional ceiling, and you were drawing from safe and familiar coping mechanisms."

Blame didn't have to be placed anywhere, even on me. This friend helped me realize the beautiful yet devastating nature of human emotion and meaningful relationships. When I hit an emotional ceiling, I shut down. That was who I am. A flawed but very real human. This realization allowed me to begin the healthy process of grief and healing.

I was not to blame. Love was not to blame. NO ONE WAS TO BLAME, and I made sure of it. Now safely inside my silent co-coon, a place to hide while the transformation took place out of sight, I began to see a new life forming. The flame that the Great Ironsmith had put me in to shape me just right for the next job at hand. I had a fourth and final career goal to achieve, and just like that, I threw myself back into the work, alone again. I would not have the strong arms of a man to run to when the subsequent loss could surely inflict mortal wounds.

We loved each other, but our timing was off. We respected one another's time and space by limiting our communication and setting a mutually agreed-upon boundary: we would not meet in person. I adjusted my Publix run cadence to prevent RomCom scenes from flooding back while I tried to hold back tears. I took a social media hiatus, not wanting to witness the potential ridicule of my life through critical social media posts. That certainly wasn't part of my nature, and I blocked people engaged in such behavior, behavior that belonged in tabloid headlines.

After several months passed, and we both felt the pain lift slightly, in a text to Love, I asked, "Do you think we will reunite again later in life?" The text bubbles faded in and out as he typed. "I would like to think so," he replied. I smiled, content to be alone for now. I texted back three heart emojis. Three hearts serving as an ellipsis, hopeful for a love story to be continued...

# Chapter 30

# Kim

*R*eader, be warned, this is a tough chapter to read. Get a tissue box and settle in to read about life's beautiful and dark surprises. The mighty fall of a flawed protagonist is told through the lens of ugly grief. A grief I had yet to experience in life. A grief that couldn't possibly be worse than losing the love of my life, but it was. And it was painful.

A love story—my love story—was over, but there was another end to something beautiful that would crash into me with such force that it knocked the breath out of me. An ending that I would witness, though it was not my ending to experience.

My next-door neighbor and childhood friend was dying. Cancer had taken every opportunity to kill her over a short period of six months. Kim was diagnosed with cancer in the spring of 2024. The prognosis was not good, but she fought with the strength and purpose that only a mother could muster up.

Remembering my Grandma Mamie and how she was determined to outlive her son, a son who would always be her child. A son not expected to live past sixteen years. With the love of his mother, they both lived a long and fulfilling life. Grandma Mamie passed away at age ninety-three. Her son lived to sixty-six. Kim fought with that same powerful determination. Her story is not one I can tell. But the impact she had on me was material. It's that impact I wish to share.

By now, in the painful weeks following Love and my failed engagement, I had regrouped and begun to process the news and the disappointment of not achieving our fourth and final goal on the timeline my team and I had anticipated. My team and I were in research mode. I was grateful for the work and the distraction.

We were now in a time of hosting post-mortem meetings and retrospectives to unpack each detail and adjust our strategic plan. Still, the feedback remained positive. I had no cause for alarm. Several factors outside of our control, including market uncertainty and the 2024 presidential election, contributed to these challenges. These were reasons entirely outside of anyone's control, especially Ellie's and my control. We were badasses, but we weren't economic miracle workers.

I spent a lot of time working behind my computer in my home office. Sitting down at my computer one December morning, I glanced out the window to take in the view of the mountains. The Appalachian mountain range came to an end right outside my front door. While working, I usually kept my phone out of reach, often in another room, to reduce distractions. A post-chemobrain behavior I'd developed to help me focus—a new, healthy boundary that kept the outside world at bay. Focus seemed out of reach on some days as I grappled with the heartache of losing my true love.

This particular morning, my cell phone was set next to my computer mouse. The screen lit up with a new text message from Kim's number. "Hi Sonia, this is Kelly. Can you come over and sit with Kathy and Kim?" I was not caught off guard. I had made it clear that I would be working from home, and if they needed me, they should not hesitate to reach out.

Kim Haynes and her mother, Kathy Haynes, often asked me to help with simple tasks, such as driving Kim's daughter to and from school. No stranger to the insurmountable number of doctors' appointments associated with a cancer diagnosis, I was happy to help when their schedules conflicted.

On this day, I was not needed for school drop off. Taking a deep breath, I left my house with a bag over my shoulder and walked down the sidewalk to Kim's house. Through the garage door, I entered. The kitchen counters were littered with medicine bottles, empty wrappers, and dirty dishes. When I looked into the living room, Kim was lying in her blueish-gray recliner. It was the only seat in the house where she could get comfortable. Weeks ago, her frailty became more pronounced, and her skin tone shifted from a sun-kissed, freckled complexion to a milky gray. She was now under the care of hospice and the gentle nurturing of her mother, a nurse by trade.

Leaning down beside her face, I whispered, "Hi, Kim." On the love seat sat one of her best friends from work, along with Kathy, Kim's mom. We engaged in a short conversation. As the friend prepared to leave, the three of us bowed our heads to pray for Kim, who lay unconscious as we prayed.

Kim had already spoken to him about preaching at her funeral. He was there talking to Kim's mom and collecting the final details he would need to prepare for such a momentous, grief-filled day. None of us knew the deadline, but we were all preparing in our own ways. The surprise date and time were coming sooner than any of us had realized, far too soon for what Kim would have preferred. Far too soon for her daughter to lose her mother. Far too soon for a family to be thrown into the pits of ugly grief.

As he left, the door opened, and another friend entered. Jocelyn Martin had driven two hours that morning to be with her best friend, a friendship that began in their college years at Auburn University. Kim made friends easily, a quality made clear by the revolving door of visitors and the outpouring of support as she continued her hand-to-hand combat with cancer.

As Jocelyn approached the living room, she stopped to greet Kim and kissed her on the forehead. A Bible was cradled in Jocelyn's arm. We didn't engage in small talk; instead, she opened up her Bible and began to read. I reached into the bag I had carefully packed with three books. Between my Bible and a daily devotional book, *The Better Mom Devotional* by Ruth Schwenk, I picked up a fictional novel. *The Stepdaughter* by Georgina Cross was one of Kim's favorites.

As Jocelyn continued to read, the wooden kitchen chair invited me over to sit. The chair was positioned next to the recliner, where Kim lay quietly with her eyes closed. Her chest rose and fell as air flowed in and out of her body. I hadn't noticed the chair when I came in. I didn't remember maneuvering around it to whisper hello. Yet, the wooden chair had been there all along. As Jocelyn closed her Bible, I moved from the couch to the wooden chair next to Kim and opened the fiction book. I took my turn to read to our friend. Reading to Kim was our futile attempt to keep her stimulated, to let her hear our voices, so she would know she was not alone.

A reader like me, Kim, loved Georgina Cross's work. She had heard Georgina speak at a Leadership Greater Huntsville event. Georgina was a local author whom we had both met and admired. Georgina and I had been friends for years, and I loved to brag about her work. I thought Kim would enjoy listening to the book, a book she had already read when she was healthy and full of life. That was the only thing I knew to do at this moment: show up, give my time, and read in an attempt to keep my friend alive long enough for her daughter to tell her she loved her one last time.

Pausing here for you, the reader, to ensure I set the appropriate tone for the remainder of this story. As I typed these words, I had to take frequent breaks because the curtain of tears blocked my view of the computer screen. This was heartache. This was ugly grief. And I had never experienced anything like it before in my forty-four years of life. This grief paralyzed me, and my tattered brain could not find the words to tell anyone how completely I was shattering on the inside, at a deeper level than I had ever felt before, and that I needed a little extra grace.

I only shared with my leadership team that my emotions were running high and that I was running on empty. I asked my team for their support, respect, and kindness as I navigated a new and unexpected challenge. My goal was to keep my emotions from coming apart on stage as our team rallied together after losing the fourth and final goal that had been so tightly within our grasp.

Time and space were all I needed to allow my brain a chance to recover from this blow that caused concussion-like headaches and dizzy spells. Cancer, a surprise lying in wait, had sprung on me at just the right time. At the time, I was riding the rocketship of my career, fueled by the successes our team had experienced in just forty-two months.

We achieved our first goal after eighteen months, which quickly led to the achievement of our second, audacious goal. Twenty-four months into my tenure as Chief Executive Officer, our team achieved the third audacious goal, only to be defeated during the fourth and final climb, at a time when heartbreak was already in motion.

My Granny Evelyn would have said it was the devil at work. Now, my Granny was not known to speak ill of anyone or engage in gossipy chatter, at least not in my presence. To quote one of her favorite sayings, a phrase to help her preserve her Southern lady appeal, she would say, "Now I don't think that person's prayers are going to make it past this ceiling." Granny Evelyn, in her wisdom and in her deep familiarity with the recipe, understood that sometimes prayers went unanswered. She was a wise woman in her own right. Still, I couldn't shake the feeling that my prayers weren't making it past my ceiling.

As we sat and read to Kim, we felt good about the comforting work we were doing. Jocelyn and I were giving ourselves feedback. The only input from Kim was the slow rise and fall of her chest as she breathed. Closing *The Stepdaughter*, I moved back to my place on the couch after reading a handful of pages. We sat in silence.

Kathy was one of my many childhood bonus moms. The moms of our small friend group had developed a close adult friendship. Their children were always surrounded by nurturing mothers, regardless of whose house we were at on any given day. Growing up, her uniform was scrubs. Her professional attire reflected her purposeful career as a nurse. I only saw her in regular clothes when our families would get together. There were four of us—Brandi, Melinda, Katie, and me—best friends from second grade through high school. Our moms tried to keep the tradition going well into our adulthood, but our annual family gatherings fizzled when we hit our mid-twenties. Between babies and careers, time seemed limited. However, sitting in Kim's home with her mother still felt familiar.

Kathy was sitting next to Jocelyn on the couch when she stood up, as if searching for something. Disappearing from the living room, she returned with a blood pressure cuff and a pulse oximeter. It was a change only the trained eye of a healthcare professional would notice. There was a shift in Kim's breathing, and her mother knew it. She recognized it after spending years working in a hospital where end-of-life medical care was provided daily.

Kathy gently placed the blood pressure cuff on Kim's right arm, so skinny from the rapid weight loss that I wasn't sure the cuff would register an accurate reading. Cancer had consumed her body and was killing her from within as it took every ounce of her strength with it. Even with my limited knowledge of blood oxygen levels, living through the COVID-19 pandemic has taught me that blood oxygen levels are a key indicator of lung function. I also knew that the number on the oximeter should be in the high nineties, if not one hundred. The greenish LED lights lit up: 83.

Stroking Kim's arm, Kathy spoke softly. "You're okay. It's okay. I'm okay. You've fought hard, and we know you are tired. Hold on. (Your Daughter) will be here very soon."

I didn't know what to do as the tears welled in my eyes. Jocelyn didn't know what to do either. As if we were synchronized dancers, Jocelyn moved in closer to hold Kim's left hand. I moved to the floor at Kim's feet, lifted by the recliner, and began caressing her legs. Unsure if she could hear us, we wanted Kim to feel our touch. We wanted Kim to know she was not alone. Jocelyn and I wanted Kathy to know she was not alone on what would be one of the hardest days of her life. Together, we sat as quiet tears streamed down Jocelyn's face and mine while Kathy encouraged her daughter to fight for just a few more minutes. Kathy knew that Kim would hear her daughter's voice one last time.

The door swung open as the family began to arrive. I sank into the background, knowing it wouldn't be long before Kim's daughter was home from school. Looking at my phone, I wondered how long I had been there. Quickly glancing at my email and Slack, I saw nothing urgent in the work chatter, so I decided to stay a little longer until Kim's house became full of friends and family. The street was lined with cars. Her daughter was finally home. This little girl with red hair and freckles looked just like her mom had as a child. This little girl with the strength of Goliath ambled up to her mom and said, "I love you." It was time for me to leave and give Kim and her family space to share those sacred moments.

The tears flowed as I walked down the sidewalk and into my house, collapsing on my couch. I fall apart off-stage, in the comfort and safety of my locked house. Not realizing I had fallen asleep, emotionally exhausted, I glanced at my phone when the chime woke me. It was around eight o'clock. The number hovering over the text message icon indicated I had a new message.

She was gone. Kim was gone. I cried alone in my house while, next door, the world of a family I loved so dearly collapsed in grief. The last words Kim's daughter spoke to her mother were, "I love you, mama."

A darkness like nothing I had ever experienced filled the room as I cried. I didn't have lived experiences to lean on—no wisdom to guide me through a moment like this. My friend, my neighbor, a young mother who was like an older sister to me, was dead, and cancer had killed her. Cancer had claimed victory in the most unimaginable way.

The weekend before Kim's passing, I invited her daughter to attend church with me and my boys. It would give Kim and her caregiving mother the time and space they needed together. Collectively, they were preparing for Kim's end of life. They both knew it wasn't supposed to be this way, and Kathy would gladly have taken Kim's place if only it worked that way. Kathy would have lived in a house with dirt floors if it meant her family could remain by her side.

Kim's daughter and Max were good buddies, and he was overly protective of her because his mom had also battled cancer and because of their age gap. Five years separated them. It was striking to see this little boy, still years away from his formative stage, show the awareness to comfort another child during her time of grief. His brain was not fully developed, and critical decision-making and emotional control still eluded his young brain.

Together, they jumped on the trampoline and played ball with our dogs out back. Max was her protector, and I knew it. He was comforting his friend, carrying heartache that he knew deep down could have been his own reality. He knew enough to understand that cancer could kill people, but it hadn't killed his mom yet. I believed wholeheartedly in my son as he, too, was beginning to show signs of understanding. He, too, knew the recipe, though he was only beginning to learn how to mix the ingredients just right.

Observing him play his video games, I knew what he was capable of when an emotional tantrum erupted. I've since patched the small hole in his wall after one of his outbursts. Careful not to dehumanize him or dismiss his emotions, I calmly waited, just like Grandma Mamie did with Uncle Carl, until his tantrum ran its course. With the calm of a mother, I would help him redirect his emotions into a more productive and healthy expression. I'm happy to report that, although it took some time, the little guy is transforming into a handsome, empathetic, respectful, and kind young man.

Kim's death was like an earthquake, shaking loose every wall I had built and bursting the cocoon I had safely retreated into following a failed engagement, wide open. I was candid with my boys as they bore witness to their mother being unable to get out of bed, put on nice clothes, fix my hair, or stop crying as I moved through this new, ugly grief. For my boys, I needed to communicate what I was feeling and how I was trying my best to process grief in a responsible, respectful, and healthy way. It was a skill set they would need as they entered adulthood, because I had the wisdom to know they would not be immune to the beautiful and dark surprises of life. Piece by piece, I crumbled to the ground—the bitter taste of defeat. Cancer didn't take my life. It took Kim's. Cancer had won, I conceded.

I'll pause again for you, the reader, to offer you a little advice. If you ever have the opportunity to sit at the feet of a dying friend, sit in stillness. Please be there so they know they are not alone at the end of life. Not everyone will have that experience, thank goodness, but for those who do, use it for good. Money can always be made. Jobs can always be secured. Life is fleeting for all of us, and we do not know our deadline. Say good riddance to people who make you small, convince you that you are unworthy, or seize every chance to bring you to your knees.

Just as I was processing my grief, two more blows struck me while I was down. Granny Evelyn died on Christmas Eve. That morning, she had gotten up, likely with plans to get a head start on Christmas Day dinner. Later, she returned to bed, fell asleep, and never woke up. After Granny's death, my mom fell very ill and had to be rushed to the emergency room.

# Chapter 31

# Granny Evelyn

*The following story is about my Granny Evelyn, my last living grandparent. Her death signified a shift in my life, an ending to a beautiful childhood, even though I was forty-four. Grandparents are special people, and mine kept me grounded in my youth. In the stillness of death, Granny Evelyn communicated a powerful message.*

My parents and I attended the Fowler Christmas lunch, which included Grandma Mamie's children, grandchildren, great-grandchildren, and great-great-grandchildren. Our family traveled in from Mobile, Alabama, and Tennessee to join the special occasion. My lunch plate was light. I wanted to save room for the delicious homemade chocolate-covered cherries that my dad's first cousin, Jasyn, always brought.

Homemade by one of his neighbors, he brought them each year, and I would devour so many that I ended up on a sugar high to carry me through our Christmas dinner and the wonderful conversation our family shared. When Mom's cell phone rang, she screamed, "What?" As we all froze, waiting for her to translate, she said, "Lynn, we gotta go. It's mom. She's dead."

At first, I thought, "What a cruel joke for Granny to play on us." It was her nature to live life on her own terms, under her own rules of engagement. Even my Granddaddy Wayne knew this, as he would often tease her about being late with preparing breakfast. After all, this was a hardworking man who needed to be in the field at dawn. Granny, in her southern style, would fire back, "If you want breakfast in bed, you'd better sleep in the kitchen." They were another perfect example of two people equally yoked in a Christian marriage.

Jasyn handed me a paper plate with a handful of chocolate-covered cherries. "Here, take these with you." He knew I would need the sugar high to carry me through the conversations I would have as I left to go to my Granny's house. I trailed right behind my parents. My mom had asked me to stop and pick up her baby sister, my Aunt Diann. My exchange with Diann was similar to my awkward emotional exchange with Uncle Larry in the hospital the day we thought my dad was going to die. Why did I find myself in this position so often?

It didn't take long for our family to fill Granny Evelyn's house for the last time. It was the end. All of my grandparents were gone. Our beloved Matriarch was gone. Before the coroner arrived, I was able to see her. I brushed her hair back and kissed her on her forehead. She was lying on her side, her right arm tucked under her pillow as if she would rise awake, feeling my touch. She didn't wake up, and I didn't cry. I smiled because I knew this was what she wanted, and it was one of the most beautiful things I had ever seen. She was reunited with the love of her life, my grandfather. The juxtaposition of Kim's and Granny's end-of-life journeys left me grappling for answers.

Granny Evelyn was always practical in her advice, and I longed for her guidance, given all the debris that lay behind me. I needed to know if I had gotten the recipe wrong. She would have the answers, but it was too late for me to seek her wisdom. In that moment of need, a moment when I needed her words more than ever, what she gave me was silence.

The stillness of her body. The stillness of the room, even with commotion all around, caused me to pause. My brain began to kick into deep thinking mode as I continued the one-sided conversation in my head.

As I said, Granny Evelyn always gave practical advice. Her last message was delivered loud and clear to me as my family moved furniture around to make room for the gurney carrying her lifeless body to the funeral home in Scottsboro, Alabama, in preparation for her final celebration.

It was our style to come together as a family for special occasions—or sometimes for no occasion at all. Now we were preparing for the final special occasion, Granny Evelyn's funeral. The church house would be packed, a testament to a life well lived. As visitors lined up, our family stood around Granny as each family member hugged every neck and thanked them for coming. The chatter of stories and memories filled the church. I was prepared to speak on behalf of the grand- and great-grandchildren. It was a privilege my cousins elected for me. I had spoken on our behalf at Granddaddy Wayne's funeral nearly five years earlier. My daddy would preach at Granny Evelyn's funeral.

As the day of Granny Evelyn's funeral arrived, the only three family members missing would be Dad, Mom, and me. While my family gathered, we sat in the emergency room at Crestwood.

We missed Granny's grand celebration because my mom almost died that very morning.

The morning of Granny's funeral, I got up a little earlier than usual. It was a big day, and I wanted to spend time alone polishing my speech before being surrounded by Granny's beloved friends and our large, loud family. My phone lit up on my bathroom counter with "Daddy" revealed as the caller. I rushed out the door, stopping only to tell the boys to get up and get ready. I would be back.

My mom was incoherent, and my daddy could not get her up. He needed my help. My mom needed my help. When I arrived, she was lying in bed. Her skin was hot to the touch. "Mom, do you know who I am?" was something I had learned to ask from watching my mom care for my grandparents. Mom was a gifted caregiver to many. Her weak voice responded. She knew my name. That was a good sign.

Mom, lying on her back, was trying to cough. For a few days, she had struggled with a seasonal cold. Unbeknownst to us, it had rapidly escalated to Flu B. As I helped her up into a sitting position, she vomited all over me, and I immediately knew we had to get her to the hospital. I didn't have to check her temperature to realize it was high; I knew the vomiting put her at risk of aspiration, and if she aspirated into her lungs, that could kill her.

We loaded her into the car, and Dad took off. I followed behind, rushing into the ER as the nurse wheeled her into triage for vitals. Following the nurse's lead, I observed the triage assessment. The nurse put the pulse oximeter on Mom's finger. I knew that device. I recalled the number ticking down each time

I passed by Kim as she lay in her recliner. Eighty-three....Eighty-two....Eighty-one.

Kathy's instincts had been spot on, and she knew Kim was nearing the end of her life. It still haunts me—the numbers, the slowed breathing, the family, Kim's daughter. I still have not fully recovered from the grief of that day, and the guilt as a cancer survivor. The pain and guilt were unbearable. If my grief was this ugly and heavy, I can't imagine the grief of her daughter, mother, father, and sister, as well as their entire family and her circle of close friends and colleagues. I wasn't alone in my grief, but I had to do the hard work to process my grief alone.

As soon as the number appeared on the oximeter on Mom's finger, a number I had not seen, the nurse reached for her walkie-talkie. I didn't have to see the number to know what the nurse knew. Before I could inquire, the triage room became crowded as another nurse and a doctor responded to the cryptic, coded walkie-talkie exchange. They moved in like ninjas, whisking my mom away before anyone could react to their swift, secret takeover. The doctor said, "Come with us, we need to ask you some questions."

Dad and I complied and answered the rapid-fire questions as our mall-walking speed kept us in a peloton with the medical team. Mom was sick, very sick. Although the medical team did not think she aspirated vomit into her lungs—that was the good news—the bad news was that my mom was going to miss her mother's funeral.

Humor has been my family's go-to coping mechanism in times of crisis. Daddy made a couple of balloon animals using hospital gloves. He was scared, and this was his way of distract-

ing himself from his fears. As we sat and talked, Mom was resting and stable. The fluids and oxygen brought her color back.
Once she was awake and talking to us, Dad and I nervously
waited for the moment she realized that today she would not be
given the opportunity for closure.

Her mom was lying in state fifty miles away at the altar of Mt.
Nebo Baptist Church, our church, surrounded by all our family
except us. Lost for words and unsure how to comfort her in this
reality, I heard the chime of my phone—a new message with two
links waiting for me to open.

"Sonia, these are the songs I chose to play at your Granny's
funeral. I thought your mom would want to listen to them." A
church friend, Beverly, stood in to ensure my Granny's funeral
was beautiful, even if we weren't there to witness it. Looking
up, I walked over to my mom's bedside. By now, she was feeling
much better, and her fever had broken. Uncertain if she was
strong enough to handle the emotional weight, I asked her if she
would like to listen to the two songs. She said yes.

Daddy stood on one side of the hospital bed, and I stood on
the other. My arms were wrapped around my mom, just like she
had wrapped her arms around me when I heard the news, "Sonia, we have a little cancer." Mom was not alone. Dad and I were
there to comfort her as she grieved her mother.

Pressing play, "Where Her Heart Has Always Been" by Alan
Jackson filled the hospital room. As our tears flowed quietly, the
next song started. It was a song I loved to hear our congregation
sing on Sunday mornings and a song I had listened to a hundred times over my forty-four years at Mt. Nebo Baptist Church:
"Beulah Land." My dad's beautiful tenor voice from my child-

hood would begin, and the congregation would follow. As the song started to play and Daddy's voice filled the sanctuary..."*I'm kind of homesick (alto softer coming in behind the tenor: 'I'm kind of homesick') for a country.*" The lyrics continued..."*To which I've never been before. No sad goodbyes will be spoken, for time won't matter anymore.*"

The fear of an unknown deadline imposed by cancer, which had driven me to rush through life collecting achievements and trophies, vanished into thin air. It took a series of hard things to make me realize that I was the one constant in my own life. The one person who would be with me until the very end, regardless of when that time came. Nothing else was guaranteed with that level of certainty. No one knew the amount of pain I had endured leading up to the day I would give up my career a second time. Sifting through and labeling the emotions was work only I could do.

On the day severance was offered to me, I was prepared to resign. It was my decision to leave, and it was mine alone to make. However, the severance came as a surprise. It provided some padding to my personal budget, so I stayed quiet, not revealing my intention to resign until my former boss, the one who had invited me to be CEO, and I hugged in the parking lot. I said, "By the way, I told Ellie that I was resigning today. Which narrative do you want me to lead with: severance or resignation?"

Rather than resign, I accepted my fate and signed the severance agreement. One person had accused me of mismanagement. I could live with that, the opinion of one person. I had experienced a successful career up to that point, and I was content with my performance. The evidence was rooted in facts that our Board and shareholders had easy access to and could interpret for themselves. The accomplishments of my team and the returns we delivered to shareholders were real, and no one could take that away from me. I had done my job, and I had done it well. I could leave my career knowing it was over, and I needed time and space to prepare for the next big thing.

Signing the severance agreement, I bought myself more time at home with my boys. It was not pride or martyrdom; this was motherhood, and it was my life with permission to do nothing for one year. With a healthy emergency fund, access to insurance, and my boys in their childhood home, I paused my career again. Only this time, at the age of forty-four and no longer afraid of cancer, I paused with the strength of a stronger, more confident woman. Reflecting on the recipe that had been taught to me by so many, I had not messed it up. With a dash of stillness, I added my own spice: pause.

# Chapter 32

# Beignets

*The following story occurred three months into my second career pause in March 2025. I was still processing a failed engagement and a series of losses. Kicking myself back to the surface, I reached out to a long-time friend to seek her wisdom.*

The young woman I had met when my career was just getting started, Jaclyn, continued to grow her career while I, too, was growing mine. After relocating to Mobile to take a new job and start fresh following a life surprise, her wanderlust inspired her to launch her first business. Photography had been a hobby, and she had turned it into a profitable side hustle that quickly evolved into a full-time career. She was great at photography and had even captured the candid shots from Jason and my wedding so many years earlier. I still have all of the photographs and memories to share with my boys. Proof that their parents loved each other and loved their boys the most.

In February 2020, just before the pandemic shut down the world, Jaclyn opened Mo'Bay Beignet Co. You can read her story and enjoy homemade beignets at her flagship cafe located on Dauphin Street in Mobile, Alabama. You can also purchase her homemade beignets at two other locations in Mobile, several franchise locations across the Southeast, and the Truist Park

Outfield Market during an Atlanta Braves home game in Atlanta, Georgia. The woman who had been responsible for guiding me early in my career, now in midlife after navigating many life surprises, was thriving.

Wait, I want to give her more credit than that. This woman is a badass who worked hard for everything she has in life, regardless of the surprises thrown her way. For all her hard work, she has a beautiful family and is faithful in prayer. Jaclyn is diligent in having little talks with Jesus. She is polished, professional, excellent at her craft, and I still want to be just like her.

Here I was, unemployed and on my second career pause, with my anxiety raging inside me. Curious to know her secret, I emailed Jaclyn, uncertain if her cell phone number was still the same. Together, we set a date for me to drive down to Mobile. As I arrived in the city, beads from the most recent Mardi Gras celebration dangled in trees above, and I parked on the street near where the GPS had instructed me to go. I got out of my gray Lexus GX and walked up the sidewalk to the coffee shop Jaclyn had raved about.

With my miniature weenie, Moo Moo, by my side, Jaclyn and I embraced with a hug that only long-lost friends could deliver. She loves dogs and was excited to see I had a little companion tagging along. Moo Moo was in her pink carrier, and Jaclyn insisted on seeing her so she could soak up some puppy love.

As soon as Moo Moo emerged from her portable carrier, Jaclyn couldn't believe her eyes. "I have a little weenie that looks exactly like her." She started swiping through photos on her phone, and with a great big smile on her face, she said, "See, look, this is my little Daisy Mae."

Laughing at the irony of how these two friends, separated by time and distance, were now reunited after many years and miles apart, we realized we had the same dog. We ordered coffee and sat down, lost in conversation.

There was so much to catch up on. We both had beautiful and dark life surprises to unpack. Each of us carefully divulged details no one else knew. After all, Lori had taught us both to be discreet with our dissatisfaction and shortcomings. Lori had trained us to be empathetic, respectful, and kind, even if we did not agree with another person's narrative or perspective. She taught us to do our jobs and do them well. Confirming our dinner plans, we parted ways, and I checked into my hotel room. The questions I wanted to ask Jaclyn over dinner buzzed in my head.

As I walked to the restaurant to meet Jaclyn for dinner, the one burning question I had was, "Why beignets?" To my knowledge, she had zero experience in food service. She began to recall the series of events that led to the grand opening of her flagship cafe. In her kitchen, Jaclyn would make homemade beignets for her family, following a recipe she had created, modified, and mastered. Around the table, she and her family would dig into puffy, sweet pastries baptized with powdered sugar, and one of her children would say, "This is so yummy." Another phrase her children would say was, "Mom, you did good."

Listening to her passion, her confidence, and the way she drew on her deep faith, I began to feel a chill, and chills appeared on my arms. Jaclyn was precisely the same person I had met all those years ago as an unpaid intern. We said our goodbyes, sure that we would do this again very soon. The next day, I rose early, checked out of the hotel, and drove to Mo'Bay Beignet on Dauphin Street. "Three beignets with a side of buttercream icing, please."

Sitting in my friend's cafe, I enjoyed a homemade sweet treat covered in a white blanket of goodness created from my friend's recipe. With powdered sugar all over my shirt and a smile on my face, I realized Jaclyn knew about the recipe. My family's recipe. It wasn't a secret. Other people were also aware of this recipe: family, hard work, and faith in God. Not everyone had been taught apathy, disrespect, and brutality. Some people, if we were lucky to meet them, were taught empathy, respect, and kindness.

Returning home from the Mobile trip, my anxiety about this second career pause vanished. I was exactly where I was supposed to be, and just like Jaclyn, I began to prepare for my next career after enjoying great success in my previous endeavors. My career had never been over. A pause was necessary to give me the time and space to heal, plan, and prepare for something bigger. Standing still in a career pause was a strategy—another divine intervention.

# Chapter 33

# Spring

*The following story is about healing. Grief is ugly, but with hard work, grief can be channeled into something productive, healthy, and beautiful. It's the Spring of 2025.*

Flower gardening has always been a hobby of mine, from childhood into adulthood. A busy schedule of an executive and a mother prevented me from gardening as much as I preferred. Still, every Spring, I made time to tend to my flowers, thinning out the ones that had outgrown their space and adding new, young plants to the mix. And every spring, the flowers rewarded me with a beautiful display of color. Dormant for the winter, their dark green leaves held the promise that new life would bloom in a few short months. The patience of a gardener rested in trusting that promise to come true.

Still grief-stricken from all the loss, winter had left me weary, tired, and numb as I began my second career pause. Signs of spring began peeking through the dirt, and my woody peony bush was preparing for its next seasonal performance. I'm always happiest when the first blooms burst open. With each passing year, it adds blooms to the count, and new light-green foliage fills the open spaces. By the way, I pronounce "peony" with the elongated charm only a Southern woman could add to such a word: "PEEEE - OWN - KNEEE." They were also my favorite flowers to give as gifts, and I'm expanding my cut-flower garden so I'll have access to more beautiful, homegrown flowers to share with friends and family.

Packing up my grief and my flower gardening tools and bucket, I walked down the sidewalk to the house that had sat empty since December 19, 2024—Kim's house. Sitting down to weed Kim's flower beds, I felt the weight of her absence. I looked up to the sky and started the conversation with a question. "Kim, what was your greatest accomplishment?" Before I could wait for a response, I fired off another question: "If you were here today, what would you aspire to accomplish?" With the sun on my face, one word landed peacefully in thought and satisfied both questions: "Mother."

Standing to review my work, ensuring every weed had been pulled, I walked over to her rose bushes and cut three blooms. Holding the handle of my garden bucket in one hand and three young rose buds in the other, I walked back to my house. The house that was my home. A home I shared with my boys, their childhood home.

Recalling the word art picture that hung in my bedroom, it read: "*A cord of three strands is not easily broken.*" The words from Ecclesiastes 4:12 resonated deeply with me. My boys and I were three strands that could not be easily broken. "Mother" was my most excellent title. It had been all along.

I'm singing in church again. Not because a fellow parishioner or my mom asked me to, but because I want to. The hard work of loss and grief strengthened my voice. I knew my granddaddy Carl would be proud. Writing has become my therapy. Although

I wasn't disciplined in daily or even weekly journaling, evidence of my desire to write was scattered throughout random places around my house. Journals gifted or purchased over the years, with little nuggets from my past. Collecting all the relics, I read what I had written over the years. It was entertaining.

The most difficult journal to open and read was the one from our trip to London and Paris. On our final day of the journey, with Love and his son safely home, our party of seven was reduced to five as I rose early. Cup of coffee in hand, I walked across the street from our hotel to find a quiet place alone. The hotel was perfectly positioned across the street from Kensington Palace and the Diana, Princess of Wales, Sunken Garden.

I had the luxury of traveling solo or with friends. It was a luxury I protected with hard work. The hard work of saving money to pay for a trip responsibly, the luxury of time since the boys were with their dad every other week, and the luxury of self-love and the love of so many wonderful girlfriends ensured that I never missed an opportunity for a planned or spontaneous trip. The conversation, photographs, and memories were enough to sustain me for the rest of my life. When I traveled with my boys, it was their time to explore. Their interests were on the agenda, not mine, although they would entertain my desire for a glass of wine or two.

This particular day in London was Anna's day. Her chosen excursion was shopping. As I sat alone in the park, she and Major hit the streets, visiting shops until they finally landed in TK Maxx, a European version of her favorite store, TJ Maxx—two teenagers, cousins, carefree, and taking in the memories. Sure to capture cute photographs, Anna would hand her phone to Major to snap photos so she would have memories to sustain her for a lifetime.

At the same time, Lane and Max requested a rideshare and traveled together across the city to a train store. I was nervous because Lane didn't always have the patience to endure the constant chatter of a history, racing, and travel enthusiast such as Max. He had the gift of gab, just like his great-granddaddy Carl and my daddy, his Big Daddy. He's such an incredible story-teller with an unpretentious humor that could leave you rolling on the floor in laughter.

Grateful for a morning alone, we had been together for eight days now, I sat on the lawn, Princess Diana's memorial garden in my right peripheral vision. Allowing my mind to wander and dream, I checked my phone for missed calls or texts and re-freshed the Life360 app. All my babies were released into the wild in a foreign country. Life360 was my way of keeping a close eye on them while allowing them some untethered time.

Sitting alone, I began to write about the love of my life and all that we had planned for our future. As I continued to write, I added details of my career and what I aspired to do in the years to come. With one last thought to ponder, I began to write about how thankful I was that I had invested my own money in a once-in-a-lifetime trip with the people I loved most.

I won't disclose the total cost of the trip, but yikes! I blew my budget on the first day, even before we had departed. My bold personality led to an unplanned expense of a one-way rental SUV so I could save the once-in-a-lifetime trip for those I loved most. Additionally, my inability to translate military time re-sulted in the purchase of seven new train tickets from Paris to

London. Way to go, badass professional woman who is always polished and on point.

The cost of those items was never disclosed to my travel companions because it was worth every penny. With money earned through my own hard work and with divine opportunities presented at the right moments, I was gifted memories captured in all the photographs I took, both candid and posed, to last me a lifetime.

Healing from heartbreak is a long and torturous process. The heartbreak of losing the man I loved and the potential of blending four children in one home had been ripped away from my heart. Kim's death left me defeated by cancer. In death, Granny Evelyn gave me peace. In the hospital room with my mom, the healing process began. Giving up my career gave me the time and space to grieve appropriately on my own, at my own pace. Hard work that only I could do, and hard work that I had to do for myself and my boys. It was the responsible thing to do.

I replayed the "do nothing" conversation from over seven years ago, and the advice still worked for me. Could it work for this amount of heartbreak? For one year, do nothing. Time was what I needed. Time was all I had. Time to be present with my boys. Time to launch a new, less demanding career. Time to find my last love, a true love, and a lifelong love. My own self-doubt and afflictions caused by my own words still left me wondering if I had messed up the recipe.

With a Realtor's "for sale" sign now placed in Kim's yard, a symbol of ugly grief, the people she loved most were left behind to navigate alone. Kim's rose bushes continue to present themselves beautifully with new blooms to welcome a new family into a home that was once filled with so much love, shared between a mother and daughter. Kathy was present every day of Kim's sickness. It was a sickness she would have gladly taken so her daughter could live a long and beautiful life as a mother. Kim was equally caring for her young daughter, like a mother always does, even when she was experiencing the hardest days of her life, which were cut short by cancer. Kim's house was on the market and would soon be filled with a new family. I would soon have new neighbors.

# Chapter 34

# Circle

*The following story describes the recipe in its entirety: family, hard work, and faith in God.*

At the age of seventy, Daddy continues to rise early in the morning to head to work. Every morning that he chooses to work, he steps onto a smaller piece of heavy equipment to dig a trench. He doesn't earn a lot of money. He's no longer a leader in a large municipality. Daddy retired from the City of Huntsville after a decorated twenty-eight-year career. He was forty-seven when he retired. Mom continues to have dinner ready when he comes in from a hard day's work.

Mom and Dad are still the first parishioners to arrive at Mt. Nebo Baptist Church on Sunday mornings. They no longer consult over a songbook; instead, Daddy sits with his Bible open, reviewing the verses selected for his sermon, words provided by a higher being. Some pew seats, once filled by my grandparents, sit empty, while others are filled with old and new family and friends.

Never seeming to be able to arrive on time as an adult, I rush into the church before the song begins to play. My boys, every other Sunday, take their preferred seat next to their cousins,

Lane and Anna, and join in the congregational singing as their Gramma plays the piano.

Sometimes I think about Love. During our short fairy tale, as equally yoked partners, he would join me on most Sunday mornings. He and his children went every other Sunday. Just he and I every other Sunday. Some Sunday mornings, I would step out, walk to the altar, and kneel in prayer. On other Sundays, I prayed silently at my pew as the invitational song played. *"Just a little talk with Jesus,"* as the old church hymnal goes, I would thank Him for sending me the strong and kind arms of a loving man. My prayer was answered. I didn't know there would be a deadline to our love. But it was love, true love. This I know.

Amanda and I don't have to think about what we'll do after church. Hopping in our own cars, we make the thirty-minute drive to our parents' house, our childhood home, for Sunday lunch. At my mom's table, we all take our assigned seats. Daddy sits at the head of the table as he shares stories about his workdays from the previous week or a recent woodworking project. My parents' house is filled with their children and grandchildren. After lunch, while Mom and Amanda clean, my dad and I walk outside to his garden. Sometimes our conversations are about his tomatoes, and sometimes they are about the recipe.

The summer of my second career pause was still among us. Max and I were spending the day together. Glancing at his wrist, I noticed the pink silicone bracelet he often wears. I had a matching bracelet, only mine was blue. On the day Kim's house was to be cleaned out, I walked down my sidewalk and joined Kathy, Jocelyn, and Caroline, Kim's baby sister. Kim's nieces and daughter were there too. As I cleaned the playroom, I came across a silicone bracelet. Inscribed on the plastic-like material were the words *#KimStrong Psalms 91:4.* The verse, from the Woman's Study Bible and New King James version, states, "He shall cover you with His feathers, And under His wings you shall take refuge; His truth shall be your shield and buckler." I placed the bracelet on my arm.

I no longer have the Unclaimed Baggage copy of *Work, Pause, Thrive.* During my minimalist phase, I developed the habit of gifting books I had read to others who might find them helpful. When my second pause began, I ordered a new copy from Amazon. I vowed to keep this copy in my home library. If I were to designate a book as a life-saver, this would be the book.

Published in 2018, I would love for the author to tackle a post-pandemic version to account for the whiplash professionals experienced when the world shut down. As the world came back to life, renewed after a pause, workplaces and workers alike struggled awkwardly in the wake of the disease and the advancements in artificial intelligence. I would read that book too, with the hope that it would help guide me through the beautiful and dark surprises that my life and my career were sure to deliver in the years to come.

The author, Lisen Stromberg, has no idea what impact her work had on me as I tried to put my career back on track after pausing to give myself the time and space to recover fully from cancer and be present with my boys as they, too, healed from our shared experience. I would definitely read a new book by Stromberg.

Big goals upon big goals were set and accomplished in my decorated twenty-year career. For the past eight years, every three months, my bloodwork told my medical team that I was a survivor. The annual bone scan and abdominal CT scan further indicated that cancer was no longer a threat at the present moment. As I sped through life, earning a six-figure salary by my mid-thirties and donning the title of Chief Executive Officer of a growing company by age forty, it was now time for me to slow down rather than struggle. It was now time for me to stop and enjoy the fruits of all the hard work.

As I tipped the measuring cup to pour the discarded sourdough "mother" into the mixing bowl, I added equal parts flour and water to the bread starter left in the mason jar. Major named the little jar "Little Mama" and the oversized mason jar "Big Mama." Now, my mother, being the Southern woman she is, drew the line when Daddy proudly announced he wanted his grandchildren to call him "Big Daddy." My mother insisted on a more refined name and title; she was called Gramma to her four biological grandchildren, and Grammy Sue to all of her bonus grandchildren. Bonus grandchildren came by the dozens because of the hard work she had put into nurturing and caring for her family and friends.

Just as the recipe for living a good life provided nourishment, I added nourishment to the sourdough "mother" to sustain her until it was time to discard a half cup and begin folding and tucking the dough. Once the dough had proofed into the ideal consistency, I placed the raw dough in the hot oven for the designated amount of time, allowing it to take shape.

Once the time in the heat was up, the Dutch oven was removed from its hot enclosure, and a beautiful loaf of sourdough was placed on the bread rack to rest. Once the bread had rested, I called for the boys. The bread knife sawed off three pieces. We all said in unison, "This is so good." And one of the boys said, "Mom, you did good."

# Chapter 35

# Fear

*The following story brings you, the reader, to the present time when my memoir was taking shape. Unsure if I should write my story, I consulted one of my trusted advisors, my Mom.*

I sat on my childhood bed flipping through photo albums with my mom. As we talked over memories, I asked her a question. "Mom, should I even write a book? I'm not sure I should. I'm not special. My story is unique to me." Anna, my niece, had made her way to where we were sitting, and she also started flipping through old photographs.

Unsure of the purpose of my story, only I could do the hard work of uncovering my purpose and using my story to fulfill it. My early career at Crestwood Medical Center shaped me into the leader I would become, thanks to the careful coaching and mentoring I received from Lori, a forever mentor and friend. She had a profound impact on me as a young professional, and I often think about what my career would have been like if I had stayed under her leadership.

My short time at BIO Alabama was equally formative. The large Board of thirty high-performing and high-demand professionals taught me that leaders are kind, supportive, and collaborative. I'm so thankful to have met all of them, and I hope that one day our paths will cross again.

The twelve years I spent with an organization to which I gave my heart and soul, during which I also lost my marriage, salary, title, and ultimately, my career, hold a special place in my heart. I am thankful for these characters in my life and book: Boss, Mentor, and Sergeant. Three men who taught me that not all men understood the recipe that my father and both of my grandfathers taught with fervor. Without their leadership, I would not be the strong woman, mother, executive leader, and survivor that I am today.

I had proven to myself that high-performing women, mothers, and executive leaders could stand up to a terrible disease, stand up to bystanders keeping score, and stand up to self-doubt that can cripple us at times. Regardless of whether the high-performing mother was a stay-at-home mom doing the vital work of shepherding her children, just as my mom had done. Irrespective of whether the high-performing woman was demoted and reduced in size as she battled breast cancer, just as I had done. The recipe was for everyone, not just me, and it was my responsibility to add my own steps and my own dash of spice. My chosen spice was to do nothing. Twice in my career, I carefully added the right amount of spice, a spice called "pause."

I didn't know what to do or how to support other women. After all, I was not unique. I was not special. My story exists in all of us. Each person is blessed with their own beautiful and dark surprises. I reflected on all the conversations I had with survivors as I traversed the decision-making landscape in and out of doctors' offices. It was stories from survivors, their deep and personal experiences, that helped me so much during my five-month battle with breast cancer and over the eight out of ten years of long-term treatment to reduce my risk of recurrence. I remember their stories and how their courage motivated and inspired me to make tough decisions. These women inspired me to fight. I thought my story might help someone, but how could I share it more broadly?

As Mom processed the question and comment combined, she was ready to give her response. "Everyone is unique and special, Sonia. Most of us are too afraid to share our story. Most of us will not put in the hard work to write our story in book form. You will write the book, even if it's just for you." She followed up quickly to say, "I want to read it, too."

My mom knew the recipe by heart, and she knew my story intimately because she had seen it unfold before her eyes. As I write this book, Mom will turn seventy in the coming year. Her lived experiences prepared her to be a mother. They prepared her to care for her daughter, hurt by divorce, cancer, and loss. They prepared her for this very moment when her daughter would need her wisdom. Her mother and grandmother had taught her the recipe. Mom followed the recipe perfectly, adding her own special touch with spices.

Fear has been a part of my life, and it's a part of most people's lives. Fear of losing a job, fear of not having health insurance, fear of a medical crisis, fear of a financial crisis, fear of losing the house that is your children's refuge. The list could go on and on. There is one fear buried deep in my heart: the fear of failing as a mother. I was aware of the risks of having children. After all, I had been young once and didn't always make the best decisions. My parents may have been disappointed in me at times, but it never lasted long. Their love for me was much stronger than any fear or disappointment.

At one of our many Sunday lunches together, I recently apologized to my parents for any disappointment I may have caused them. Daddy didn't even look up from his food as he prepared another bite. "You never disappointed us," he said. With this book, I also want my boys to know this is true of them. There is nothing they will ever do to lose my love, and I will always show up for them, even if they, too, feel as though they messed up the recipe.

Standing in the kitchen together, Major cooked his lunch after a hot and long football practice. He still had the energy and awareness to ask his brother and me if we wanted anything. He would cook for us. The man of the house. A role he was thrown into at the early age of eight while his mom fought breast cancer. As Major announced lunch was ready, all three of us were in the kitchen together. Now, both teenagers, my boys stood there in their childhood home. The home Jason and I wanted to keep for them as their lives turned upside down with the divorce. My Great-Aunt Gail understood the recipe, too, as she honored the hard work of her mother by keeping her son in his home following her death.

No longer silenced by the author of this book, I was ready to embark on my next career. After all, my job was important to me, and I was eager to get back to work. There was a new, unfamiliar barrier in the way. A barrier not encountered during my twenty-year decorated career thus far. I had no idea how to write a book, let alone publish one. I wasn't sure if readers would be interested in an honest and raw story told by a flawed protagonist and written by a real, raw, and flawed human like me.

Even though I planned to be on pause for twelve months this time, my anxiety caused me to browse Indeed and begin applying for entry-level jobs three months into this second career pause. In total, I was invited for three different interviews, each with an organization highly regarded in our community, places where my strengths could truly shine. With each interview, I heard the word "no." The entry-level roles were not for me. Entry-level roles were the catalyst for young women just starting in their careers to shape their own professional lives, just as I had done twenty years ago.

The conviction to write a book, even if it was just for my boys, mom and me, led me to begin my research. I found her on Facebook and opened the Messenger app. As I began to type the message, a smile appeared on my face. The fog of grief started to lift. The message was to Georgina Cross, author of six published books, whom I had read. Confessing my desire to write a book, Georgina responded with an invitation. This time, the invitation from a wise, seasoned, professional woman was to join the next session of "The Word," a group she had started to help other aspiring writers. As the rain poured down, I drove to the library where the meeting would take place. I had taken the first step in writing a book—the first step in building the next layer of my beloved career. My career was not over; it was just beginning. My second act, as I had been told.

I began to write. Initially, it was bullet points, which evolved into more detailed points that expanded into complete sentences. Short stories appeared on my computer screen in their own right, but incomplete pieces as a whole. A pencil and notepad were always with me to capture random thoughts that I didn't want to escape my brain—a brain struggling with medically induced menopause. I had been in a state of medical menopause for eight years now, and it was taking its toll on my memory, recall, and quick thinking. If I didn't have a pen and notepad handy, I would open the voice recorder app on my phone to capture my thoughts, which I would later dictate into a Google document on my computer. A book—my book, about my story—was taking shape.

Unable to attend most of the writing group meetings due to my boys' schedule, I continued to read the emails that Georgina sent out to the group. In one email, she suggested that we all consider attending an upcoming writing conference. It was the Third Annual Athens State University Writing and Arts Summit, and admission was free. Since I was on a career pause, I didn't have the extra cash to pay for a conference, and Athens was just a short forty-five-minute drive away.

The morning of the first day of the conference, I loaded up my computer bag and drove to Athens. I was unsure of what I would learn, but I knew I would meet several local, success-ful authors and hear their stories as I sat and listened to them speak. One advised, "You need a flawed protagonist." Check, I had that, and she was here with me. It was me. Another sug-gested that you had to keep the momentum going, stating that he often woke up at four or five o'clock in the morning to get in two hours of writing, only to have another writing session in the evening, totaling four hours a day, give or take. Still, yet an-other advised, "You have to write the book. You have to get to 'the end'."

It would be a serendipitous conversation with two of the event attendees that took my breath away. As we engaged in small talk, the typical question in a business atmosphere came

up: we asked each other about our careers. All three of us unknowingly gave the same answer. We were all on pause.

Each of us was on a career pause for very different reasons.
One of these new fast friends I had made at the conference
confessed, "I retired from my long-term career, divorced, and relocated to Athens, Alabama, to be close to my son, daughter-
in-law, and grandson." The other new friend confessed that she
had been caught up in a recent reduction-in-force due to a
business merger. It wasn't uncommon, given the economic environment of early 2025, to experience downsizing or a reduction-in-force. It was my turn to confess, "I left my beloved career
to write a book." These two new friends would not know the actual reason I had left my career, severance due to allegations of
mismanagement, until they read my book.

Using the discretion taught to me by my early-career mentor,
I spoke nothing about the events, words, or actions that had led
to my being offered severance. Severance was a bonus for the
hard work, the return to investors that my team and I had generated, and the success we had achieved together as a cohesive
team.

These two new friends and I exchanged numbers, unsure if
we would attend the second day of the conference. Vowing to
stay in touch, I did not plan to attend on Friday because I had
gotten exactly what I came for: inspiration and motivation to
put in the hard work to write a book, just as I had received from
breast cancer survivors as I prepared to put in the hard work to
fight cancer. Furthermore, the feedback and guidance I received
from Linda before my first career pause was to do nothing for
one year.

Friday morning arrived earlier than usual for me. I woke up at 5:00 a.m. without the aid of an alarm. Opening up my computer, my stream of consciousness filled page after page. Not realizing how long I had been writing, how long my brain had stayed engaged and focused, my dogs snapped me out of a trance. It was time for their morning walk, and they were growing impatient.

Once each dog was leashed, we went out the door for our morning mile walk around the neighborhood. It's one of my dogs' favorite things to do, in addition to playing ball in the backyard. Chase, the Australian Shepherd and oldest; Piper, the doodle mutt; and Moo Moo, the miniature weenie and youngest. Three dogs, each with their own unique personality, whose combined personalities match my own. Chase was the anxiety-stricken shepherd trying to keep everyone together. Piper was a relaxed, free-spirited individual who enjoyed life. Moo Moo, even with her tiny stature, was big and bold in everything she did. Once our walk was over, I sat back down at my computer and continued writing. For a two-week sprint, my story came together. Now it would be someone else's to read.

As I prepared to type the final two words of my book, I sat in the light of reflection. I wanted to give my boss, the man who invited me to take on a Chief Executive Officer position, a big hug and say thank you. My courage came from his harsh criticism, hostility, and demanding demeanor. Cancer gave me the courage to fight for a life worth living boldly. I realized that while I would have loved to have a husband by my side through all of this, I did not need a man to stand me up. After all, I had never let anyone in to explore and learn each crevice of my mind and experience the emotion deeply buried inside. Everything I needed was there—a perfect blend of my mom and dad. They were equal parts of my grandparents. And even still, my grandparents were equal parts of my great-grandparents: a legacy, a recipe to be passed down to each new generation.

I'm unsure if I will ever have the opportunity to lead a team and share my executive leadership style again. I'm uncertain whether my brain will ever be healthy enough for a high-performing, high-demand role again in my career. I already sold my 2024 Lexus GX, a luxury car suitable for an executive, because the expense was not justifiable while I was on a career pause. Using a portion of the profit from the sale, I purchased a 1977 Ford F-100 Ranger, one just like my Granddaddy Carl used to ride me around in when we spent time together during my childhood. A vehicle more fitting for me at this new stage in my life.

Ever since my diagnosis with cancer, I have had a burning desire to do more to help cancer patients, specifically high-performing executive women and mothers who received the dreadful notice of a cancer diagnosis or other life-altering surprise. Mothers who are navigating the cold world of business as they forge ahead to create a good life for themselves and their children. I want them to know that they will not only survive life but thrive if they put in the hard work and add the right amount of spice to the recipe: family, hard work, and faith in God.

# Chapter 36

# The Will of a Mother

*D*ear Reader, thank you for reading my story. It is my hope you walk away with one nugget of wisdom to help you on your personal journey. In conclusion, the following story connects the dots of all my lived experiences up to this point in life.

Going back to the story that started this book, Grandma Mamie had the will of a mother to live a long life. She found purpose in her children, especially her son, who was her forever child. Grandma had a recipe to follow, and she followed it carefully, step by step. She followed it perfectly and added her own spice.

Ellie and I were scheduled to have coffee. It was a time for us to catch up and chat about our dreams. I was excited to share the news of my book with her. We made it a habit after I left the paid workforce on January 13, 2025, to meet for coffee every four to six weeks. Before this cadence began, we gave each other three months of space to process and heal from our own experiences in the same reality.

We had both been accused of mismanaging the company we were entrusted to lead, as well as a company we had led to financial success. The two of us were equal participants in researching, planning, and implementing a strategy that, with consistent positive feedback, had been implemented to the absolute best of our combined ability.

The fourth and final goal could not be achieved or destroyed by one individual. The failure to reach the fourth goal overshadowed the success of attaining three audacious goals. We were proud of our work and could live with the feedback from one critic. We were a team. As we began another conversation over coffee, we kept our focus on productive, healthy, and forward-looking topics. We shared dreams of our next career and the latest shenanigans of mom life. Still unsure, we occasionally reflected on the challenges we had overcome to reach this point in our careers and lives. Another friend placed perfectly in my path at the right time: a forever friend, mother, and badass executive woman.

If Love chose to read my book, he would discover the realization for the very first time. I didn't have the heart to tell him to his face or even in a text. It was too painful for me to reveal publicly until now. The realization that I forgot his birthday and the butterfly effect of my actions. How can any of us truly understand the butterfly effect of a simple action, such as forgetting to say "Happy Birthday"?

Realizing I had forgotten his birthday, I aimed to make amends for my transgression that only I knew about. Between work, research, and meetings, I rushed to Edgar's Bakery for a red velvet cake. When they asked if I wanted to personalize it, I said, "Yes, please. Happy Birthday!"

Once I had the cake, I rushed to Party City for a balloon bouquet, a mix of red balloons with the number "47" in black, plus silly streamers for the kids to use as we sang "Happy Birthday" in joyful laughter on the back porch. Our four children and I doused Love with silly streamers, and we all laughed together. We were happy. We were a family.

His birthday celebration was our last night together, all because I was so overwhelmed by a career goal and the negative, unproductive opinion of one person, and a villain called cancer—so microscopic that it took electromagnetic radiation to even be seen by the human eye—that I neglected the people I loved most.

Our love story ended because I was so focused on proving cancer wrong. It was all my fault. If I had just confessed to Love that I had forgotten his birthday, rather than trying to be the perfect executive leader, flawless lover, and present mother, he would likely have been bringing me a cup of coffee as I wrote my book. We would likely have been husband and wife, actively participating in the blending of our family. Love and I would have been planning our future together, including a trip to London and Paris, as we had promised to do again later. A trip I couldn't wait to take with my bonus daughter. If I had just confessed to my mom that I had forgotten Love's birthday, her wise words would have cleared my headspace. Still, I was silent.

Reflecting on my sister's young, inexperienced manager—a person who, in her own right, had been trained to be a people leader, but did not understand the butterfly effect of her actions. Amanda lost access to the doctor who saved her life. The actions of her manager sent her into a deep and dark depression because no one believed her pain and sickness. The disbelief was so great that she was placed on three months of paid administrative leave, funded with taxpayer dollars, as an investigation diverted valuable resources within a government municipality to prove one person's narrative. In hindsight, as a leader, I wish I had coached my sister differently. I wish I had told her to "do nothing." It could have saved her from ugly grief if only I had given her those two words: "Do nothing."

Jason and I hadn't comprehended the butterfly effect of divorce and how we fought like hell to be great parents, teaching our boys the recipe. Neither of us knew the boys might need a mom later in life—the ripple effect of our decision to divorce brought Maria into our lives.

My countless family members, mentors, friends, and trusted advisors would never know the impact they had on my life unless I told them in my own words. To anyone mentioned by name in my story, or if your name is redacted in my book, rest assured, you made a positive and impactful impression on my life. Some chose words and actions with empathy, respect, and kindness, while others elected apathy, disrespect, and brutality. Two different recipes were taught. Only I had the responsibility to choose how I would plate either recipe for the nourishment of my emotions and mentality. It was hard work, but it paid off in the end.

Still further, the reflection continues as I'm back in that coffee shop where I wanted to scream, "I QUIT" to the boss who delivered the fatal blow with a salary cut and title demotion. He, too, hadn't realized the butterfly effect of his decision. While I continued to do my job and do it well, in the quiet stillness, I planned to pause.

This same gentleman was unaware of the butterfly effect of his actions and words when he delivered the final blow that would end my beloved career with severance. Not even I had a preview of the results of that butterfly effect. It's too soon to know. However, I did gain wisdom through lived experiences, with proactive planning and preparation, learning to "do nothing" and sit still during a second career pause.

None of us can appropriately comprehend the ripple effect of our words and actions. Not even cancer. Cancer took its final shot and was victorious. Cancer didn't take my life, but it took my career, my true love, and my neighbor. The fight was far from over, and I had to get ready to battle, kick myself back to the surface, and fight for a life worth living—not merely surviving, but living bigger and bolder than ever before.

Kim is not here to bear witness to the butterfly effect she had on my life through her death. Neither were my great-grandparents and grandparents. They all taught me the recipe. The proof that they followed the right recipe was evident in the church house, which overflowed as people they had impacted spilled out into the hallway and out into the yard. One day, I, too, hope Mt. Nebo Baptist Church will burst open as people gather for my grand celebration of life. Only I can do the hard work to follow the proven recipe: family, hard work, and faith in God. I believed I could because of my historical performance in life.

The series of losses I experienced in late 2024 began with Love, all because I ignored the smallest detail, the mundane detail of life: a birthday. Like the date placed on one's tombstone with a dash separating it from the end date, our love story died that day. All we would have left was the date of our first conversation at Greenbus Brewery and the date of our demise, separated by a dash. A dash, we had lived well together in our short three-year romance. A dash, two of them tattooed on my body one with ink and the other with a scar, leaving me with memories that must sustain me for the rest of my life, no matter how long that may be.

To prove that cancer had not taken my career, accomplishing the final business goal at the organization I led as CEO was for me and no one else. The financial upside certainly motivated me. The economic gain would pad my children's college fund and my retirement fund. Yes, my colleagues were growing in the process as they learned new knowledge, skills, and abilities.

Stakeholders were engaged due to our financial success. I was not the only one who benefited from the hard work. That also made achieving this goal important. But the most potent motivation pushing me to achieve this goal was the satisfaction of looking cancer in the eye and saying, "You did not win. You did not take my career from me." But my team and I would never celebrate the fourth and final goal.

In the dark days of grief, I remained silent, venting my frustrations to my mom only. After all, silence is a powerful form of communication. My Granny Evelyn had taught me that loud and clear as she lay silent in her bed on the day she died, Christmas Eve 2024. No one knew about my fight because I never spoke a word of it. Only occasional, discreet details were shared in the confidence of trusted advisors—individuals placed in my path at the right time and for the right duration.

Life was about hard work, and sometimes you had to do the hard work alone in silence. It was no one else's responsibility. Equally, I was not responsible for others' words, actions, or the butterfly effect that would ripple, unknowingly, through lives in its wake. Only I could do the hard work for myself. Only I could follow the recipe taught to me.

In the case between Love and me, the evidence was clear, and I had no defense. Love was absolutely right when he defended his position. I had lost Love, my neighbor had been murdered by cancer, my grandmother died, my mom almost died, and my career was over. Signing my severance agreement, I knew I would likely never receive half of the severance money agreed to in the legal document. It was a sunk cost, and I would have to leverage the equity I had worked hard to build—equity I had intended to use to create a new life with Love, but now to be used to rebuild my own life.

To begin the recovery process after a series of devastating losses, I placed one of my bamboo towels out in the grass in front of my house. Lying down and looking up at the sky, I pressed play and listened to *Man's Search for Meaning* by Viktor Frankl. He had the will of a father, husband, and a man with faith in God. Frankl credited his survival to his ability to be useful through hard work and to create purpose in his life, even while suffering insurmountable physical, emotional, and mental pain.

While my lived experiences do not compare to the horror Frankl witnessed and endured in not only one but four Holocaust camps, his work in psychology fascinated me as I studied his ideology and philosophy. Frankl believed that in the face of suffering, individuals can discover purpose and resilience by actively choosing their attitudes and finding meaning in their experiences. The author's story was delivered beautifully and with complete emotional control. Coming from a brave Holocaust survivor, I believed every word he wrote.

As the days began to add up in my second career pause, peace began to come over me. My boys were thriving. They could now survive losing their childhood home, having gained a better understanding of the recipe. I wasn't so sure I wanted to keep this house, their childhood home. It felt like a home built for survival rather than a home built to thrive with a life of purpose. It felt like a home where my boys and I had to fight for financial stability, health insurance, and a sense of normalcy. The three of us needed a fresh start in a new home.

Discreetly, I began planning and preparing in silence for a new career, new home, and new true love. A love directed toward the one person who was guaranteed to be with me the rest of my life, regardless of the deadline: me. A love directed toward the two young men who had been right by my side through each sad, fearful, and devastating blow. This book is my voice. My way of unapologetically saying, "Fuck you, cancer," because I was still hopeful that I had a lot of life to live. I knew I would not live in a house with dirt floors.

This book is my way of teaching my boys how to use the recipe responsibly—to lead with empathy, respect, and kindness by modeling the behaviors through my words and actions. Because I know there is an alternative recipe waiting for them if I don't pass down my family's recipe. The other recipe is full of discontent, hurried complacency, and sadness. It's a recipe that's being taught equally.

Two additional people who taught me the recipe were always there to help guide me as I worked in my own kitchen, following the instructions carefully: my parents. They were with me through divorce, cancer, loss, both of my career pauses. I didn't have the strong arms of a man who intimately knew my curves and scars; I had the caring arms of a mother, father, and two beautiful boys, like a warm, homemade quilt. I had never been alone.

My story serves as a message to mothers, executive leaders, and women: lead with empathy, respect, and kindness. None of us is immune to the beautiful and dark surprises of life, most of which are entirely outside of our control. Stand up to behavior that is apathetic, disrespectful, and brutal. Offer grace to individuals in their transgressions. Above all else, love one another and treat people as you want to be treated, especially when they may be fighting a Goliath that kills. Sometimes the recipe gets messed up, leaving a person to start all over again. It may result in a bitter taste, and the fruits of your labor may have to be discarded, but trust the process, trust the recipe, and start from scratch.

Now, at my midlife point, if I'm lucky enough to live a long life like all of my grandparents, I'm no longer in crisis but instead firmly rooted in my purpose. No longer struggling with ugly grief and paralyzing fear, I just needed to add two specific spices, a perfect mix of my boys—two people I love the most and who love me the most. Major and Max have been by my side as I fought cancer, fought for financial stability, fought for health insurance, fought to keep their childhood home, and fought not merely to survive life, but to live life responsibly and respectfully. My parents taught me the recipe well. I would never be alone because I was a mother.

This is my story, told from my perspective. I have been careful with each word I've chosen—words to foster empathy, respect, and kindness in every reader. A risk assessment, including a book pre-mortem, was prepared with the same care and caution applied to each career pause plan. I wanted to be ready for the beautiful and potentially dark surprises that might result from sharing an honest and raw story about a flawed protagonist, myself.

It is the will of a mother, the will to live a long life, to be able to teach my boys the recipe. If my final deadline comes sooner than expected, my boys will know how hard their mom fought for them for a very long time. This book is for them, so that they may have memories of their mother to sustain them for a lifetime.

My Uncle Carl outlived his mother, and it is my prayer that my boys will outlive me. The recipe is simple, although it is not easy: family, hard work, and faith in God—adding in a dash of spice that only I could add to enjoy the sweet, sweet taste of life.

As I prepared to type the final two words, "The End," I had another little talk with Jesus.

The one-sided conversation filled the room. I was sure my prayers had already been answered because I had an editor and over a dozen peer readers to review my work. My prayers did make it past my ceiling, and I believed this because He had already answered so many prayers—not all of them in the way I had hoped. But there was one prayer He answered so boldly that it gave me the chills to this very day. He sent my boys another mom, Maria. God provided my boys with a back-up mom, a co-mom, a mom who loves Jesus. My boys would not only have one mom, but they would have two. Major and Max were the bonuses in life to those who love them most, including me. Grandma Mamie's recipe, which she passed down to her daughter, Granny Ruth, was now being passed down to my boys generations later.

**-THE END-**

# Epilogue

It was a Friday, and I rose earlier than usual. With a warm cup of coffee in my palms, I thought about the day ahead of me and the final walk I would take down the sidewalk and into Kim's house. This particular Friday was the Estate Sale, where all of Kim's earthly material belongings would be on display.

Walking through the threshold of the garage door, I greeted my bonus mom, Kathy, and bonus baby sister, Caroline. Caroline had already placed a "SOLD" sign on a few of the items I had selected. My boys would later help me move them down the sidewalk and into our home, their childhood home—a home I wasn't so sure I would keep.

As shoppers began to fill Kim's home, I realized Kathy and Caroline understood the recipe, too. They knew the recipe better than I did and with the same faithful pursuit as my great-grandma, Mamie. Only the roles had been reversed. Kathy would outlive two of her daughters. She would have lived in a house with dirt floors if it meant her daughters were still here. Even through ugly grief, Kathy comprehended the recipe: family, hard work, and faith in God.

# Acknowledgments

Writing this book was energizing and good medicine for my soul. Thank you to all of my friends and family, mentioned by name in this manuscript, for your blessing in allowing me to publish my story. Thank you for allowing me to share the recipe. I have been careful not to divulge any proprietary secrets or offer any disparaging words. This is my story, and only I could tell it. Our family's recipe is worthy of the world.

To Major and Max, being your mother is my greatest accomplishment, and you will always be my greatest achievements. Your father and I serve as your safety net. Our arms will always be the safest place for you to take refuge when you may feel like you, too, have messed up the recipe.

To Daddy and Mama, Lynn and Susan, thank you for raising me in a Godly home. Growing up, I never questioned your priorities because they matched perfectly with the recipe: family, hard work, and faith in God. As my parents, you have always been my safety net. Seeking refuge in your presence, you have always been gracious in your words of wisdom and in your pointed advice, leaving it up to me to accept or decline. I like to think that I accepted your advice and guidance more than I declined it.

To my sister, Amanda, for being my built-in best friend, gifted to us by our parents. You are my companion in this life. I'm proud of you for finding your voice and standing firmly in your truth when no one else believed you. I wish I had your strength.

To Jason, we didn't get married only to end it. Divorce wasn't part of our plan when we started building our life together. Today, we make a great co-parenting team. Thank you for being an extraordinary father. Thank you for always taking my call when I needed you.

To Maria, my co-mom. I prayed my children would have a mother. God answered my prayer and provided my boys with not one, but two moms. You are my equal in raising our two young men. The care and concern you have for Major and Max are what only a mother could provide. Thank you for loving them. They are yours.

To my career, we had a great run. I'm thankful for all the people I met along the way, even if I questioned their motives at times. I'm especially grateful for the failures and the lessons neatly packaged in uncomfortable emotions. Unwrapping each of them revealed the hidden treasures of growth and wisdom. I thought I needed you to be worthy of this life. It turns out I didn't need you. I wanted you.

To cancer, sure, you scared me, but you did not take my grit, toughness, and discipline, qualities that my earthly and heavenly father instilled in me throughout my childhood. I was His child, and you had no authority over me. I only give you credit because you were an incredible teacher. It's because of you that I slowly discovered my true worth and found my voice.

To Crystal, Jennifer, Steve, and Ellie, thank you for the opportunity to lead with empathy, respect, and kindness. Our four years together were a career highlight. Ellie, for our one year of serving together, at least we looked and played the part well.

To Love, for showing me that I was worthy and capable of building a life with you. I, too, would like to think so. Our timing was off. I love you.

To Kim, for all the wisdom you revealed to me through your short battle with cancer. Even in death, cancer did not win. Your legacy—your daughter—will continue. I would trade all the wisdom I've been given for another opportunity to sit with you on the back porch, rocking as our kids played. On the day Jocelyn and I read to you, touched you, and prayed over you, you were not alone. Throughout your battle, you were never alone.

To Meredith, for interpreting my vision for the cover art perfectly and beautifully.

To all the readers, you now have my family's recipe. With the two words Linda gave me, they now belong to you—your permission to do nothing when you, too, hit a new emotional and mental ceiling. You can do nothing for one year or take as long as you need to rest, because you will rise again with grace. It's your permission to pause.

# About the Author

Sonia S. Robinson's background encompasses college, career, cancer, and motherhood. She earned a bachelor's degree with a concentration in Public Relations and an MBA from the University of North Alabama. Over the past twenty years, Sonia has worked in three industries: healthcare, human

*Credit: Sarah Ashley Swain*

capital management, and biotech nonprofit. She has intentionally paused her career twice—first after her breast cancer diagnosis and again after completing her first experience as a Chief Executive.

Sonia founded Mamie Ruth & Co., a personal brand powered by legacy and a belief that the pause in your story is not the end. It's the turning point. Mamie Ruth & Co. helps high-performing women reflect, rest, and reclaim their path forward, especially when life interrupts their momentum.

Named after her great-grandmother, Mamie, and her grandmother, Ruth, the brand blends vintage warmth with modern wisdom, honoring the strength of the women who came before while forging new pathways for those who are still becoming.